D0122301

The Lost Cyclist

BOOKS BY DAVID V. HERLIHY

Bicycle: The History

*The Lost Cyclist: The Epic Tale of
an American Adventurer and
His Mysterious Disappearance*

The
Lost Cyclist

The EPIC TALE
of an
AMERICAN
ADVENTURER
and His
MYSTERIOUS
DISAPPEARANCE

David V. Herlihy

Houghton Mifflin Harcourt
BOSTON   NEW YORK
2010

For information about permission to reproduce
selections from this book, write to Permissions,
Houghton Mifflin Harcourt Publishing Company,
215 Park Avenue South, New York, New York 10003.

www.hmhbooks.com

Library of Congress Cataloging-in-Publication Data
Herlihy, David V.
The lost cyclist : the epic tale of an American adventurer
and his mysterious disappearance / David V. Herlihy.
p. cm.
Includes index.
ISBN 978-0-547-19557-5
1. Lenz, Frank G. 2. Cyclists—United States—
Biography. I. Title.
GV1051.L463H47 2010
796.6092—dc22 [B] 2009028857

Book design by Melissa Lotfy

Printed in the United States of America

DOC 10 9 8 7 6 5 4 3 2

Photo credits appear on page 314.

To my mother, Patricia Herlihy

Contents

III: Epilogue

Prologue

ALTON, ILLINOIS

October 28, 1952

PAUL COUSLEY LOOKED UP from behind his crowded desk and stared incredulously as an elderly man strolled into the pressroom of the *Alton Evening Telegraph*. Moments later, the veteran editor bounded toward the stranger with an outstretched hand. "Will Sachtleben?" he blurted. "Well, I'll be!" The visitor beamed, delighted that someone in this small town by the Mississippi River had recognized him after an absence of fifty years.

"Time was when Will Sachtleben was a popular hero in Alton, known to everyone," Cousley reminisced in the paper the next day. "His fame was nationwide, and wider still, because of his daring deeds." The editor himself fondly recalled the day, back in the spring of 1893, when Sachtleben and a college chum, Thomas G. Allen Jr., sailed into town on "safety" bicycles, prototypes of the modern machine. The intrepid pair had just completed what one newspaper pronounced "the greatest journey of this century, or perhaps of any century": a three-year, fifteen-thousand-mile romp across Europe, Asia, and North America. Incredibly, they had eclipsed a similar journey by Thomas Stevens, made a few years earlier atop an old-style "high-wheeler."

The American public, caught up in the great bicycle boom, relished Sachtleben's harrowing tales of adventure and hardship in exotic lands astride the wildly popular vehicle. Two years later, his fame grew even greater as he embarked on a second, no less daring mission: a trip to eastern Turkey to unravel the mysterious fate of another famous cyclist, Frank G. Lenz of Pittsburgh, who had disappeared toward the end of his own global circuit designed to set new milestones while validating the inflatable tire. Sachtleben's timing was impeccable: the ancient Ottoman Empire was on the verge of collapse, and American newspapers were rife with reports of widespread massacres of Armenians in the very region where the young wheelman had vanished.

The two old-timers sat down for a long chat about the good old days, when the bicycle was the fastest vehicle on the dirt roads and an exchange of letters could take months. Asked why he had come back to Alton after all those years, the retired theater manager and longtime Houstonian explained that he and his nephew, Charles King, had just driven to San Diego to visit Sachtleben's younger brother, Charles, the last of his four siblings still alive. They were on their way back to King's home in Columbus, Ohio, and Sachtleben wanted to revisit his boyhood home, a rambling Victorian on the corner of Seventh and Langdon.

"I have often thought of Alton," the eighty-six-year-old confided to Cousley. "Of my loving mother, also born here, who left us children so early in life, and of my self-sacrificing father, who said to me as we walked down the hill to the Chicago & Alton railroad station the day after my graduation from Washington College: 'Well, son, stay away until you get your fill.'" Added the aged adventurer with a sly smile: "I reckon I did just that."

The veteran newsman, ever on the alert for a good story, coyly mentioned that one of his retired writers was preparing a series of articles on colorful Altonians at the turn of the century. Sachtleben had barely agreed to submit a detailed account of his search for Lenz, the lost cyclist, when he noticed the time. "Now if you'll excuse me, Mr. Cousley," he interjected softly as he rose to his feet, "I really must be on my way."

I

On the Road

1

PITTSBURGH, PENNSYLVANIA

May 30, 1887

H E RIDES WITH a dash and daring that can almost be called recklessness." So marveled the *Bulletin's* sports columnist, describing Pittsburgh's newest wheelman, a nineteen-year-old prodigy named Frank George Lenz. Perched atop a massive, spidery wheel measuring fifty-six inches in diameter, the precocious Lenz, the reporter noted, "surmounts curbstones and dashes over objects with an ease and abandon that calls forth admiration from even old and experienced riders."

Young Lenz in fact cut a dashing figure on or off his wheel, with his sandy blond hair, boyishly handsome face, piercing blue eyes, and muscular five-foot-seven frame. His ever-flashing grin, easygoing manner, and cheerful company quickly made him as popular with the public as he was with his peers.

A decade earlier, at the dawn of American wheeling, this bookkeeper from a modest German American family might have seemed a bit out of his element. The pioneer wheelmen were predominantly eastern elitists who practiced medicine, architecture, law, and other prestigious professions, while emulating the predilections of their English counterparts. But the sport's popularity had grown considerably in the interim, as Americans enjoyed greater prosperity and increased leisure time. Cycling welcomed respectable, up-and-coming young men like Lenz, driven by ambition.

In Pittsburgh alone, the nation's twelfth-largest city with a population around a quarter of a million, the local fleet of wheelmen had grown from about twenty-five hearty riders to about three hundred, including a handful of lady tricyclists. The national figure, meanwhile, had surpassed 100,000. Numerous clubs flourished across the country, and a handful of manufacturers operated in the East and Midwest.

The impressive growth of the cycling industry in the 1880s was due in large part to the vigorous efforts of Albert A. Pope, the pioneer American manufacturer and the maker of Lenz's Columbia bicycle. This Boston businessman helped to quash the public's initial misgivings about the big wheel and to establish the sport as a healthy and gentlemanly pursuit, albeit a risky one reserved primarily for the young and athletic. Among other successful initiatives, Pope helped launch the League of American Wheelmen (LAW), a national lobby that pushed for better roads while promoting racing and touring.

The prospects for further growth were downright rosy, thanks to the newly introduced Rover "safety," which had already induced a few women and some older men to take to the wheel. Developed in England, it was the latest in a long line of two-wheeled challengers designed to remedy the high-wheeler's chief drawback: its unfortunate propensity to hurl the careless—or unlucky—pilot over the handlebars whenever the big wheel hit an unforeseen obstacle, an all-too-common occurrence known in cycling parlance as a "header." These dreaded spills could inflict serious injury and even, on rare occasion, death. The new pattern promised fewer and softer spills, and it was the first alternative bicycle to gain any real traction in the marketplace. Notwithstanding its solid rubber tires, the safety bicycle was a radical departure from the norm. It featured two small wheels of similar size, the rear one powered by a chain and sprocket. Some even said it was the bicycle of the future.

But to fanatics like Lenz and other athletic young men the world over, it was no substitute for the "ordinary." An offshoot of the original "boneshaker" of the late 1860s, the high-wheeler had long delivered to a select few an irresistible mix of speed, exercise, camaraderie, and adventure. Affirmed one early devotee: "I have passed some of the happiest hours of my life on my bicycle." It boasted light and springy metallic wheels, a backbone of tubular steel, and joints turning on smooth ball bearings. It was a modern mechanical miracle on a par with the telephone, the typewriter, and the elevator.

Nor were purists seduced by the prospect of a safer ride. On the contrary, as one enthusiast explained, "The element of safety is rather distasteful to a good many riders who prefer to run some risk, as it gives zest to the sport." To them, the big wheel was an asset, not a liability. It effectively absorbed road shock, gave an optimal gear, and retained the boneshaker's direct action cranks, the simplest and most efficient propulsion scheme. It also placed the rider directly above the pedals, allowing him to apply his full weight when pedaling. From that lofty vantage point, comfortably seated above the dust of the road, the rider enjoyed a view comparable to that of a horseman. Even average riders could easily cover one hundred miles in a single day over the roughest of dirt roads.

Before buying his first bicycle, Lenz had saved for many months, putting aside a portion of his $1,200 annual salary with A. W. Cadman and Company, a manufacturer of brass fittings located in Pittsburgh's strip district on the southern bank of the Allegheny. At last, he scraped together $125, enough for a Columbia Expert, an entry-level roadster weighing a hefty forty-five pounds. He joined the Allegheny Cyclers, a club based on the other side of the river in what was then the distinct city of Allegheny. With a membership of about thirty, it was the largest of the three bicycle clubs in the immediate Pittsburgh area.

Before long, the young clerk was spending nearly every free moment on his bicycle, escaping the unhappy home he shared with his tyrannical stepfather William and his dear but doting mother Maria Anna. On weekdays, before or after his dreary workday, he would cycle at least five miles. On weekends he would roam the hilly countryside alone or with any club mate who dared to chase after him. He loved the sensation of flying into the distance as he churned his smooth pedals and plunged ever deeper into nature's lush sanctuary. He had no qualms about returning in the dark, with his trusty gas lamp suspended on his front hub.

Lenz soon earned a reputation for gritty outdoor adventures. In June 1887, he accomplished his first "century" run to New Castle, Pennsylvania, and back. Leaving home at four in the morning, he proceeded over miserable roads. On his return, his handlebars snapped in two. Despite the jolting and jittery ride, he continued to pedal, arriving home at midnight, sore but satisfied. Two months later, Lenz recorded his first long-distance tour, spending his two-week vacation cycling to New York City and back.

Recognizing his extraordinary speed, stamina, and verve, Lenz's numerous friends urged him to give amateur racing a whirl. Throughout the cycling season, from May to October, various bicycle clubs in Pittsburgh and nearby cities organized high-wheel races, which were generally held on weekends and holidays at outdoor tracks before a paying public. The events typically covered between one-half and two miles, with the winner collecting a token prize, not to mention the crowd's adulation.

That Decoration Day, in 1887, Lenz entered his first cycling contest, witnessed by a festive crowd of one thousand. He had traveled by train to Beaver Falls, a small town thirty miles northwest of Pittsburgh. Facing several competitors, he was to make four circuits to complete a mile. "He undoubtedly would have won the novice race," the *Bulletin* reported, "had it not been that the track was slippery and his wheel slid from under him on the first lap." He did manage to prevail in the consolation race, finishing a mile in four minutes less eighteen seconds.

A few months later, in August, Lenz tried another variety of competition: a twenty-mile road race outside Pittsburgh hosted by his own Allegheny Cyclers. The scorching heat had reduced the field to six, including the two favorites, the brothers William (W. D.) and Albert (A. C.) Banker. These club mates were widely considered the strongest wheelmen in western Pennsylvania, and they relished their stature. The family ran a bicycle store in Pittsburgh that specialized in Victor products (Columbia's chief rival), as well as a riding school in Allegheny.

"Lenz was sick before he started," the *Bulletin* reported, "and those who had hoped that he might give W. D. Banker a hard tussle, saw that the condition of their man precluded any such ideas." The challenger nevertheless gamely fought off cramps and gave the Bankers chase. The *Bulletin* relayed the remarks of an old lady in De Haven, who had stopped to watch the men fly by five miles into the race: "Them fellers is fools to race on a day like this," she scoffed. "Why, my old man had to knock off harvesting, it is so hot." To no one's surprise, W. D. finished first, in 1:44.5, followed by A. C., a mere second behind. Lenz arrived six minutes later, in fourth place.

By the close of his inaugural season, Lenz had begun to deliver on his considerable promise as a racer. In October, he entered a two-mile race in Pittsburgh starring A. C. Banker, who was a few months older and an inch taller than Lenz. "The day was inauspicious on account of the high wind that prevailed, raising clouds of dust and rendering anything like fast time impossible," the *Bulletin* reported, "but the prizes were an incentive that nerved each contestant to do his utmost."

Still, no one anticipated a shocking upset. "This was a genuine surprise," the *Bulletin* affirmed. "Everybody thought that Banker was a sure winner, but Lenz made a great effort on the finish and won by three yards." A stunned and humiliated Banker vowed that he would never again lose to an "inferior rider" and promptly hired a personal trainer to ensure that he avenged himself at the next opportunity.

In 1888, at the start of his second season, Lenz upgraded to a fifty-three-inch Columbia Light Roadster, which was a good twelve pounds lighter than his original mount. His performances improved markedly. For the first time, he nearly climbed Pittsburgh's Irwin's Hill, a two-hundred-yard stretch where the road rose fifty feet. That June he needed only eleven hours to make another run to New Castle and back, this time without incident. His results on the track were even more striking.

That July, before six hundred fans, Lenz took on the revenge-minded A. C. Banker. The *Bulletin* described the half-mile contest as "one of the best races between local men ever seen here," adding that "the pace was for blood from the word go. Banker was looked upon as a sure winner, though Lenz received all the encouragement." Amid deafening cheers, the popular upstart crossed the tape just ahead of his rival, registering a time of 1:33 and pocketing a pair of opera glasses. For good measure, Lenz also edged out W. D., winning the two-mile race by half a wheel.

Remarkably, Lenz was still employing a relatively heavy model designed for road use. "If Lenz gets a racer," the *Bulletin* columnist mused, "he will undoubtedly do much better than on the roadster he now rides, with a cyclometer swinging from the hub." Bowing to peer pressure, Lenz obtained Columbia's lightest model, which weighed a scant thirty pounds, just in time for the follow-up races three weeks later. In the quarter-mile open, he again made a furious spurt down the stretch in a bold bid to eclipse A. C. Banker. But this time Lenz's foot slipped, and he flew off his precarious mount. The bicycle began to flip over and over, before breaking into pieces. For his part, Lenz badly bruised his knee. He decided to go back to his trusty Light Roadster.

Despite the setback, Lenz was assuredly, as the *Bulletin* proclaimed, a "rising luminary in the racing field." But he was not satisfied being a mere local celebrity. He was, after all, a proud denizen of Pittsburgh, a city known for producing overachievers of international repute. The steel magnate Andrew Carnegie, for one, had started out as a bobbin boy in a local cotton mill and was now the world's richest man. The financier Andrew Mellon and the coke magnate turned art collector, Henry Clay Frick, had likewise amassed vast personal fortunes from nothing, not to mention George Westinghouse, the electrical pioneer who ran the factory where Lenz's stepfather labored as a machinist. To no one's surprise, when Lenz spotted an opportunity to vault into the national limelight, he seized it.

That summer, Lenz eagerly read up on a four-day cycling extravaganza scheduled to take place in Buffalo that fall in conjunction with the International Industrial Fair. Grandly billed as the "World's Cycling Tournament," the program was to feature a vast variety of safety and high-wheel track races, ranging from one-quarter of a mile to five miles in length. Effused one reporter: "There is not a champion for any distance in any country that will not be there."

The culminating event—the one that caught Lenz's eye—was to be a one-hundred-mile road race from Erie to Buffalo. As fast as he was on the track, Lenz knew well that his strong suit was long-distance racing on regular roads. In his first two seasons, he had amassed over four thousand miles riding outdoors—more than anyone else in rugged western Pennsylvania. He could just imagine himself arriving in Buffalo on the specially built track at the fairgrounds, making his victory laps while thousands of fans in the grandstand roared their approval. Where exactly a victory would take him in life he did not know. But he was certain of one thing: both cycling and fame were intrinsic to his destiny. He vowed to prepare diligently for the race.

The ambitious program was the brainchild of Henry E. Ducker, the veteran cyclist turned promoter who, earlier that decade, had introduced untold Americans to the towering "English" bicycle of his homeland. His annual tournaments in Springfield, Massachusetts, were lavish affairs that for several years drew top international talent and thousands of fans. And now he aspired to work similar magic in Buffalo by making the proposed tournament an annual event. The Queen City, whose proximity to Niagara Falls ensured a constant flow of tourists, was in fact a shrewd choice for a new cycling capital. A number of local firms were pumping out large numbers of safety bicycles, and Buffalo already boasted an expansive network of asphalted, tree-lined roads as well as several bicycle clubs, including one just for women.

The great road race, designed to bring the sport straight to the people, was the main attraction in Ducker's inaugural program. Admittedly, the idea was not entirely novel. Nearly twenty years earlier, in November 1869, James Moore had rumbled some eighty miles from Paris to Rouen atop a primitive, eighty-pound bicycle with a solid iron frame and wooden wheels. His time—nearly eleven hours—was widely considered a stunning achievement and a compelling mandate to improve bicycle construction. Five years later, the newly formed bicycle clubs of Cambridge and Oxford Universities hosted a lively intercampus race, signaling the advent of high-wheel road racing. Covering a comparable distance on a vastly improved mount, the victor required a mere eight hours. Even Americans—relative newcomers to the sport—were occasionally treated to road races. For the past several seasons, Boston-area clubs had been running an annual century race, the record time standing a shade under seven hours.

Still, Americans had never seen an outdoor cycling contest quite as enticing as the one Ducker proposed, which was destined to feature the best amateur cyclists in the land as well as posted telegraphic reports to keep the crowd at the fairgrounds apprised of the racers' progress. Their dramatic arrival on the track and a possible struggle to the finish over the final laps would provide thrilling theater unlike anything ever witnessed in the annals of American cycling. To all but guarantee that the affair would end with a new world's record, Ducker routed the course over one of the country's best highways, the flat shore road skirting Lake Erie.

At last the big day arrived. In the wee hours of September 8, Lenz boarded a train bound for Erie. Reaching the starting place, the corner of Seventh and Sassafras, he found several hundred curious citizens of Erie jammed into every accessible niche, despite the ungodly hour and the pounding rain. Obviously, neither he nor anyone else would be smashing records on this miserable day. Still, should the contest come off, the courageous winner would no doubt enjoy even greater glory. Meanwhile, to pass the time, the bare-limbed Pittsburgher, seemingly oblivious to the deluge, bantered with the crowd.

The six o'clock hour struck. The starting gun should have sounded an hour earlier, but all one could hear was the relentless rain and the murmuring of the restless crowd. The organizers were huddling together, debating whether to spring the poor devils loose into a quagmire of mud. For their part, the wheelmen quashed any talk of postponement, insisting that they would not linger another day in Erie. They all had jobs to get back to come Monday morning, and some had long train rides ahead of them. Either the great race would come off that morning or not at all.

Of course, the racers were eager to get a move on. These were, after all, the "sturdy fifteen," as one reporter pronounced the diminished field. These were the hearty ones who had refused to shy away from "an awful trial of physical stamina." They did not "dread a drenching," nor were they afraid of a little "heavy wheeling." They could do without sensational times or lusty roadside cheers. All they wanted was a clean shot at glory and the shiny gold medal offered by *Bicycling World*.

A loud cheer erupted at a quarter after six, when the organizers announced that the race was on. The cyclists dutifully scurried out from under their cover to reclaim their wheels, stowed under an expansive tarp. They were all ordinaries, except for three. One was a Star, an innovative American design that reversed the order of the large and small wheel for greater stability, and another a safety tandem. Only one, belonging to Peter J. Berlo of Boston, was a Rover pattern bicycle. That past season, its third on the American market, the "dwarf" had continued its surprising surge. And thanks to a series of refinements, the safety had considerably narrowed the performance gap. Many old-school riders now grudgingly conceded that the upstart might indeed suffice for the faint of heart. For them, however, the ordinary remained the paragon of elegance and efficiency—the only sensible choice of wheel for the serious cyclist.

As the racers took their positions, several girls scampered about handing each competitor a cup of lukewarm coffee and a small basket filled with broiled chicken and stale bread. Should the racers need more nourishment along the route, they could procure sandwiches from any of three designated roadside hotels. For any other assistance, they could appeal to the timekeepers at the six checkpoints.

Lenz felt extremely confident about his chances. For the past few months, he had been training hard, riding up and down freshly paved Forbes Avenue, zipping past horse-drawn vehicles and their irate drivers. He knew this road well, having taken it on his return from New York, and he was used to riding in rain and mud. The *Bulletin* had also voiced its confidence, affirming: "There's good stuff in Lenz, and his friends do right in expecting much of him."

The Pittsburgher was nevertheless a decided underdog, blithely dismissed by *Bicycling World* as a "delicate youth." He would indeed face stiff competition, since all the favorites remained in the running. Twenty-six-year-old Fred Eldred, the captain of the Springfield (Massachusetts) Bicycle Club, had just ridden his high bicycle twenty miles in one hour over the level roads near his hometown. The strapping and explosive Robert Gerwing of Denver was one of the top guns in the West. The swampy course seemed tailor-made for G. A. Tivy of St. Louis, nicknamed "Mud Horse." Frank Dampman, a five-foot-five dynamo rumored to relish moonlit rides over the roughest of roads, had brought along two teammates from the fabled Wilmington (Delaware) Wheel Club to pace him to victory. Among the wildcards were the local boys George McIntire of Erie and Roy Blowers of Westfield, New York.

At last the gun sounded. Lenz pushed his bicycle forward, planting a foot on the small step at the base of his bicycle's backbone. His small wheel instantly sank several inches into the mushy ground. He gamely vaulted onto his saddle and stood up on his pedals, applying all his weight and might. The stubborn creature lurched forward, just fast enough to avoid a nasty spill. Miraculously, it picked up momentum and straightened itself out as it emerged from a murky pool of water.

The racers spurted en masse toward Lake Erie. The townspeople along the way had been warned by their newspapers to expect an invasion of cyclists that morning. Had good weather prevailed, the locals would no doubt have lined the roadside to absorb the spectacle and lend their cheers. As it was, the smattering of spectators offered only faint applause. No matter. The racers would be showered with accolades soon enough, should they reach the sheltered compound in Buffalo.

Eldred, the favorite, quickly charged to the forefront and set a surprisingly fast pace. He was anxious to distance himself from the three Wilmington boys so that they could not gang up on him. Upon reaching the shore road, however, the pack was still at his heels. Eight miles out, at Harbor Creek, Eldred nursed a slim lead over the top five, with Lenz occupying fourth place, about thirty seconds off-pace. The stragglers had already fallen at least ten minutes behind.

As the vanguard approached North East, the second checkpoint fifteen miles out, the rain finally stopped. But that was small consolation since the terrain was mushier than ever. Several racers had already suffered severe spills, and all had stopped at least once to remove fistfuls of mud from their wheels. A reporter on hand got the distinct impression that the "travel stained" men were now riding "for something other than pleasure." By the time the caravan reached Ripley, the third checkpoint twenty-one miles out, the three safety riders had already abandoned the race, leaving a dozen competitors.

Just after Ripley, Eldred, too, dropped out. "He was in condition to finish," his hometown newspaper, the *Springfield Union*, would insist, "but it would have been a mere act of bravado for which there was no call. The glory of having pushed through 100 miles of mud and clay he sensibly deemed insufficient recompense for the physical disabilities that might result."

The lanky Gerwing surged to the forefront. As he passed the struggling Dampman, the cocky Denver giant ordered his diminutive challenger to "cheer up" and advised him to follow in his wake if he wanted second place. Dampman ignored the taunt and stuck with his teammate Frank McDaniels. The other Wilmington pacer, Steven Wallis Merrihew, who had suffered a mechanical mishap, soon rejoined his mates. Lenz, meanwhile, clung to fifth place, two minutes off-pace.

At Westfield, a large crowd cheered the local boy, Blowers, who was mired in the back of the pack. By Portland, thirty-six miles out, the scrappy Dampman had overtaken the deflated Gerwing to claim a narrow lead. Lenz, who seemed to be pacing himself for the long haul, continued to hang on to fifth place, though his deficit had grown to five minutes.

Nine miles later, at Fredonia, Dampman held on to his slim lead. Just behind him were his two teammates and the pesky Gerwing. Lenz continued to hold fifth place, six minutes off-pace. By Silver Creek, fifty-seven miles out, Dampman had widened his lead over his teammates to two minutes. But Lenz had suddenly sprung to life, blowing past the fading Gerwing, and was now just a minute behind the Wilmington trio.

Four miles farther on, at Irving, Lenz surged ahead to claim the lead for the first time. With less than forty miles to go, he could already taste victory. Indeed, to onlookers the fresh-faced Pittsburgher seemed like a sure winner. The roads, however, were at their soggiest, causing yet another round of tumbles. The brave few who remained in the contest were now doing more walking than pedaling. Lenz failed to pad his slim lead.

Compounding the racers' ordeal was a lack of sustenance: the promised sandwiches never materialized, and the desperate men had gone for miles without food or water. One heartless spectator emerged with a pail of milk and tried to sell drinks. He did not realize that the racers had no change in their pocketless woolen tights. Responding to their pleas, some of the spectators hopped on their own bicycles to fetch water and food. Despite their relatively fresh state, however, they were unable to deliver the goods to the contestants.

At Evans Center, about thirty miles from the finish, Dampman pulled even with Lenz. A distant third was the Star rider, who had emerged out of nowhere. Dampman's pacers, meanwhile, had seemingly fallen out of contention. McDaniels in fact had seriously damaged his machine after jumping full force onto its backbone to avoid a header. The race appeared to be coming down to a fierce duel between Lenz and Dampman.

As the racers approached Bayview, eighty-one miles out, the checker gave a sigh of relief. Unaware of their late start and underestimating the weather's toll, he had expected them a good two hours earlier. Dampman was the first to pass the checkpoint, followed closely by Lenz. But in an ominous twist for the Pittsburgher, the two Wilmington pacers, working together, had somehow managed to rejoin their leader. Lenz's situation improved slightly when Merrihew faltered once again (he would later blame his hunger), but it would still be two against one going down the home stretch.

At that point, Dampman coyly suggested to the Pittsburgher that they let McDaniels set the pace. Lenz, having noted McDaniels's damaged vehicle and exhausted state, saw no harm in that arrangement and allowed the Wilmington pacer to spurt to the forefront uncontested. As soon as McDaniels was out of their view, however, Dampman suddenly burst forward to rejoin his teammate. Lenz, ever-confident of his superior stamina, failed to react with a surge of his own.

Once Dampman regained his teammate, the two co-conspirators began to work in tandem, furiously swapping positions as they pushed themselves to the brink of exhaustion. Gradually, they widened their lead over their unsuspecting rival. Not until Lenz reached Limestone Hill, the final checkpoint ten miles from the finish, did he realize his tactical blunder. He had fallen a good eight minutes off-pace with precious little time to catch up.

Still, all was not yet lost. From that point to the fairgrounds the road was level and smooth. Drawing on his natural speed and ample reserve, Lenz knew he could still catch his treacherous rivals. But he desperately needed help. Fortunately, at this very point volunteer pacers were allowed to jump into the fray to assist the contestant of their choosing.

Lenz frantically scanned the faces of the dozen or so newcomers, hoping to find his rescuer. His pounding heart sank. Here he was, the most popular rider in all of Pittsburgh, waging the race of his life. Where the hell were his friends at this critical juncture? Where were the Banker brothers, confound it! Blind with rage, Lenz made a wrong turn, quashing any hope for a comeback victory.

Dampman and McDaniels, meanwhile, approached the fairgrounds utterly spent but with an insurmountable lead. The only question remaining was which Wilmington man would take the gold. All things being equal, McDaniels, the stockier of the two and the better sprinter, figured to prevail. But his wheel was badly damaged, and the persistent Dampman was not about to yield to his pacer without a struggle.

The animated crowd of fair goers, which numbered twenty-five thousand, braced itself for a thrilling finish. There was, however, one last snag: the track where the men were supposed to finish was utterly decimated after days of relentless rain and hard use. Ducker had made a last-minute adjustment: the racers would forgo the track and finish with a lap around the road encircling the fairgrounds.

The fans spilled out of the grandstand and planted themselves alongside the ring road, fixing their eyes on the horizon at the point where the racers were expected to appear. A Buffalo paper, the *Lightning Express*, described the chaotic scene. "Occasionally some smart Aleck would raise the cry of 'here they come' and everyone would crane his neck and strain his eyes for a sight of the vanguard." After repeated false alarms, the crowd was getting increasingly anxious.

At last, at precisely 3:42 according to a report in *Bicycling World*,

> a murmur of voices was heard in the distance, which gradually swelled into cheers, announcing that the leader was in sight. Half a hundred excited wheelmen came tearing down the road shouting and demanding a clear track. Then came a couple of the sorriest looking objects it has ever been my fortune to see: McDaniels, and right on his little wheel, Dampman. The men and the wheels they rode were one mass of mud.

As McDaniels staggered to the gate, one reporter related, he was "rapturously cheered and smiled all over. But when told that he had to continue his journey around the Park Meadow and return to the bridge his look of joy vanished in an instant." In fact, the pacer had nothing left. Dampman blew past his spent teammate and never looked back, crossing the finish line at four minutes after four—just under ten hours since the gun had sounded in Erie. His dejected mate gamely crossed the line three minutes later.

Bystanders quickly pried the groggy Wilmington men from their bicycles and carried them to awaiting cots. There the racers were at last given badly needed food and water. A Buffalo reporter noted that McDaniels was especially "fagged out," adding: "He was a pitiful sight. There was little left of his tights, and the boys threw a blanket around him to cover his nakedness."

Seven minutes after the Wilmington pair had reached the gate, Lenz appeared at the same spot. One reporter found the resigned Pittsburgher "as white as a sheet," but everyone agreed he looked much fresher than the two men from Wilmington. Informed that he had to loop around the park road, Lenz was nonplussed. This was, after all, merely a ceremonial lap, for he was comfortably ahead of the two remaining stragglers.

As Lenz methodically circled the ring road, he heard the deafening cheers directed at the Wilmington pair. It pained him to think that he would have been the object of their adulation had he run a smarter race or received a little help down the stretch. Crossing the finish line, a frustrated Lenz hollered: "Where do I go now?" The Banker brothers made a belated appearance, lifting their teammate off his bike and laying him down on a cot. While the Bankers gave him food and water, their masseur began to work on his stiff legs.

The barbaric contest had left all the entrants badly bruised and cut; one had even temporarily lost consciousness after a terrible tumble. Still, the race was a smashing success. A reporter with the *Pittsburg Times* affirmed that it was "the talk of the bicycling world." Indeed, the champions assembled in Buffalo regarded it as the "greatest feat of human endurance ever performed on a wheel." Marveled the *Springfield Union:* "No other race was ever run, or probably ever will be run, under such conditions." Many found it unfathomable that the winner could have plowed through that frightful sea of slime averaging over ten miles an hour.

For Lenz, however, the aftertaste was bitter. Although the *Bulletin* insisted that he had "covered himself in glory" and would have won had he been "better coached," he felt only the pangs of failure and betrayal. Aggravating his misery, the package he had sent from Erie, containing about $60 worth of valuables, failed to appear, leaving him without a change of clothing, a coat, or a watch. He found himself in the humiliating position of having to borrow money from the disloyal Bankers, of all people, so he could pay for new clothes and a night in a hotel room.

Fortunately, Lenz enjoyed a much-needed pick-me-up the following morning when he examined the historic bicycles on display at the industrial exhibition. He stood mesmerized before the "velocipede" of Pierre Lallement, the oldest bicycle in existence, dating back to 1865. Here was the ingenious breakthrough that had given rise to the magnificent high-wheeler. As crude as this vehicle was, it had established the surprising principle that a slender vehicle on two wheels could be steadily and continuously propelled by means of the cranks protruding from its front hub.

Ironically, given its relatively low profile, the quaint relic more closely resembled the latest Rover safety than the ordinary it had spawned. Perhaps Lallement had the right configuration after all, Lenz mused. An English writer had recently predicted that the ordinary "would soon be relegated to the place where all obsolete machines go." Of course, not everyone accepted this startling prognosis. Retorted *Bicycling World,* "The Ordinary will never be an obsolete pattern; it has far too many splendid qualities for that."

Thanks to his profuse reading of cycling literature, Lenz was well aware of Lallement's personal saga. In July 1863, the Frenchman completed a bicycle prototype in the Parisian workshop where he built baby carriages and carts. After mastering his new steed in a long corridor, he rode it along the boulevards, to the astonishment of onlookers. Two years later, in search of greater opportunity to exploit his invention, he left Paris for New York, toting the makings for an improved machine—this very bicycle.

Lallement settled in Ansonia, Connecticut, where, in the fall of 1865, he made the first bicycle ride on American soil. The following spring he rode his creation around the New Haven green. His curious gyrations attracted an investor, and the two secured the world's first patent describing a basic bicycle. But the hapless pair failed to enlist a manufacturer, and a dejected Lallement retreated to France, unaware that a velocipede craze had already erupted there in his absence. It would soon spread around the world, sparking high hopes that the long-coveted practical mechanical horse was at last at hand.

A mere toddler in early 1869 when the great velocipede craze exploded, Lenz had been too young to remember that brief episode. Indeed, the vehicle quickly lost favor once it became painfully apparent that it was not about to serve as the "people's nag" anytime soon. Nearly a decade would pass before the ordinary, developed primarily in France and England, partially filled its void. Unlike the discredited "boneshaker," the new bicycle made no practical or popular pretensions. It offered a recreational ride, pure and simple, to young, athletic males. Still, it validated the principle of the bicycle and opened a promising path for development.

Lallement himself made little from his patent, having sold it to an American maker at the peak of the craze for a fraction of its worth. Years later the patent wound up in the hands of Albert Pope, who used it as the cornerstone to a lucrative monopoly controlling domestic high-wheel production. In 1888, a few years after his patent expired, Lallement himself entered Pope's employ and was now working as a lowly mechanic in Pope's elegant Boston headquarters on Columbus Avenue—further proof, Lenz concluded, that the inventor himself rarely profits from his audacity and sweat. Lenz, who took great pride in his own mechanical ingenuity, hoped someday to meet the reclusive Frenchman.

Even more intriguing to Lenz was the nickel-plated Columbia Expert, reminiscent of his own first bicycle. It belonged to his idol, Thomas Stevens, the world-famous "globe girdler." Between 1884 and 1887, Stevens had ridden and trundled his way across three continents, covering about 13,500 miles in all. After riding from San Francisco to Boston, Stevens received the bicycle on display from Albert Pope himself and then rode it across Europe and Asia.

Lenz had eagerly devoured Stevens's firsthand accounts published in *Outing*, a monthly dedicated to sports and travel. The Pittsburgher knew all about Stevens's harrowing adventures in distant and exotic lands, his joyful encounters with foreign dignitaries, missionaries, and fellow wheelmen, and his narrow escapes from hostile men, beasts, and elements. In fact, while riding in the countryside, the young clerk would often imagine himself as Stevens, plunging into a thick Indian jungle in search of the next thrilling adventure.

Lenz simply could not fathom how any pursuit could be more exciting or satisfying than touring the world on a bicycle. Life post-tour would not be bad either, he surmised. Stevens was about to release a two-volume book set entitled *Around the World on a Bicycle*, and he was in high demand as a travel writer and lecturer, making appearances across the country. Anytime he wanted to embark on a new adventure he could afford to do so. Certainly, Lenz would rather be a famous cycle tourist than a miserable book-keeper, toiling his life away in the bowels of a dingy factory, juggling meaningless figures for a callous boss. If only he, too, could engineer such an envious arrangement, he would be off in a flash.

Shortly after Lenz returned to Pittsburgh, his lost package miraculously surfaced. As it turned out, it had never left Erie, owing to a faulty address. His elation over the return of his possessions quickly dissipated, however, when the ugly Banker affair spilled into the press. A well-meaning journalist blasted the Bankers for their failure to help out their own club mate, "a good man who is honest in his riding." The reporter alleged that A. C. Banker had even admitted that he would have helped Lenz had the latter been riding a Victor, the make the Bankers rode and sold.

Banker angrily denied the charge. Partial to the Victor, he insisted that he had merely jokingly suggested to Lenz that he would have prevailed had he been riding one, given its superior quality. In no way did he mean to insinuate that he had withheld assistance on account of Lenz's mount. Banker explained that he and his brother were unavailable simply because they were scheduled to race the next day and could not risk tiring or injuring themselves. He added that they had done all they could for Lenz, taking care of him on the fairgrounds and spotting him cash, though "not one word of thanks was vouchsafed by the object of our solicitude."

Lenz did his best to put the Banker affair and the Erie debacle behind him. Two weeks after that bitter disappointment, he entered another cycling contest in his hometown. His preparation, however, was lax. In the two-mile state championship, he finished behind both Banker brothers. In the one-mile open for amateurs, won by the reigning national champion, William W. Windle of Millbury, Massachusetts, Lenz again finished third. Although Lenz's performances were eminently respectable given the competition, they could not mask his waning enthusiasm for competitive cycling.

To be sure, Lenz still loved attention. And he knew he could hold his own with the very best on either the track or the road. Yet he always seemed to finish second-best. Perhaps he could redouble his efforts and break through to the top. But what future did racing hold for him anyway? Training was hard and time-consuming, the opportunities for glory were limited, and the material rewards were meager. Even if he became a professional, he could hardly expect to make a decent living from racing alone. Perhaps touring was his true calling after all. He loved to ride at his own pace, taking in the scenery, visiting distant cities, and meeting new people.

As the winter of 1888 set in, Lenz began to think more seriously about traveling full-time on his bicycle. If he could just persuade a publisher to send him on a world tour, he could indulge in his favorite pastime while still enjoying the respect and admiration of his peers—indeed, of the public at large. Of course, he knew that his poor mother would bitterly object to the scheme. As it was, she constantly implored him to focus on getting ahead in the workplace. She begged him to settle down and find a good girl he might want to marry someday, but Lenz refused to relinquish the idea. However far-fetched it might be, he was convinced that it offered his best, if not only, chance to roam the earth while he was still a young, unattached man.

In the spring of 1889, Lenz discovered a second love, one that would cement his transition from racer to tourist and bring him a step closer to realizing his pipe dream. Reported the *Bulletin* that April: "Lenz created quite a sensation last Sunday when he appeared out Forbes street with a big camera case and tripod strapped on his back, which has the appearance of an elongated knap-sack." Noted the columnist: "The outfit makes a considerable load but Lenz thinks he is equal to the task."

The alluring concept of a roving photographer on wheels was as old as the bicycle itself. Twenty years earlier the *Illustrated Photographer* had gushed: "A practical two-wheeler would be a great boon to an amateur, as he could go about the country with great ease and pleasure to expose his plates." Of course, the primitive bicycle was hardly ready to facilitate that romantic notion. Nor was the camera. Photographers at that time typically employed a complicated "wet" process that involved immersing glass plates in an assortment of chemicals just before exposure—in the dark no less.

Even though a few daring pioneers did in fact manage to cart all the necessary equipment on primitive bicycles, the lengthy setup time precluded anything approaching snapshots. One man who was painfully aware of this drawback was the photographer who had attended the Gettysburg address in November 1863. Having just endured a two-hour monologue by Edward Everett of Massachusetts, he felt no pressing need to start preparing his plates when the president stepped forward. "We all supposed that Lincoln would make a rather long speech—half an hour at least," recalled one witness. Two minutes later, after reading three paragraphs, the concise chief marched away from the podium—leaving the crowd hushed and the idle photographer dumbfounded. "Were the scene to be re-enacted today," reassured a contemporary journal, "the photographer could easily secure a dozen or more exposures."

In fact, thanks to simpler "dry" processes and improved wheels, cycling photographers were no longer mere abstract concepts but rather proud members of a small but growing fraternity. After joining their ranks, Lenz routinely sped off into the countryside with his wooden Blair camera and glass plates, measuring five by eight inches. Whenever he spotted an attractive scene, he dismounted and took the shot within a matter of minutes.

In August 1889, Lenz again rode to New York City and back, but this time he brought along his photographic gear. The *American Athlete* recapped his adventure:

> Lenz, recently returned from a three weeks' wheel tour, reports that he made about 150 exposures, photographing scenery of every description, towns, cities, street scenes, public buildings, bridges, canal streams—everything that looked at all inviting. His method, after making 12 exposures, was to unpack the holder, re-

fill it with fresh plates, and ship the others home by express. The big pack which contained camera and plates created no end of comment. He was taken for a peddler, drummer, and [itinerant] quack doctor. The total mileage for the trip was 836 miles, and the weight of the knapsack that burdened his broad shoulders is exactly 35 pounds.

Lenz was confident that his world tour would become a reality once he had perfected his skills as an amateur photographer. Whereas Stevens had merely sketched the passing scenery from memory, using pen and paper, Lenz was prepared to record his trip in a plethora of stunning photographs. In the meantime, he resolved to spend his month-long summer vacations taking ever-longer and more ambitious tours on his wheel. Sooner or later, he firmly believed, he would be off on "a wider flight."

2

ATHENS, GREECE

January 4, 1891

O N A B R I G H T but cool Sunday morning, two young Americans hastened up the interminable stony steps to the Pro-
pylaea, the crumbling gateway to the Acropolis. For William Lewis
Sachtleben and Thomas Gaskell Allen Jr., both steeped in the classics at Washington College in St. Louis, entering that bastion of
antiquity was no ordinary treat. "Here are the soul-inspiring monuments of the first Republic that breathe freedom," Sachtleben effused in his diary that evening. "Even the least educated person
would gaze on these remains with awe. How much more deeply
must they impress those who have studied the life of the ancient
Greeks, who have read of their heroic deeds in their own sweet
language?"

Reaching the hallowed grounds, the awestruck pair stopped to
gape at the Parthenon's gigantic marble columns rising gracefully
into the radiant sky. The men pondered how glorious this temple
must have been in the age of Pericles and wondered aloud how
the ancients could have erected such a massive structure at these
heights. "It is impossible to record my thoughts on first seeing the
ruins," gushed Sachtleben. "I looked upon them with something
akin to veneration. One has such opportunities so rarely in a lifetime that they are all absorbing when they do come."

After a leisurely stroll, the pair picked out a grassy spot by the temple of Nike Athena. There they spread out their picnic lunch, a feast of bread, figs, oranges, cakes, and sweets. They gazed at the metropolis below and the bustling port of Piraeus. In the distance, they could make out the sparkling Saronic Gulf, a smattering of islands, and the silhouette of the Peloponnesos Mountains. "One could sit among the ruins and moralize, sentimentalize, and philosophize for hours," Sachtleben noted. In fact, that was precisely their program on that unforgettable afternoon.

They began their erudite exchanges by contemplating why the cultural influence of the ancient Greeks, so pervasive some four centuries before Christ, ultimately gave way to that of the mighty Roman Empire. From there, the discussion turned to the rise and fall of great civilizations. "Then, with even greater eagerness," recounted Sachtleben, the two young men asked themselves: "How long would be the space between the acme of Roman grandeur to that of the next culminating epoch in our world's history?"

Such profound musings naturally stirred their deepest patriotic sentiments. For while the old European powers, with their vast colonies, still held considerable sway over world affairs, the youthful United States was manifestly on the rise. "Our thoughts turned proudly to America," recorded Sachtleben, "the land of freedom and progress. To it we looked and hoped to give birth to an age grander than that of Pericles, more splendid and powerful than that of Augustus." Sachtleben's conclusion was uplifting: "Greece, Rome, America, three gigantic steps in the development of civilization."

These two philosophers in fact were out to make a little history of their own. They planned to register the first "round the world" tour on safety bicycles, by now the acknowledged successor to the high-wheel bicycle and an object increasingly in demand worldwide. To that end, over the previous six months, they had already logged nearly four thousand miles apiece, riding through Great Britain, Ireland, and continental Europe. They had come to Athens to wait out the winter and restore or replace their battered bicycles before attempting the most difficult part of their journey: a seven-thousand-mile trek across Asia. Such a feat would eclipse, in both distance and daring, that of the great Thomas Stevens and doubtless secure their own places in the pantheon of cycledom.

Although they traveled in tandem, there was no mistaking the architect of this madcap scheme. At twenty-five years of age, the dark and dashing Sachtleben was a good two years older than his cohort. Moreover, with his fit 150-pound body on a 5′7″ frame, Sachtleben looked downright Olympian beside Allen, who was an inch shorter and fifteen pounds lighter. "So great is the difference between the two," remarked one astonished reporter, "one involuntarily wonders how Allen could hold his own with his more athletic friend." In fact, Allen was a determined trooper willing to follow his charismatic leader to the ends of the earth.

Sachtleben, the eldest son of a wealthy clothier in Alton, Illinois, had long enjoyed a reputation in his hometown as a feisty fighter and a free spirit prone to energetic excesses. As a boy, he excelled at baseball and marbles. He eagerly devoured Daniel Defoe's *Robinson Crusoe* and became a hearty outdoorsman himself. The summer after his sophomore year at college, he enticed four local boys to travel with him by train to Minneapolis, where they boarded a sixteen-foot raft to cruise down the Mississippi River back to Alton. One stormy night, stranded in Quincy, Illinois, the boys sought refuge in a paper mill. The alert night watchman spotted them and telephoned the police, who hauled the vagrants off to jail. The next morning the lads got an earful from the judge, much to the embarrassment of their well-heeled parents.

Allen, the only son of a county judge from St. Louis, was barely fifteen when he met Sachtleben at Smith Academy, Washington College's preparatory school. At that time, Allen was despondent, having just lost his nine-year-old sister to a sudden illness. Some years later, he would describe the tragedy in an award-winning essay published in *Student Life*, the Washington College review: "Little did I think as we strolled home from school together one June afternoon, talking of the vacation soon to come, that it was for the last time. We were playmates, she and I. Together we wandered in the woods and glens in quest of flowers. We gathered cherries from the branches which were now shading her little grave."

Sachtleben, no stranger to youthful tragedy, having lost his mother at age ten, consoled his distraught schoolmate and gradually cracked the boy's sullen shell. The two developed a special bond that carried over into their college years. They frequently studied together, and at one point they jointly managed *Student Life*. Though they began college several years apart, the precocious Allen eventually caught up to his buddy, and the two were together during their final year, when they jointly discovered the safety bicycle.

Pedaling around the world was a wildly ambitious and dangerous quest, however, even for the likes of Sachtleben and Allen. They were destined to encounter Asiatic peoples who had never even seen Westerners, let alone their strange flying machines. There was no telling what perils or hardships they might face along the way, and for that matter, there was no guarantee that they would come home alive. Nor did their proposition meet with universal approval. "You have to be an American to come up with an idea like that," scoffed one French observer after interviewing the latest pair of self-anointed globe girdlers.

To be sure, for four centuries the West had been producing and idolizing fearless explorers who routinely risked their lives, and those of their followers, to plumb the unknown. The present generation was relentlessly canvassing the last uncharted corners of the globe in Africa, the Amazon, and the Arctic. And just like those explorers, these cyclists would have to rely on their hearts and wits to survive beyond Western civilization. The explorers were courting disaster, however, for a noble scientific cause: the mapping of every square inch of the human domain, the raison d'être of the fabled London Geographical Society. To critics, the cyclists' mission lacked any such redeeming scientific value, especially since Thomas Stevens had already demonstrated that both man and machine could withstand a jaunt around the globe.

At least the young Americans would fulfill one time-honored role: educating the public about distant lands and cultures through travel writing. As Stevens himself had put it, readers would benefit from "the theatre of their experiences" without "the trouble of wandering all over the earth themselves." Long popular as a form of escapism, this genre was increasingly relevant with the rise of leisure time and disposable income combined with ever-faster means of transportation and communication. Indeed, as the twentieth century dawned, the idle rich were rapidly losing their stranglehold on international travel.

In truth, the cyclists had had no plans for such an audacious adventure when they docked in Liverpool on the fourth of July in 1890. They merely intended to tour select cities in Europe and Asia and to put a "finishing touch" on their liberal educations. (They held the only two bachelor of arts degrees issued to their graduating class of fourteen.) Figuring that bicycles could at least partially fulfill their transportation needs, they immediately purchased a pair of hard-tired Singer safeties for about $80 apiece— nearly half the going rate at home.

Mounting their forty-pound wheels, loaded with an additional fifteen pounds of gear, the pair proceeded south to the charming medieval city of Chester. After visiting the famous castle of Caernarfon in Wales, they rode to Holyhead on Anglesey Isle, where they sailed to Dublin. They then made a clockwise loop around the northern tip of the Emerald Isle, passing through the famous Giant's Causeway where rows of basalt columns meet the North Sea. From Belfast, they sailed to Glasgow, whereupon they slowly made their way south toward London.

By mid-August, the two young tourists had already cycled more than one thousand miles. Sachtleben would later characterize this stretch as the highlight of their entire journey. They felt quite at home in the birthplace of the modern bicycle, where wheelmen were ever-present. Everywhere they enjoyed fine roads, gorgeous scenery, good food, and restful nights at cozy inns.

Although the joys of cycle touring had far exceeded their expectations, they still entertained no thought of girdling the globe on their wheels. That idea dawned one evening after a chance encounter at a village inn in Galashiels, Scotland, near the English border. There the Americans met two English travelers who had just returned from Constantinople. In gory detail, the Britons described the bold Armenian uprising they had witnessed in that city on July 15 and the brutal response of Turkish soldiers. The cyclists listened intently, feeling both revulsion and fascination. Ever the adventure seekers, they resolved to include Turkey in their travels.

And then it occurred to Sachtleben: why not bicycle all the way to Constantinople upon reaching the European mainland? After all, they had enjoyed cycling so much—why stop? Moreover, as he had discovered, "it is easier to travel by bicycle than with bicycle." For that matter, if they could get as far as Turkey, why not keep going all the way across Asia to the Pacific coast? From there, they could catch a steamer to the West Coast. At that point, all they would have to do to complete a global circuit à la Thomas Stevens would be to pedal across the United States.

True, they would face strange languages and cultures, not to mention poor roads, hostile citizens, and extreme hardships—but why not have a little youthful fun?

Settling in London in early September, the pair began to set their wild scheme in motion. First, they struck a series deal to help cover the projected costs. The *Penny Illustrated Paper* (*PIP*), a popular weekly, agreed to pay for periodic progress reports. John F. Walters of the Iroquois Cycle Company furnished two of his Minnehaha safeties featuring light nickel-plated frames, blue rims, and the latest "cushion" tires—hollow rubber tubes designed to give a soft ride. With Walters's help, they also designed, patented, and procured leather bags customized to fit neatly inside the central triangle of their bicycle frames.

Though novices at photography, they were determined to record their exploits on film. They had heard about the new Kodak film camera, a remarkably compact wooden box introduced with the slogan "You press the button—we do the rest." In fact, once a roll was completed, the owner sent the entire camera back to the factory to have the film developed and reloaded.

Paying a visit to the London sales office of the manufacturer, the Eastman Dry Plate and Film Company, they met William Hall Walker. This American inventor, in collaboration with George Eastman, had designed Kodak's roll holder. The cyclists purchased two Kodak No. 2's, the latest model, which sold for about $35. With every roll, it took up to one hundred circular, black-and-white "snap shots" measuring three and a half inches in diameter. Walker showed the young men how to load and unload the film in the dark, but explained that they would have to send the rolls to the factory for development.

To secure travel papers, the cyclists called on the embassies of the four foreign powers whose territories they would be traversing: Turkey, Persia, Russia, and China. The incredulous Ottoman and Russian officials would do no more than write letters of introduction, deferring any decisions to their colleagues in Constantinople and Teheran, respectively. The Persian minister demanded to see their bicycles and gear. The Chinese minister was the most uncooperative of all, warning that he could not vouch for their safety. Nor would he even consider the bizarre request without a letter of introduction from the American minister in London.

The lads thus paid a visit to Robert Todd Lincoln, the only surviving child of the assassinated president. The bewildered minister fetched several enormous atlases from his bookcase to study their proposed route. He quickly surmised the foolhardiness of their venture. "Do your fathers know what you're up to?" he demanded at last. Sachtleben responded with a "good old-fashioned Alton fib," adding that they planned to proceed with or without papers. The exasperated minister reluctantly wrote out a letter to the Chinese minister requesting his cooperation. Handing it to Sachtleben, Lincoln muttered: "I would much rather not have written it."

The young men purchased maps and joined the Cyclists' Touring Club (CTC), the popular London-based organization that promoted two-wheel travel. Although they were headed well beyond its reach, they identified with the club's ideals. "Traveling always by first class," Sachtleben explained, "is like staying in your own country. There is such a thing as too much convenience. For our part, we have long since tired of trains and artificial, modern hotels. We love to roam on our bicycles, unfettered, among the scenes of unsophisticated nature and the common people."

As summer drew to a close, the lads went public with their plans. *PIP* published a studio portrait of the aspiring globe girdlers seated on their loaded bicycles. Their compact luggage carriers held all their modest gear, which included "a complete change of clothing, toilet fittings, revolver, writing materials and a Kodak camera." Noted the paper: "The whole outfit, including valise, weighs exactly 36 pounds, being 20 pounds lighter and much stronger than their earlier mounts."

On September 16, 1890, the newly famous pair headed to the port of Southampton, escorted by fawning members of the Catwick Bicycle Club. At Newhaven, they were delighted to learn from the manager of their CTC-approved hotel that Thomas Stevens had slept there on his tour. Before retiring for the night, they gave their first in-depth interview to a reporter from the Associated Press. The next day the cyclists took the overnight ferry to Dieppe, where they started their tour of continental Europe.

After a weeklong romp over the verdant hills of Normandy, they reached Paris. They spent ten days in the capital city, exploring its sites and cavorting with members of a cycling club. They quickly became almost as comfortable and conversant in France as they had been in Great Britain. The day of their departure their French friends escorted them south to the cathedral town of Chartres for a boisterous farewell banquet.

Arriving in Bordeaux in mid-October, they were heartily received by the staff of *Velo Sport*, a cycling weekly. The editor, an experienced cycle tourist, admired their tenacity, audacious itinerary, and lightweight gear. He questioned, however, the wisdom of traveling without brakes or lanterns. He also talked them out of going to Spain, just then afflicted with an outbreak of cholera. Following another lively banquet, the lads proceeded toward Italy via southern France.

Over the next few weeks, the cyclists collected a host of pleasant memories, many captured on film. Near Perigueux, they watched peasants harvest grapes. Farther along, a marquis served them a lavish meal at his country estate. While crossing rugged central France, they took in breathtaking natural scenery. At Garabit, they admired Gustave Eiffel's newly constructed viaduct, the world's highest bridge, spanning a canyon some five hundred feet below. At Nimes, they toured the ancient Roman arena and the famous Maison Carrée. They lingered at the papal palace in Avignon before reaching the magnificent Mediterranean coast.

Passing into Italy early on All Saints' Day, the first of November, the travelers were suddenly disillusioned. The roads were markedly poorer, and the carriage drivers were loath to yield to the rare cyclist. Streaking through small towns, they drew cold stares as women looked up from their chores and men eyed them from their gambling tables. To the cyclists' disgust, they discovered that many cities forbade cycling in the streets. "The fact is, the bicycle of today is a form of nineteenth century progress and cannot be barred or restricted," Sachtleben huffed in his report to *PIP.* "It is only a question of time before some form of it will be as common a vehicle as the modern carriage."

But soon they began to feel at home in the sunny land celebrated for its warm hospitality and fine cuisine. In Genoa, they met with members of the local cycling club, who gawked at their svelte wheels and cushion tires. Their friends gave them a tour of the town, showing them the house of Christopher Columbus. When the Americans finally set off to cross the Apennines, they were told that it would be "impossible" to pedal for the first fifteen miles. Undaunted, the pair managed to reach the highest village without dismounting, and just in time for lunch. Afterward, they charged down the mountains at breakneck speed, resting their feet on the footrests while their pedals spun furiously.

Entering the Po Valley, the cyclists veered northward through

Brescia. They passed the southern shore of the spectacular Lago di Garda, Italy's largest lake, with its five sparkling island jewels. In Milan, the cyclists had an enjoyable meeting with fellow wheelmen who had read of their presence in the newspapers. From there it was smooth sailing to Verona, the legendary home of Romeo and Juliet. Passing through Padua, they reached Venice. There they treated themselves and their wheels to a gondola ride, drawing quizzical looks. Zigzagging their way down the boot of Italy, they rolled through fertile plains to Ferrara and Bologna.

Heading to Florence, they again crossed the Apennines, but this time the going was much tougher. They had to walk many miles between mountain villages, at times in total darkness. In mid-November, the cyclists reached the city of David, where they stopped for a few days to take in the numerous treasures of art. One afternoon they rode their bicycles in Piazza della Signoria, only to find themselves being marched to the local police station in step with two officers and hundreds of curious citizens. The offenders elected to pay hefty fines rather than languish in jail for a night.

The cyclists charged over the hills of Chianti country, visiting Sienna and Viterbo. In Rome, they rode freely about town and even made laps within the Coliseum. On their last night, some forty members of a local bicycle club hosted a banquet in honor of the Americans at their elegant clubhouse. Rolling down the Mediterranean coast past olive orchards and orange groves, the cyclists reached Naples in mid-December. Resident cyclists led them through the city's narrow streets and took them on excursions to Mount Vesuvius and Pompeii before throwing a ball on the eve of their departure.

The lads again crossed the Apennines, heading east and braving the cold. They spent Christmas Day in Foggia as guests of an American engineer. A man on a donkey told them in perfect English that he had worked in New York as a blacksmith for three years, making $2.50 a day. He longed to go back, for in Foggia he barely made a fifth of that sum. At Bari on the Adriatic coast, Sachtleben's crank axle snapped, forcing the pair to take a train to Brindisi. On New Year's Day, they sailed to the Greek isle of Corfu. After a day of sightseeing, they took another ship to Patras. There they boarded a train to Athens, skirting magnificent coastal bluffs.

In the ancient Greek capital, they settled into a modest hotel and quickly adjusted to local life. Their smattering of modern Greek, as well as their French, came in quite handy. Typically, they started their day at a café, sipping thick coffee and devouring heaps of doughnuts sprinkled with honey. In between errands to the bank, post office, and grocery store, they visited libraries and museums. Sachtleben often rode their one working bicycle in the city, drawing enormous crowds. In the countryside, he relished a good race against farmers driving mule carts. In the evenings, the cyclists holed up in their quarters and exercised their fountain pens.

"It seems as if we can never finish writing," Sachtleben groused. In addition to their numerous letters home, the cyclists penned reports to *PIP*, which the Coventry review *Wheeling* pronounced "remarkably particular as to trifles." They tallied their riding days in Europe: seventy-five in England, forty-four in France, and sixty-one in Italy. Their daily totals ranged from forty-two to fifty-two miles. Of the four thousand miles they traveled in all, the pair trudged some five hundred on foot. The miles they covered with assistance included one hundred by rail, fifteen on horseback, ten in carriages, and five in a gondola. Their financial accounting was no less precise. Each cyclist had spent over $600, including minuscule offerings to street musicians and church beggars.

Despite their routines, the Americans' days in Athens were anything but predictable. Shortly after their visit to the Acropolis, on January 6, 1891, they were surprised to find everything shut down. They soon learned that it was the Greek Christmas. They were better prepared for the corresponding New Year's Eve, when they donned costumes and wheeled their way around the revelers. The next day they awoke to the sound of cannon volleys. Following a military band, Sachtleben arrived at the royal palace just as a bevy of elegant ladies spilled out from a reception. He marveled at "all the gold lace, silk, satin and jewels," adding: "I saw plenty of bare arms and low necked dresses, but no pretty faces."

Once, Sachtleben spotted an ornate carriage as it pulled away from the palace gate. He managed to get close enough to the royal couple to snap a photograph and was elated when the young monarch turned his head back to smile and wave. Not all surprise encounters, however, were as pleasant. One afternoon Sachtleben was passing by a café when chairs suddenly began to fly through the air. He watched in horror as two men came to blows. One brandished a knife, while the other produced a pistol and began firing at his overmatched foe from point-blank range. Fortunately, the police soon arrived, rescued the wounded man, and took both combatants into custody.

One day the young men watched the elaborate state funeral of Heinrich Schliemann, the famed German archaeologist who, twenty years earlier, discovered Homer's lost city of Troy in modern-day Turkey. He had died the week before in Italy, and per his arrangement, he was about to be buried in his beloved Greece. "It seemed as if all Athens was out from the number of carriages," Sachtleben noted. "We followed the procession a piece to the graveyard, but turned back before reaching it, the crowd was so thick." On the way back, they saw a simpler, but no less striking, funeral led by chanting priests. "You could see the dead body and face," Sachtleben recalled. "She was dressed in white garments and her hair was flying loose in the wind."

Everyday people often provided curious spectacles as well. Several times Sachtleben observed frantic firemen, wearing cumbersome coats, as they dashed off to duty with overflowing pails. The workmen restoring ruins were methodical, though woefully ill-equipped. Sachtleben's favorite street character was an industrious milkman who employed a "slow, curious but good way" to deliver fresh milk. His goats at his side, he "knocked at the doors of his customers and inquired how much they needed. Forthwith, he milked out the requisite amount and handed it over."

No mere passive observers, the cyclists enjoyed an active social life. Naturally, they were quick to introduce themselves to resident diplomats. The American minister to Greece, A. Loudon Snowden, took an instant liking to the young men and regularly invited them to dine at his luxurious home, where a large American flag flew over the doorway. His son, a budding cyclist, was surprised to learn from Sachtleben that the mile record for the low mount stood at a mere 2:30, nearly half a minute faster than the comparable high-wheel record.

The cyclists also became friendly with the American consul, J. Irving Manatt, a former professor of Greek archaeology who had left a comfortable post at the University of Nebraska in order to be closer to his beloved ruins, bringing along his wife and their five children. Unlike the Snowdens, however, he was no conversationalist. "As soon as one gets outside the range of his own life, that is, Greece and antiquities, he is not much good," Sachtleben lamented, adding, "He impresses me as a man not very well fitted for his position."

Athens being quite cosmopolitan, the cyclists quickly met a host of colorful characters, none more so than Serope A. Gürdjian, an Armenian American who had graduated from Bowdoin College fourteen years earlier. Charismatic and cerebral, he spoke fluent English, Turkish, and Persian, as well as several other languages. A trained photographer, he was especially drawn to their Kodak cameras, but he also admired their bicycles and was full of travel advice. The trio began to meet at cafés in the daytime and in their respective hotel rooms in the evenings to talk for hours on end.

One night, while playing host, Gürdjian delved into his trunk and pulled out photographs from his college days in Maine. He loved his adopted country, he explained, and could easily have found good work in Washington as a bureaucrat. But his heart was in his homeland, and in December 1878 he had set sail for Constantinople to found a college for Armenians. After that effort fell through, he reluctantly retreated to the United States. Four years later, he managed to return to Turkey, where he had pursued various mining projects until his recent removal to Athens.

At that point, the boys were in for a shock. "We found out that our Armenian friend had been one of the ringleaders of the July 15th rebellion in Constantinople," Sachtleben scrawled in his diary. Indeed, Gürdjian utterly despised Sultan Abdul Hamid II, the despot who had seized power fifteen years earlier and revoked constitutional reform. Declared the refugee: "I wish his damned carcass would rot in a place worse than hell." Recorded Sachtleben: "Gürdjian proudly declared that this was the first rebellion that had ever taken place in the capital of Turkey. Then, with a wicked twinkle in his small black eyes, he said it wouldn't be the last."

His true identity revealed, Gürdjian launched into a hateful tirade. "The Turk embodies all the lowest attributes in the human race," he ranted. "Selfish, brutal, and cruel he hesitates at nothing. If he thinks he can gain by committing a murder, he will do so." Sachtleben reflected: "I believe Gürdjian would have every Turk murdered, if he had his way." Still, the cyclist understood why his friend harbored such blind animosity, observing: "We at home in America little dream of the atrocities that are being enacted by the Turks against the defenseless Armenians."

According to Gürdjian, the Islamic faith as practiced by the Turks perpetuated both the "rotten hulk of the Ottoman empire" and the oppression of the Armenians. Fumed the rebel:

> Nothing will ever improve as long as the Koran is taught as at present. The book itself is not bad but it is wrongly construed and interpreted. They consider everyone who does not profess Mohammadism an Infidel. "There is but one God and Mohammed was his prophet." This is their cry and has always been. Under the fanaticism infused into them from childhood they march to certain death with calmness. With this cry on their lips they feel composed to any fate, feeling sure of a reward in heaven.

One evening, as the young Americans sat in rapt silence, Gürdjian lit a cigarette and recounted his recent arrest in Constantinople:

I had rented a suite on the third floor and was giving lessons to a young Armenian named Grigor. The porter came up and told us some friends wished to see me. He had been instructed not to mention that they were three policemen, one officer and one secret detective waiting to seize me below.

"Who is it?" I asked.

"Some friends who cannot come up."

"Well I won't go out tonight. If any one wants to see me, let him come up."

So in a few moments, with a great rattling of swords, the five came in and told me to come along. I refused to go. They were going to take me by force when I jerked away and went into the next room and brought out my passport. "Do you see that?" I cried. "I am a citizen of the U.S. You have no right to take me out at such a time of night. Go to the U.S. Embassy and get an order from the Minister."

Unfazed, the officers seized the suspect and dragged him half-naked to the local police station. Continued Gürdjian:

I protested again and showed my passport a second time, again to no purpose. The officer said I must go to the head office. So I was marched through the streets with two soldiers on each side. I was brought before an officer who ate and drank, although the Koran forbids the drinking of wine. This officer asked after a long pause:

"Where do you come from?"

"From America," I replied.

"Where were you born?"

"In Caesarea in Armenia."

Then I protested against this ill-treatment and again held up my passport and claimed the right of American citizenship. "Let's see that passport" said the piggish officer. Taking it, he threw it without a glance to one side and ordered me to be imprisoned.

Gürdjian was then dumped in a "cold and damp" dungeon "built entirely of stone about five square feet with an iron door. Here, without any covering, I had to pass my time in utter darkness. This gave me a bad cold and brought me the illness of which I am still suffering. In the morning my trouble was lightened. Mr. Hirsch [Solomon Hirsch, the U.S. minister] had learned of my predicament and demanded my immediate dismissal. This frightened the Sublime Porte and he hastily sent an order for my release."

The Americans became so attached to their Armenian friend, and he to them, that the trio decided to rent a large room together. Gürdjian and Sachtleben promptly went out and purchased, after some haggling, a little coal stove. From then on, the three dined in, and every evening they gathered around a pan of hot coals to read and discuss classical works such as Thomas Moore's *Lalla-Rookh*, an Oriental verse-romance. Their conversations touched on everything from the latest news to eternal questions such as "is there anything in man besides material substance?"

The men became quite comfortable in their cozy confines. On one occasion, the cyclists took turns cutting each other's hair. "The result was two handsome young fellows, of course," Sachtleben recorded. "Allen, however, made a miscue and cut my hair a little irregularly, so that I had to keep my cap on to obscure it." One day, when Allen's feet hurt so badly that he could barely walk, he nonchalantly employed what Sachtleben termed a "quack remedy": soaking his feet for hours in bovine intestines. "What miraculous powers that pot contained I didn't have faith to see," confessed Sachtleben. "Still, Allen said he felt better afterwards."

One night Gürdjian brought over an Armenian friend who spoke no English. The conversation turned to developments in American politics since Gürdjian's departure eight years earlier. Allen vividly recounted the infamous Haymarket affair of May 1886, when a demonstration in Chicago in favor of an eight-hour workday took a violent turn. Someone in the crowd hurled a bomb, and when the fumes and mayhem subsided, seven police officers lay dead on the street. Eight anarchists were arrested and tried, and four were eventually executed.

As Gürdjian began to translate Allen's remarks for his friend, the two Armenians suddenly burst into a shouting match and nearly came to blows. When they finally calmed down, a mystified Sachtleben asked Gürdjian what all the fuss had been about. "I'm afraid he's an anarchist," Gürdjian explained. Taken aback, Sachtleben turned to the man to ask, in French, if that was true. The Armenian glared back and retorted: "You have plenty of money, why haven't I?" A stunned Sachtleben confined his reaction to his diary: "You had better not come to America, my friend, or you, too, might decorate a scaffold someday."

The cyclists also met Basilios Georgiou (B. G.) Kapsambelis, whose family had made a fortune in the fabric industry. Sachtleben described their initial encounter:

> I had no sooner sat down at a café with Gürdjian when a Greek gentleman, young and well-dressed, came up to me and said "Excuse me, but do you teach how to ride a bicycle?" I laughed and replied that I was not in that business. He asked how long it would take me to teach him. I said I could teach any one who tried hard in 15 minutes. He asked me to come up to his house at 40 Socrates street in a quarter of an hour.

The American innocently agreed, without fully realizing what he was in for.

As soon as Sachtleben entered the residence, several servants ushered him into an elegant parlor. B. G. promptly appeared with his brother, a lawyer, and the siblings led their guest to a room containing two bicycles, one a safety, the other a high-wheeler. B. G. explained that the wheels had arrived from England two weeks earlier, but the brothers had yet to master the art of cycling. "They were in a pretty fix," Sachtleben concluded.

While the American was examining the pristine wheels, a servant handed him a glass of cognac. After taking a few reluctant sips, Sachtleben announced that he would be happy to teach the brothers how to ride the safety. He volunteered his own mount to serve as the second steed. The brothers acceded, and off the trio went to the seashore. "In a half-hour both rode quite well,"

Sachtleben recorded, adding that the brothers "expressed their heartfelt thanks."

One evening the Kapsambelis family invited the Americans to their seaside mansion in Piraeus. Recorded Sachtleben:

> Our dinner consisted of beef, ham sausage with salad, a soft boiled egg and dessert of fine rice pudding. Besides we had bottled beer, red wine, and cigarettes. We passed a very pleasant hour at the table and then were ushered into the sitting-room and treated to music. Their eldest sister and brother played a duet on the piano accompanied by another brother on the violin. The trio played very well indeed and reminded me of home.

Vying with Gürdjian for the attention of the American cyclists, if not their affection, was a German expatriate named Anton von Gödrich. Formerly an army officer with impeccable bourgeois credentials, he had abandoned a diplomatic career to indulge in his favorite pastime: riding his beloved high-wheeler. Four years earlier he had chosen Athens as his base, and two years earlier he had founded the city's first cycling club. At present, he was earning pocket money by advising a major cycle manufacturer in Dresden while producing a steady stream of articles for German cycling magazines.

This man, too, they had met on the streets, after Gödrich spotted the Americans clutching their one functional wheel. Sachtleben recorded the episode: "He came up, shook us by the hand and proceeded to rattle away at me in German. I understood all, but Allen, only a sentence now and then. He was short (fully 3 inches shorter than us) and stout. He was evidently a cyclist judging by his dress. Looked as if he was a strong rider."

He was indeed. The year before, Gödrich had propelled his high-wheeler over common roads some three hundred miles in a single day—a new world record. He also loved to tour foreign lands on his big wheel. In fact, he was something of a globetrotter himself, having cycled all over Europe, North Africa, and Asia Minor. Gödrich boasted that he knew useful phrases in a dozen languages, and he planned to cycle in virtually every country over the next few years.

Sachtleben quickly sized up the diminutive German, however, as a hopeless curmudgeon who "clung to his big wheel, when the whole world was turning to the safety." The American was also put off by Gödrich's obsession with clubs and all their rigmarole, so patently out of tune with the new independent spirit of cycling. "He proudly said he was a member of the General Union of Veloci-pedists, the largest cycling organization in the world," Sachtleben noted. "When we told him that we didn't care two cents for any kind of Union his countenance fell."

Despite their common passion for bicycle touring, their phi-losophies were as disparate as their chosen vehicles. "This fellow, German-like in his thoroughness, started to do every country on a bicycle," Sachtleben related. "From what I could glean, he was not going in a direct line but jumping around here and there. He had been at it three years and was still unknown in London, the great-est place for cycling in the world. His trip will consume a dozen years at that rate."

Even Gödrich's admirable policy of learning phrases in the local lingo wherever he roamed had little appeal for Sachtleben. "What good all the petty languages of Egypt, Palestine, Turkey, and Asia will do for him I don't see," the American huffed. "These countries play such an insignificant part in the world's affairs that I am even in doubt sometimes whether it pays to travel through them."

What irked Sachtleben most about the German, however, was his massive ego. After professing surprise that the Americans had not read about him, Gödrich proceeded to monopolize their con-versation. "We couldn't mention a town or city or country where he had not been," Sachtleben grumbled. "Otherwise it was impos-sible if he had not seen it. When we politely informed him that we were on the same arduous enterprise [going around the world], he could not have been more astonished."

In Sachtleben's estimation, Gödrich was an insufferable know-it-all, a species foreign to the average American, who is "subjected to such sharp competition in all lines that he soon finds out he can be perfect only in one, and even that with difficulty." That Gödrich happened to be German was something of a letdown to Sachtleben. "Being to a certain degree German myself," he wrote in his diary, "I had always thought the Germans were a modest, unassuming people. This chap knocked my belief sky high." Upon further reflection, Sachtleben conceded: "Perhaps I myself am a bit troubled with a little of this same failing. If so, I shall endeavor to keep my mouth shut unless my experience is desired."

Still, for all his flaws, Gödrich was nothing if not friendly. The day after their initial encounter, he called on the Americans at their apartment and insisted that they visit his clubhouse for an evening of entertainment. "It consisted of two small rooms in Northern Athens," Sachtleben reported,

> decorated in German fashion as nearly all the members are Germans. Greek wine, German songs and music constituted the program. We drank but little wine and smoked no cigars. Four Greek ladies, two old and two young, were present. The gentlemen had no regard for them, smoking before them with perfect nonchalance. These girls remind one of wooden posts put up for ornament. They are stiff, ill at ease, and never utter a word or smile unless in a whisper between themselves. They would be termed wall-flowers in America.

Against their wishes, the Americans soon found themselves the center of attention—and forced to defend their choice of wheel. "Gödrich had imbued all the members with a love for the high wheel," Sachtleben recounted. One "thick-skulled German" even insisted: "There's more fun in the high wheeler. It is more difficult to learn and when you fall, you fall harder." Sachtleben resisted the urge to snicker. To him, it was obvious which pattern represented the machine of the future. When fully loaded, the German's big wheel weighed a hefty seventy pounds, nearly as much as the two Minnehahas, with gear, put together. And while the German strapped his bulky luggage to his handlebars, the Americans' luggage was "neatly packed away between our knees in the frame of the machine." Still, "the German had the audacity to tell us point-blank that his machine was superior. It was amusing."

Compounding their discomfort, Gödrich disparaged their plans to cycle through Asia Minor come springtime. "You can never go where I have been in Turkey," he insisted. "I had to obtain special permission from the bandits, who let me pass safely." The German's misgivings were grave and numerous. "Gödrich gave us the most frightful description of the road we were going to follow. We listened as politely as possible while he chattered away. In the first place, the season was bad. The mud would be a foot deep. We would have to swim swollen streams and fight brigands. We would lose our way and a dozen other objections. He concluded that we simply could not do it." Gloated Sachtleben: "It remains to be seen if his 'impossible' is the same as that Italian word."

Finally, at midnight, the beleaguered Americans made their escape. They would keep their vow never to return to that clubhouse. Still, Gödrich would have the last laugh. That spring, after the Americans left Athens, he would fire off numerous letters to European cycling journals denouncing the Americans as frauds. Read one litany: "During their stay in Athens they were rarely seen on a bicycle, nor did they associate with the local cyclists. In fact, they spoke quite snidely about amateur sport, stating it was useless to be a member of an association." Gödrich charged that the Americans were riding simply to promote their cushion tires and absurdly light bicycles. "They speak quite boldly about cycling around the world," he seethed, "but mostly they travel by train and ship. Showmen like these are an insult to true sportsmen and a menace to cycling."

After that unpleasant evening, Sachtleben and Allen chose to ignore Gödrich altogether. But they could not so easily dismiss his dire warnings about the road through Turkey. They appealed to Gürdjian, who knew the area well. Alas, he affirmed that the territory was utterly lawless, adding that the Russians had just expelled a fresh wave of desperate Circassians who were now stalking travelers along all the major routes of Turkey. Fearing that they might "strike Turkey at the worst possible moment," the cyclists began to consider a safer and shorter route through Alexandria, Cairo, Jerusalem, and Baghdad.

Either way, they would need new, sturdier bicycles. In fact, they were ready to dump Walters. It had taken him two weeks to send a new axle, and when it finally arrived, they had to pay extra postage. Then they discovered that it was too short. They had to track down a blacksmith who could make the necessary washers. "I have determined to go on my own resources hereafter and not depend on Walters for one single thing," vowed an exasperated Sachtleben. "He does not slight on purpose but has the constitutional failing of never tending to affairs promptly."

The tourists decided that Allen should travel back to London by train to settle matters with Walters. At the same time, Allen was to seek more favorable terms with both the journal and the Eastman company. Recounted Sachtleben: "We drew up two contracts in the most lawyer-like manner to present to the *P.I.P.* editor and to Walters. If Walters failed to sign, we intended to drop him and his bicycle altogether. And if *P.I.P.* would not pay our expenses we also intended to drop them and take to another paper. Besides this, our arrangement with Walker (of the Eastman Film company) would necessarily have to be altered."

On the morning of February 4, Allen busily prepared for his departure. To avoid any potential embarrassment, Allen elected to mask his identity. He shaved off his mustache, dyed his eyebrows, and donned an elaborate disguise courtesy of B. G., who had supplied a suit, a high silk hat, spectacles, and a cane. Sachtleben, meanwhile, grabbed his bicycle and dashed over to the American consulate to obtain a form granting Allen power of attorney.

Reaching the office, Sachtleben found Manatt at his desk. The consul promptly produced a form for the cyclist to fill out. After collecting the fee, the bureaucrat dutifully stamped the document. Sachtleben stashed it in his valise and made a move toward the door. Just then, Manatt cordially invited the cyclist to return later that afternoon to join him on a tour of the nearby American School. Sachtleben was little enthused by the proposition but accepted it so as not to offend the dull but sympathetic official.

At the train station, Sachtleben barely recognized his companion, who was standing beside the tracks chatting with B. G. Their Greek friend had come to give his regards to Allen and also to ask Allen to make inquiries in London on his behalf regarding his plans to import British bicycles. Just then, Allen's train steamed in from Piraeus. The Greek vigorously shook Allen's hand. Sachtleben followed suit, fighting back tears. "For the first time in nearly eight months," he recorded that evening, "Allen and I were to be separated for more than a few hours."

As soon as the train pulled away, a somber Sachtleben dashed over to the Manatt residence to keep his appointment. "I was astonished when the door was opened by Manatt's lovely daughter of 19," Sachtleben recorded that evening. "She was dressed in an entirely black dress with low cut neck. I lost my command and could hardly say anything bright or original. I soon rallied, however, and wound up gallantly." Stowing his bicycle in the flowery courtyard, the cyclist learned that Winnie was the name of this petite brunette with sparkling blue eyes. "But I was not granted much time to spoon. Mr. Manatt was quickly prepared and off we went to the American School."

Sachtleben soon found himself in a classroom with half a dozen students who sat in a semicircle, semiconscious. At the head stood an elderly professor who was droning on about ancient Greek battlefields. "The subjects were dull and uninteresting, as well as the manner of delivery," concluded Sachtleben. At the school, he met a number of students of both sexes from all over the United States, but his thoughts were still firmly fixed on winsome Winnie.

The cyclist politely excused himself and headed back to the

Manatt residence to retrieve his bicycle. "I wished not to draw any attention," Sachtleben professed in his diary,

> but the vigilant eyes of the Consul's lovely daughter were on the alert. Consequently, I had a private interview with her in the back yard. It is impossible for me to recall the many sweet and foolish things I said in her angelic presence. She, and of course I as well, talked of what a fine time we could have making short excursions on a bicycle. I informed her that I should be delighted to teach her how to ride, and that seemed to tickle her very much. But she expressed the deepest regret that it would be impossible for her to obtain a ladies bicycle in Athens. She then hinted how fine it was to be on the Acropolis in the moonlight and how sentimental such a walk would be one fine evening. But I failed to propose a trip up there, for what reason I can hardly say.

As the days passed by, Sachtleben was increasingly tempted to act on Winnie's romantic overtures. He was lonely without Allen, and tiring of wintry Athens. "Surely I would enjoy such a sweet, lively American girl by myself," he confessed in his diary. Still, he hesitated to embrace the opportunity. At best, theirs would be a harmless dalliance, but a blot on his gentlemanly record nonetheless. And what if he really fell for her, or she for him? Soon Allen would return, and the globe girdlers would be off once more to face their destiny. The physical and emotional toll from so long a journey would be onerous enough—he had no need to risk unnecessary heartache.

3

PITTSBURGH

August 9, 1891

F RANK LENZ STOOD beside the trolley tracks at the entrance
to the Smithfield Street Bridge, a massive iron structure
spanning the Monongahela River and connecting Pittsburgh's
downtown to points south. With one hand, he steadied his Columbia Light Roadster, which was loaded with about twenty pounds of
gear distributed in two compact packs, one strapped atop the handlebars, the other just below the seat, on the backbone. On his own
back he carried a bulging camera case, which, when full, added another twenty pounds to his burden.

Standing beside Lenz that misty morning was his constant companion, Charles H. Petticord, who was holding up a laden high-
wheeler of his own. Completing the lineup of wheelmen were the
youthful Friesell brothers, H. Edmund ("Ned") and Frederick C.
("Charles"), both clasping hard-tired safeties, and John Ward, another defender of the increasingly obsolete ordinary. On cue, the
quintet spun around to face Lenz's mounted camera. They raised
their caps and cracked faint smiles while a small crowd of well-
wishers looked on and cheered. Moments later, the cycle tourists
were rolling across the bridge.

Lenz and Petticord were off on a twelve-hundred-mile excursion to New Orleans, calculated to last the balance of the month.
Their entourage would accompany them only as far as Browns-

ville, thirty-five miles southeast, where the party would retire that evening. The long-distance tourists would then continue east over the Alleghenies on the National Pike, the country's oldest highway. At Hagerstown, Maryland, they would veer southwest and traverse the lush Shenandoah Valley before heading to the Gulf Coast. After a few days touring the Crescent City, they would return home by steamship and train, via New York City.

Lenz had carefully designed this route, which would include some remarkably rugged and scenic terrain, to enhance his growing reputation as a long-distance tourist and roving photographer par excellence. As soon as he returned to Pittsburgh, he planned to fire off a barrage of letters to magazine publishers describing his latest cycling and photographic feats. He would then pitch his long-cherished scheme to girdle the globe with wheel and camera.

Stevens's continued post-tour success only strengthened Lenz's resolve to make a global circuit of his own. In recent years, the original globe girdler had accomplished three more astonishing adventures: a ride across Russia on a mustang, a dash into Africa to rescue the rescuer Henry Morton Stanley, and a recently concluded six-month tour of European rivers. Stevens had published two more books recounting the first two of these adventures, and he was busy writing an account of the third. He had just announced his intention to settle in the United States, where he would offer his services as a lecturer. "I've collected no end of unique and interesting material," he explained to a journalist. His advertisements noted that each of his three "stereopticon entertainments" featured "over sixty graphic scenes of Moving Life."

Yes, Stevens was Lenz's idol. Here was a man who had traveled in twenty-five countries, surviving, by his count, just as many "exceedingly narrow shaves." Boasted Stevens to *The Wheel:*

I've seen about everything abroad worth seeing. I've about touched the top and bottom and both ends. I've met the Tzar, the Shah of Persia, and drank coffee with the Sultan of Zanzibar. I've run up against all sorts, conditions and races of people. I've stood in the shadow of Masai spears, Afghan bayonets, Russian prisons and the torches of Chinese mobs. I suppose I ought to be glad I'm alive and cry quits. Anyway, civilization will be good enough for me from this time forward.

Lenz could only imagine the rewards awaiting the man who eclipsed Stevens's cycling performance, and he knew that now was the ideal time to enlist a sponsor for a world tour of his own. Cycling had never been more popular, thanks to the safety bicycle. The national population of cyclists was approaching the one million mark. In Pittsburgh alone, some 1,500 practiced the art, about five times as many as when Lenz had taken up the sport four years earlier.

Lenz was certain that an alert editor would recognize the broad appeal of another serialized "round-the-world" tour, especially one profusely illustrated with photographs. Of course, a sponsor would no doubt demand that Lenz himself ride a safety, to ensure an element of novelty, not to mention relevancy. As a longtime cyclist, he did not favor the diminutive mount. In fact, many of his peers from the early days had quit the sport altogether, so put off were they by its sudden popularity. But Lenz was realistic, and he was not about to sacrifice his shot at a world tour to defend an obsolete pattern. He was fully prepared to transition to the safety whenever the circumstances demanded as much.

In the meantime, if this trip to New Orleans was indeed his last hurrah on his beloved high-wheeler, Lenz was poised, with Charlie at his side, to make the most of it. "No twins were ever closer" was how one journalist described their mutual dependency. They had been utterly inseparable since the spring of 1890, when Charlie lost his brother and cycling partner John to "inflammatory rheumatism." Charlie hardly knew how he could carry on. Lenz immediately showed his sympathy, designing and executing the club's embossed memorial resolutions with a penmanship the *Bulletin* pronounced "faultless." The sunny Lenz soon filled an enormous void in Charlie's life, and he, in turn, became the brother Lenz had never had.

They made a curious pair. "Long Charlie" towered over his chum by a good six inches. And his rail-thin body had none of Lenz's muscular padding. Petticord, with his closely cropped hair and bushy mustache, looked considerably older than his boyish pal, even though he was in fact the junior partner by a good two years. Charlie acted older too. He had a deliberate, almost sleepy, way about him, in contrast with the impetuous Lenz, who always seemed revved for action, no matter how rash.

They took their first tour together on the weekend of July 4, 1890. Along with another pal, Warren T. McClarren, they boarded a night train for Cleveland, then spent the holiday riding through the city parks and cruising around Lake Erie on a steamer. The next day they rode forty miles to Akron, where a reporter noted their arrival: "Three dust covered bicyclists wheeled into the city at 2 o'clock and created something of a sensation. They were attired in black tights and gave every indication of having been on a long journey. One of the trio had a square awning erected above his head and a Kodak strapped to his back."

After a hearty lunch at a hotel, the young men rode another twenty-five miles to Canton. To their great surprise, they bumped into three hometown friends also on a cycling holiday. The next day the six Pittsburghers teamed up with eleven members of the Canton Bicycle Club for a fourteen-mile run to Congress Lake, where they all took a refreshing dip. And to think that only one member of the party rode a "jigger" (a derogatory term for the safety)! How times had changed in little more than one year.

The previous August, Lenz and Petticord had cycled to St. Louis, timing their visit to coincide with the largest cycling tournament ever held out west. Although the rains had reduced the National Pike to a shallow, muddy river, their spirits never flagged. The Dayton Ramblers found the chirpy pair "as brisk as spring roosters and as happy as larks." The road gave out entirely in Illinois. Still, they managed to stage a triumphant arrival at the meet, minutes before the opening event.

Later that month, the tanned pair traveled to Niagara Falls to attend the eleventh annual LAW national meet. They witnessed a safety race that marked the American debut of the pneumatic tire. Recently introduced in Ireland by the veterinarian John Dunlop, it promised unprecedented speed and comfort. Indeed, the unheralded winner sailed to an easy victory, amid howls of protest. Lenz, ever the engineer, instantly realized that the ordinary was indeed doomed if these inflatable tubes—ideally suited for a bicycle with two small, equal-sized wheels—proved practical.

The trip to New Orleans promised to be Lenz and Petticord's greatest joint adventure yet. On the second morning out, they climbed the rugged Alleghenies, walking much of the way. Anticipating a wild fourteen-mile plunge into Cumberland, they had equipped their front wheels with "coaster" hubs, which allowed them to keep their feet stationary on the pedals. Reaching the Chesapeake and Ohio (C&O) Canal, they abandoned the pike for the smooth towpath. At one point, the canal entered a tunnel nearly a mile long. After a few feet, the cyclists found themselves in utter darkness. They wisely dismounted and proceeded on foot. Enjoying clear weather, they spent one night in the open air.

At Hagerstown, the thriving bicycle club gave them a royal reception. The next day they cruised into the Shenandoah Valley. At Martinsburg, West Virginia, they found themselves gleefully leading a circus parade. That night they reached Woodstock, Virginia, having covered an impressive seventy-three miles during the day. Two days later, they had gotten as far as Staunton before a deluge hit. From then on, they struggled to make twenty miles a day over the spongy Virginia red clay. With few towns along the way, they subsisted primarily on their own supply of bacon bits, corn, and stale biscuits. At Lexington, they stopped to admire the newly erected statue of Stonewall Jackson, whose cold stare seemed to symbolize the South's enduring and unapologetic defiance. They swam in a nearby pool two hundred feet below the famous Natural Bridge.

At Wytheville, near the Tennessee border, Lenz's big wheel suddenly collapsed, and he narrowly avoided serious injury. The accident compelled him to order a new wheel by telegraph before he proceeded by train to Chattanooga. Petticord, meanwhile, carried on alone, bumping over the ties spanning the Louisville and Nashville (L&N) Railroad. His tire became loose, forcing him to tie it down with a string. He sought refuge that evening in an abandoned shack. When he heard Lenz's train rumble by around midnight, he deeply regretted his ill-advised decision to go it alone.

Reuniting in Chattanooga, Lenz and Petticord trudged up nearby Lookout Mountain, where they enjoyed a magnificent panorama. After Lenz reclaimed his repaired wheel, the pair continued merrily on their way, heading into territory where the bicycle was as yet an anomaly. As Lenz would later recall, the locals stood by the roadside gaping "with open-mouthed wonder." In Trenton, a tiny town in the northwest corner of Georgia, the entire populace came out to inspect the strangers and their bizarre vehicles. Lenz further startled them when he jumped off his wheel and, rather insensitively, started flashing his camera in their direction.

As the cyclists approached the dense forests of northern Alabama, the locals warned them to go no farther. A notorious moonshiner was supposedly hiding out there with his ruthless band, and the lawmen were about to smoke them out. Undaunted, the pair spent the next five days fighting their way through the thick brush. Fortunately, they emerged unscathed. At Fort Payne, they were astonished to find a ghost town with an impressive assortment of new buildings, including several banks, two mills, and an opera house—all abruptly abandoned when the local iron and coal deposits had failed to live up to expectations.

Perhaps the most memorable moment of their southern swing was their clamorous appearance in Birmingham. As a New Orleans paper recounted: "They arrived in the Magic City shortly after 1 o'clock, and marched right into the crowded dining room of the Florence Hotel dressed in their dusty and dirt-begrimed garments, creating something of a sensation among the swell diners dressed in their Sunday best. But the cyclers were looking for dinner. They had forded three rivers and numerous creeks, and did not stand on style or ceremony." Indeed, as another paper related, "they proceeded to eat a very hearty dinner, attracting a good deal of attention from persons desirous of knowing who the strangers were and whence they came."

One reporter chastised the young men for their bold breach of protocol: "Messrs. Petticord and Lenz should remember while traveling through the South not to leave their manners at home." Deploring their "soiled, dust-covered, skin-tight professional paraphernalia," which he deemed "an insult to every lady and gentleman," the reporter huffed: "It is hard to believe they would have entered any first-class dining room in Pittsburgh in such a costume. The respectability of the South will not stand any such exhibition of boorishness, gall, and lack of respect for respectable people."

Having fallen several days behind schedule, and with their tires worn to the rim, the unrepentant duo decided to take a train through Mississippi. After crossing the viaduct into New Orleans, they were warmly received by members of the Louisiana Bicycle Club. Their escorts took them through the French Quarter, where they visited the old parish prison. That evening the club held a reception in their honor. "Lenz has quite a number of photos taken in this city and en route," reported the secretary. "He swears by the town, and says it is beautiful, and the climate delightful."

As the Pittsburghers boarded their ship to New York, they were already making plans to cycle to California on their next summer vacation. And if by then Lenz had enlisted a sponsor for his world tour, Charlie promised to continue on with his buddy as he sailed from the West Coast to Asia. Although they would be reversing Stevens's course, Lenz maintained that an east-to-west movement offered distinct "climatic advantages."

Back in Pittsburgh, Lenz began his letter-writing campaign. He proposed a tour studiously designed to eclipse that of Stevens. He anticipated cycling and walking a minimum of twenty thousand miles within two years. Moreover, unlike Stevens, who was turned back at the Afghanistan border for lack of papers, Lenz would at all costs cross the daunting and hostile continent of Asia. Nor would he ever resort to trains, as Stevens was allegedly wont to do. Lenz would take ships only to cross the "briny spots."

If any American was up to this Herculean task, all agreed, it was surely Frank Lenz, the twenty-four-year-old captain of the Allegheny Cyclers. True, he had not raced in nearly three years, but he had lost none of his formidable form. In St. Louis the previous summer, he had astonished the locals when he kept pace with a pack of scorchers while riding a fully loaded wheel. "For strength and endurance," marveled one reporter, "I doubt if Lenz has an equal in America. Just think of carrying a 20-pound camera on your back, over all sorts of roads, from Pittsburgh to St. Louis, in addition to other luggage on the backbone and handle bars."

Lenz had also retained his legendary nerve. The St. Louis reporter admired the reckless way the Pittsburgher charged downhill at breakneck speed. He removed his feet from the furiously spinning pedals, slipped his lower legs under the handlebar, and slouched back until he was almost completely horizontal, thereby minimizing wind resistance. Lenz insisted that he could still bring his machine to a full stop if ever the need arose. One could only shudder at the prospect.

Just a few months earlier, in fact, Lenz had once again shown his fearlessness. He and McClarren had taken a train out to the popular resort of Ohiopyle. After frolicking on the massive rocks beneath the spectacular waterfall, the pair wheeled down the railroad side path over the mountains toward Connellsville. "The scenery for the entire distance is wildly picturesque," reported the *Bulletin*, "but it requires skilful and plucky riding to retain one's equilibrium. A single waver to one side would have hurled a careless rider and wheel upon the rocks fully two hundred feet below—into the boiling Youghiogheny River. Track walkers stated that this pair were the first bicyclers that had ever attempted this dangerous ride."

Lenz had other qualities befitting a globe girdler, like tenacity. Once, returning from Butler, he and McClarren tried to cross Pittsburgh's Seventh Street Bridge. The toll collector demanded five cents apiece. Lenz refused to pay, arguing that it was unethical for the company to charge on Sundays. The collector finally let Lenz pass, on the condition that he meet with the company president the next day to argue his case. True to his word, Lenz called on Mr. Orr. "As in past interviews of a like nature," the *Bulletin* reported, "Mr. Orr was obdurate though courteous." He told Lenz point-blank that he would not change the policy and "did not want the patronage of wheelmen." Even the reporter had to question the point of challenging the rule, obnoxious though it was, considering that one could either walk the bicycle over the bridge and pay only one cent or use an alternative bridge and pay nothing at all.

Above all, Lenz was resourceful. He devised an ingenious method to photograph himself riding his wheel. He would rest his camera on a ledge or secure it to a tripod, then choose his background through the finder. He would then grab the bulb at the loose end of a thirty-six-foot rubber hose, the other being connected to the camera, and strategically place it on the road. When he rode over the bulb, it triggered a snapshot. At that moment, he often looked straight at the lens to register a smile or a tip of his cap.

To overcome inclement weather, Lenz also devised a special umbrella that attached to a thin pole mounted atop his camera case. As he explained in a letter to *Bicycling World*, it was designed to provide "excellent shade in the hot sun" and also protection from "light rain." His buddies laughed it off, but they could not help but admire Lenz's imagination and ingenuity.

Despite all these compelling credentials and qualities, Lenz was convinced that his window of opportunity to circle the globe by bicycle was rapidly closing. Every day newcomers were taking up the sport. It was only a matter of time, he believed, before someone else with greater means embarked on a similar mission. He had to find a sponsor while the idea still held some novelty and appeal, or forever relinquish his dream.

Compounding his sense of urgency was Lenz's gnawing feeling that he had reached a crossroad in his life. His new club mates were getting younger by the day. Some, like Ned Friesell, were mere teenagers who favored the safety. Many of the old-timers, like McClarren, had either drastically curtailed their cycling or hung up their wheels altogether to start careers and families. Perhaps, if he failed to find a backer, it was time for him, too, to settle down to the business of life, just as his mother constantly implored him to do.

One way or another, Lenz knew he had to move out of his parents' house. For despite his cheerful public persona, he was increasingly miserable inside. In fact, he had never known a happy home. He had no recollection whatsoever of his biological father, Adam Reinhart, who had emigrated with his mother, Maria Anna, née Schritz, from Malsch, Germany, in late 1865. A year later, the couple settled in Philadelphia, where Adam found work as a cigar maker. But Adam soon died, and Anna and her toddler moved to Pittsburgh. When Frank was six, his mother married the German-born William Lenz. Though he gave the boy his name, he never truly accepted Frank as a son. Lately, their relationship had become even more strained. William often came home from work reeking of alcohol. Frank could not bear to watch his stepfather mistreat his mother, a loving, strong-willed woman who, like himself, deserved a far better existence.

Several weeks after returning to Pittsburgh, while awaiting his replies, Lenz decided to enter the annual Keystone Road Race. He was curious to see how his big wheel would fare against the latest pneumatic safeties. The fifteen-mile route started in De Haven, about ten miles north of Pittsburgh, and continued over the Butler plank road just beyond Bakerstown, at which point the contestants were to turn around and retrace their route. The course included a steep hill, making the event, according to the *Press*, "more of a hill climbing contest than a road race."

Still, the paper looked forward to the showdown, noting: "Mr. Lenz is the only rider of note who remains true to the grand old ordinary. He is always out with the best safety riders, but has no trouble showing them his little wheel." Lenz planned to do exactly that in this race too. As a warm-up the previous Sunday, he had reeled off 162 miles—a new regional twenty-four-hour record. Concluded the paper: "Lenz will be looked upon as a dangerous man against the pneumatic, though he will have to do good work to win."

On the afternoon of the race, about 150 animated cyclists, one-sixth of them women, met at the clubhouse of the Keystone Bicycle Club to cycle en masse to the starting line. Thirteen racers presented themselves, including Lenz, the lone high-wheel entrant. The handicapper awarded Lenz a three-and-a-half-minute head start, but the indignant cyclist refused to accept it. The gun sounded. Lenz surged forward but soon struggled over the hill. Meanwhile, several competitors overtook him. He finished a disappointing fifth. His time of 1:23 was a good six minutes off the best pace. The humiliating loss to inferior riders only underscored what he already knew: it was time to switch to a pneumatic safety.

Coming home from work a few weeks later, Lenz found a thick envelope marked *Outing Magazine*, 239 Fifth Avenue, New York City. Opening it with trembling fingers, he retrieved a letter from James Henry Worman. The distinguished publisher expressed a keen interest in Lenz's proposal, provided the cyclist agreed to ride a Victor safety bicycle. Lenz was ecstatic. He immediately dashed off a letter to convey his wholehearted acceptance of Worman's terms.

The forty-seven-year-old German-born editor, a short, balding man with a bushy white mustache, was a former professor of classics and linguistics who had made a fortune penning French and German grammar books. Four years earlier, he had purchased *Out-*

ing, a richly illustrated monthly glamorizing outdoor life. Despite a robust circulation of twenty thousand, it had been struggling financially—until the exacting editor and a succession of harried underlings managed to turn things around.

Worman knew well that Stevens's series had been hugely popular, and he had even briefly retained the celebrity as his cycling editor. Worman anticipated that his readers would eagerly devour Lenz's reports as well, especially if they were illustrated with Lenz's own photographs. The editor was already convinced that Lenz had all the necessary skills to complete his self-appointed task. Still, before accepting the proposition, he wanted to vet the intriguing young man who had declared in his first letter: "I will go if I have to go alone and unaided; the world I will see."

At the close of 1891, Worman sent his young assistant, Robert Bruce, to Pittsburgh to interview Lenz. Years later, Bruce would recall how he was accosted by both Mrs. Lenz and A. W. Cadman, the owner of the brass manufactory where Lenz worked. "Both requested me to exert any influence I might have to discourage the scheme," Bruce reflected, "but I think that Lenz would have gone anyhow, as he was entirely wrapped up in the idea."

Bruce gave Worman a favorable report, pronouncing Lenz "an unusually keen observer" and "no mean philosopher." In fact, Bruce was deeply impressed by Lenz's wanderlust and idealism. "The whole world is man's heritage," Lenz had asserted, "and as long as I am on this earth I shall feel as much at home by the banks of the Euphrates as by the Monongahela." True, Bruce conceded, the cyclist might not be a gifted writer. But at least he was sincere, as there was "nothing in his nature suggestive of the artificial." Besides, Bruce could tend to the heavy editing.

In early 1892, wanting to meet the young man himself, Worman summoned Lenz to his office. There the Pittsburgher cheerfully described his upbringing, recounting how he had sold newspapers as a boy to help with family expenses. He had diligently pursued his studies, earning the favor of his high school principal. He had put himself through business school, where he learned accounting and exquisite penmanship. While still a teenager, he had secured an enviable position as a bookkeeper.

Yes, Worman liked Lenz's persona all right. Here, before him, was the quintessential plucky American boy, of modest origins but bent on making something of himself. In fact, the editor saw a bit of his own younger self in this ambitious and hearty wanderer. At the age of sixteen, Worman had run away from his home in Germany to enlist in the Union Army. The authorities, however, got wise and sent the lad back to his homeland. After studying at the University of Berlin and the Sorbonne, he had returned to the United States a few years later to start a distinguished academic career.

In early April 1892, Lenz and Worman worked out the final details of their pact. The editor would cover up to $2,000 in traveling expenses, nearly twice Lenz's annual salary. Worman also agreed to take out, in secrecy, a $3,000 insurance policy on Lenz's life, payable to his mother. For despite his ever-cheerful and confident air, the wheelman knew well that he would be risking his life and potentially depriving his mother of not only her pride and joy but also her financial pillar.

For his part, Lenz stood by his bold plan to traverse North America, Asia, and Europe. He would send reports and photographs every other month. Although he would aim to complete the journey within two years, he would not race time. Rather, he would observe the world at his leisure, with an intimacy only a cyclist could enjoy. He would start May 1 from Pittsburgh, pass through Washington to collect his passport, then stop in New York City for his official sendoff, at which point he would begin his journey in earnest.

Their deal struck, Worman and Lenz traveled by train to Chicopee Falls, Massachusetts, to visit the sprawling plant of the Overman Wheel Company, makers of the Victor. Settling into the president's plush office, they conversed with Albert H. Overman. A decade earlier, the Illinois native had established a small factory in Hartford, Connecticut, that specialized in tricycles. He soon moved the thriving enterprise up the Connecticut River to western Massachusetts, becoming Pope's chief rival. An early advocate of the Rover style who imposed the highest manufacturing standards, Overman was happily presiding over a booming business. Some one thousand employees struggled day and night to meet the seemingly insatiable demand for his safety bicycles.

After some consultation, Lenz placed an order for a customized nickel-plated bicycle he deemed strong enough to withstand the rigors of a world tour. To ensure a reasonably comfortable ride, even over rough roads with a heavy load, he requested a well-sprung and elongated leather saddle and massive springs acting on the front fork blades. He also ordered two sprockets on the rear hub so that he could flip the wheel to engage either a high or low gear, in accordance with the terrain. In a bold gamble, he opted for the latest pneumatic tires rather than the puncture-proof cushion variety.

Returning to Pittsburgh, Lenz promptly resigned his position at Cadman's, which he had held for seven years. His boss graciously accepted the inevitable and even promised to hire Lenz back upon his return. Frank's mother, however, was distraught, having a premonition that her only son would never return alive. "But, Mother," Frank insisted, "I shall see things and accomplish deeds to remember until I am eighty years old." He did his best to console her, promising that he would write every week until he returned home.

While awaiting his bicycle, Lenz took care of some paperwork. He sent his passport application to Washington, declaring his intention to return to the United States within two years and pointedly listing his occupation as a bookkeeper in the past tense. He also took one more discreet measure on his mother's behalf. Somberly seating himself at a large wooden desk in a lawyer's office, he methodically wrote out in his beautiful cursive a two-page will. In the event of an untimely death, he specified, everything he had was to go to his dear mother. If she was already gone, his estate was to go to his "beloved" Annie Leech, his Irish Catholic girlfriend from the neighborhood who worked as a dressmaker. She, too, feared for his life. But Lenz had promised her that he would settle down upon his return and the two would enjoy a happy and comfortable life together.

Up to this point, Lenz was still counting on Charlie to join him on his great adventure. But Petticord was having second thoughts. He was reluctant to leave his sister Amelia, with whom he lodged, and he had just received a good offer for a clerking position he had long coveted. Charlie bowed out, though he promised to join his friend in Europe for the final leg. Lenz turned to Ned Friesell, who would later reflect: "I had a hard time deciding whether to go to college or around the world with Lenz." Dental school won out.

Having resolved to go it alone, Lenz carefully selected his gear to minimize his load. He packed a change of clothing, a spare inner tube, a handful of tools, a collapsible aluminum tripod, his homemade umbrella, and a leather belt with pouches to carry his watch and cash—what he jokingly called his "time and money." He allowed himself several small harmonicas with which to entertain company or break the long stretches of solitude. Lenz also acquired a trunk to store a stash of inner tubes, parts, and other provisions, as well as mementos gathered en route. He planned to ship it ahead of himself to strategic locations.

And of course, he would continue to carry a camera in a case strapped to his back. To save weight, however, he bought a new film-loaded camera manufactured in Rochester, New York. The latest Kodak would have been even lighter and more portable, but he considered that a mere toy. Mindful that people in certain cultures were averse to having their pictures taken, for fear of compromising their souls, Lenz devised a timer from the parts of a music box so he could set up his camera and allow a delay of five, ten, or fifteen seconds—enough time to get himself into the picture.

Lenz borrowed a friend's bicycle and began a crash course on safety riding, suffering what the *Chronicle Telegraph* described as a "narrow escape from death." Elaborated the paper: "He was speeding down Fifth Avenue on a new solid rubber tire wheel when, just in front of our office, he struck a rut and was almost thrown in front of a cable car coming at full speed. Lenz was badly scared."

In early May, Lenz was set to go, but the non-arrival of his bicycle forced a two-week delay. In the interim, the Allegheny Cyclers held a farewell banquet. Mayor Kennedy gave a rousing speech at the clubhouse, and the festivities lingered into the early morning. Several days later, the Keystone Bicycle Club held another emotive affair. Recounted one attendee: "The rooms of the club were filled with happy people, all the prominent wheelmen of hereabouts being present." Lenz was presented with an engraved silver Smith & Wesson revolver to take with him for protection.

At last, on May 9, Lenz received his shiny new Victor. Hundreds flocked to see it hanging in the window of the sporting goods dealer A. G. Pratt. The *Bulletin* attributed their fascination to the growing popularity of cycling, marveling: "A few years ago, a man on a wheel in our town was a target of criticism [and] a universal curiosity. But to-day, the solitary wheelman has become two thousand of his kind." The paper expounded on the magnitude of Lenz's mission:

> Mr. Lenz's trip is of interest to everybody who admires courage and manly strength. When he gets home two years hence, provided he survives, he will no doubt have plenty of marvelous traveler's stories to tell, and he should have a rousing welcome. When we reflect that a very few years ago many parts of the globe over which he will travel were terra incognita to white people, the contrast between then and now will strike us with irresistible force. Truly, the world moves, and the bicycle is responsible for much of that motion.

Finally, Lenz's big moment was at hand. Early Sunday morning, May 15, some eight hundred animated well-wishers, including scores of wheelmen, gathered by the central post office in downtown Pittsburgh, where the world tourist was due to appear. For six straight days rain had fallen, but at last the sun poked a hole through the dense clouds. Suddenly, a transfigured Lenz appeared with all his gear, amid shouts of joy.

A broad smile brightened Lenz's cherubic face. He sported a natty dark blue uniform and a cap with raised golden letters spelling out OUTING. Of course, his faithful camera box rested on his back. Hanging over his handlebars was a canteen and a small sack, while atop his rear rack sat a large satchel, sandwiched between two cylindrical cases, one holding his tripod and the other his umbrella. Obscuring the top portion of the rear wheel, on either side, were placards announcing himself and his mission, to be changed periodically to stay in sync with the local language.

Those who were unfamiliar with the man of the hour were startled by his youthfulness and short stature. In fact, he did not look even his twenty-five years, despite the newly grown blond mustache intended to age his appearance. His muscular physique notwithstanding, he hardly looked the part of a superhuman. Still, as one witness recounted, "everyone seemed to think that he was quite a novel person—one possessed of great pluck, energy and determination to even think of starting out on so long a journey."

As Lenz dutifully waited for the nine o'clock hour to strike, the bystanders fired off a barrage of questions:

"How heavy is your load?" asked a small boy.

"About 240 pounds," Lenz replied instantly. "My camera [weighs] about 13 pounds, and I have another 25 pounds of gear. The bicycle weighs 57 pounds and I weigh 145."

"Will you encounter any danger?" queried a young lady.

Without flinching, Lenz allowed: "I might have trouble in China and Turkey, the two countries most difficult to tour in."

"What if they don't like Americans?" shouted another lad.

Lenz cracked a smile. "That's no problem! They can consider me German. I speak the language fluently."

"Are you sure you'll make it back?" pressed a young man.

Assured Lenz: "I shall succeed if it takes a lifetime. I have nothing but the most pleasurable anticipation of my trip abroad. Besides, I have never encountered anything yet that I have not overcome."

Asked about his diet, Lenz, an avowed teetotaler, asserted that "daily plain living is the best kind of preparation." He said he had no intention of making any drastic alterations in his eating habits. He would continue to enjoy a hearty meal whenever he was sure it would do him good. He also stated that he would avoid sleeping outdoors, except as a last resort. But he acknowledged that he would face so many "unusual circumstances" along the way that it would be "useless to say now exactly how I will live."

At last, at the appointed hour, Lenz straddled his bicycle and took off amid a fresh round of cheers. He sailed past Kaufman's department store looking, as one reporter put it, "extremely happy." About one hundred wheelmen were supposed to follow him that day to "Little Washington," where a banquet was scheduled in his honor. As it was, however, only three—one of them, of course, being Petticord—chose to do battle with the heavy mud. The rest would take a ferry the next day to Brownsville, where they would meet up with Lenz and his party for one last celebration.

The next afternoon, after all the hoopla finally had subsided, Lenz found himself on the National Pike heading east, with only Petticord at his side. Together they reached Uniontown, a manufacturing center at the base of the Alleghenies. There, after a satisfying lunch full of good cheer, it was time for wrenching goodbyes. The two friends embraced, then headed in opposite directions.

As he crossed the toughest stretch of the Alleghenies, Lenz was alone for the first time since starting off—but not for long. In Hagerstown, the local bicycle club once again extended its hospitality. This time a dozen members took Lenz out to lunch, and afterward three escorted him on the pike as far as Frederick. There they decided "to tarry the afternoon" in the old town, visiting its "peculiar streets and quaint old buildings." Lenz took several photos, including a snapshot of the grave of Francis Scott Key, the revered author of "The Star-Spangled Banner."

The next day, in the nation's capital, Lenz met Bruce, his "business manager." When the pair stopped by the Washington Monument to take a photo of themselves, Bruce observed firsthand the wheelman's verve. "A dozen colored toughs thought to have a little sport at our expense," recalled Bruce, "by standing in such a position that any picture of us two would include them also." Without a moment's hesitation, Lenz "jumped into the midst of them, putting the whole crowd to flight."

The pair then called on the secretary of state himself, James Blaine, who furnished Lenz's passport and a letter of introduction addressed to foreign authorities demanding that Lenz be well treated in their territory. The official queried Lenz about his plans, before offering the wheelman a warm handshake and a hearty "good luck to you!"

Ten days out of Pittsburgh, Lenz entered Baltimore. He sailed past "hundreds of negroes building cable lines who shouted with delight." The local wheelmen took him around the city, and he photographed the inner harbor and a few historic buildings. The next morning he started for Philadelphia, his native city, via the bucolic Lancaster Pike. Three days later, he wheeled through the leafy suburbs of Bryn Mawr and Ardmore before bumping along the cobblestoned Lancaster Avenue to his downtown hotel. A journalist on hand noted that Lenz's bicycle was already "patched up with decorations of hard yellow clay." The next day Lenz visited several bicycle clubhouses, as well as Independence Hall.

Leaving his native state once again, Lenz pedaled through Camden, reaching Trenton for the night. The next day, May 30, he arose at dawn to catch the Irvington-Milburn road race, held every Decoration Day. Along with the Pullman race near Chicago, it was the country's premier amateur cycling contest. Lenz passed wheelmen "by the tens and twenties," all headed to the same destination. Arriving at the starting line just before the 11:30 start, he joined thousands of spectators. One hour and seventeen minutes later, Hoyland Smith triumphantly rode in on his pneumatic safety. He shattered the record for the twenty-five-mile course by ten minutes, vindicating Lenz's choice of tire.

The tourist wheeled on to Newark for lunch, then Jersey City, where he caught a late afternoon ferry to New York City. He rode

to the *Outing* office in midtown Manhattan, where Worman anxiously awaited. The editor warmly received his intrepid correspondent, who seemed to grow in stature with every revolution of his
pedals. In two weeks, Lenz had already covered 555 miles, according to his odometer. Not a torrid pace, to be sure, but a respectable
one, given the poor roads and bad weather.

After a brief rest, Lenz was set to make his official departure.
On the morning of June 4, he rode to the steps of City Hall, leaving his bicycle and gear with a few friends. He then slipped off
with a few intimates for a hearty lunch. Returning that afternoon
for the sendoff, Lenz happily discovered that his bicycle had been
covered with cards and flowers. Meanwhile, the crowd was swell-
ing so fast that Lenz decided to forgo the official photograph and
make his way at once to the corner of Chambers and Broadway, behind a wedge of policemen. There he patiently awaited the three
o'clock hour.

Taking advantage of the lull, a reporter from *The Sporting Life*
sprang forward to confront the wheelman about the practicality of
his inflatable tires. Lenz calmly explained that he had tested them
thoroughly and was fully confident that they would prove their
merit. Besides, he would have plenty of spare tubes and tires in his
trunk should he need them.

The skeptical scribe scoffed the next day in his column: "Anyone
who knows anything about cycling is aware that Lenz's trip is impossible upon any form of pneumatic ever made. Granting the tire
should escape puncturing—a thing almost impossible—the mere
wear and tear of so long a journey will destroy a dozen or more
of them, which will make touring an impossibility in any foreign
lands beyond communication with European civilization." The
journalist was equally critical about Lenz's naive scheme to ship
a trunk ahead of himself. "Any one who has toured either in this
country or abroad," he huffed, "knows the fallacy of ever expecting
to have any sort of baggage follow or precede him."

The journalist challenged the very validity of the mission. "I'm
blessed if I can see what the object of the trip is," he fumed, "except

for Mr. Lenz to earn the money that *Outing* is foolish enough to expend." He denounced Lenz's entrepreneurial spirit, labeling him a "perambulating sandwich man" after "gingerbread glory." And he derided Lenz's comical appearance, likening the overloaded wheelman to "one of those stalking musicians who play a dozen instruments at the same time." His harsh conclusion: "What benefit is to be derived from this trip? It is not a new idea."

Lenz merely shrugged off such criticism. Admittedly, he was not the first globe girdler on wheels. Nor would he be the last. But God willing, he would go down as the most memorable of the lot. And he had his defenders. "Lenz is a plucky young fellow for undertaking such a long and perilous trip," wrote one cycling journalist. "He should be encouraged by the cycle papers, instead of being dismissed with a few lines like the winner of a country race." Moreover, he had a noble purpose: to prove, as he put it, that the safety bicycle offered "an easy and healthful manner of traveling and sightseeing."

At last it was time for Lenz's departure. A reporter described the dramatic scene: "Promptly at 3 o'clock, Lenz clambered slowly on his machine. He settled himself carefully into the middle between the humps of baggage behind and before, which made it look like a veritable ship of the desert, and then he trundled away up Broadway." Scores of men and women looked on and cheered from sidewalks, while others leaned out their windows and waved handkerchiefs.

At Madison Square Park, Lenz veered onto Fifth Avenue. A few blocks later, he looked up at the *Outing* office and waved to the cheering staff. Yet another enormous crowd awaited him at the Manhattan Athletic Club on the corner of Forty-fifth and Madison. He pulled over and mingled with his admirers. At four o'clock, he pushed off again, accompanied by one hundred wheelmen who would escort him all the way to Tarrytown, where he would spend the night.

The vast assembly gaily spun through Central Park. Upon reaching the iron bridge spanning the Harlem River, Lenz turned around to glance one last time at the fading metropolis and the barely visible spire of Trinity Church. His mind raced ahead to the distant day when he would make his triumphant return. He knew he would face countless hardships and perils before then. But for now he was content to savor the moment as he pedaled along the shady banks of the Hudson, surrounded by a sea of goodwill. After all those years of dreaming and scheming, his epic journey was at last under way.

Shortly after concluding his deal with *Outing* in April 1892, Frank Lenz struck this studio pose, probably in Chicopee Falls, Massachusetts. This was not the equipment he would actually use, but it served for this publicity shot.

St. Louis Tournament August 16th. 1890.

F.G.LENZ—PGH

Lenz, an avid amateur photographer, superimposed three
images of himself in distinct moods.

Lenz lounges with his friends during a ride near Pittsburgh, about
1890. Left to right: Charles Petticord, Warren T. McClarren, Lenz,
and an unidentified man. Note Lenz's homemade sunshade, attached
to his camera case.

Top: McClarren, Petticord, and Lenz ride through Glenshaw, near Pittsburgh, about 1890. *Bottom:* The same trio (Lenz in center) poses in Cleveland's Wade Park, July 4, 1890, the same day Allen and Sachtleben arrived in Liverpool to start their world tour.

Petticord and Lenz stop in Collinsville, Illinois, en route to St. Louis, August 1890.

Lenz (under his sunshade) leads his buddies and members of the Canton Bicycle Club, July 9, 1890. Petticord is on the far left.

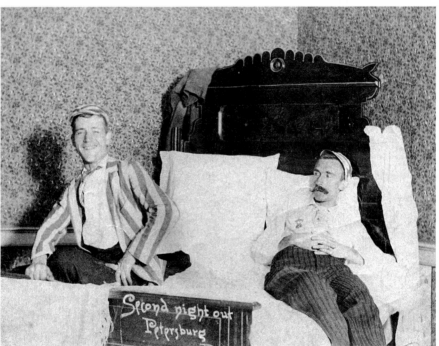

Top: Lenz (far left) and Petticord (middle) on Pittsburgh's Smithfield Street Bridge, August 9, 1891, departing for New Orleans. Between them is Ned Friesell, who considered going with Lenz on his world tour. *Bottom:* Two days later in Petersburg (now Addison), Pennsylvania, Lenz and Petticord share a bed.

En route to New Orleans, Lenz surveys the rugged road across the Alleghenies.

On the same trip, Petticord stands ready to greet the citizens of Trenton, Georgia, while Lenz takes the photo. Petticord would later call Trenton "a bum little town."

Petticord and Lenz take in the view from Lookout Mountain, Tennessee.
Note the cable Lenz is using to snap the photograph.

The pair reached New Orleans in September 1891. Lenz took this view
of Canal Street.

Thomas Allen and William Sachtleben pose in a London studio in September 1890, shortly after announcing their plans to circle the globe. Their light bicycles had cushion tires.

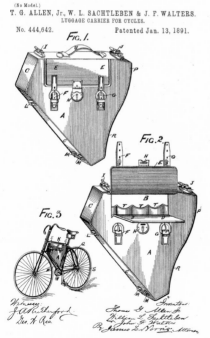

(No Model.)

T. G. ALLEN, Jr., W. L. SACHTLEBEN & J. F. WALTERS.
LUGGAGE CARRIER FOR CYCLES.

No. 444,642.   Patented Jan. 13, 1891.

FIG. 1.

FIG. 2.

FIG. 3.

Above: Early ad for a Kodak camera. *Left:* U.S. patent taken out by Allen, Sachtleben, and Walters, the maker of their bicycles. The leather bags were designed to fit within the central triangles of their bicycles.

Scenes from Allen and Sachtleben's European tour, fall 1890, taken with their Kodak cameras. *Left:* The Maison Carrée in Nimes, France. *Right:* The Coliseum in Rome, where the pair pedaled freely.

Left: Portrait of Serope A. Gürdjian while he was a student at Bowdoin College in Maine, c. 1877. The Armenian rebel befriended the boys during their stay in Athens in early 1891. *Right:* The Manatt family aboard a steamer. Winnie, Sachtleben's flame in Athens, is on the far left. With her are her siblings (dressed in traditional Greek garb), her mother, and her father, the American consul.

On Summit of Mt. Ararat.
JULY 4th, 1891

17,250 ft.
above sea level.

July 4, 1891. A year into their epic journey, Allen (raising a bottle of champagne) and Sachtleben (firing his revolver into the air) celebrate their arrival at the summit of Mount Ararat. Shortly thereafter, they entered Persia to resume their ride across Asia.

Allen and Sachtleben raise their pith helmets to the crowd gathered in front of a gate to Teheran, October 5, 1891, as they head for the holy city of Meshed.

A map of their route from their book *Across Asia on a Bicycle,* published after their return to the United States in the spring of 1893. After some hesitation, they decided to cross northern China via the Gobi Desert.

Messrs. Allen & Sachtl
Tai yuen fu, Shansi, North C

"Rwnd the World" bicigclysts.
Oct 18 1892.   Chu-yuch-um

The cycling review *Bearings* celebrates the return of the globe girdlers.

Sachtleben (third from left) and Allen (far right) on an outing with the Los Angeles Bicycle Club in January 1893. They are riding new Victors, their fourth set of wheels but their first with pneumatic tires.

Preceding pages: Allen (left, steadied by photographer) and Sachtleben pose in Taiyuan, capital of the Shanxi province, two weeks before their arrival in Peking. Sachtleben's cloth banner identifies the pair as "traveling scholars."

4

PEKING, CHINA

November 3, 1892

CHARLES DENBY HAD SEEN many unusual sights in Peking during his seven-year stint as the American minister to China, the world's most populous nation. But nothing had quite prepared the sixty-year-old lawyer from Evansville, Indiana, for the stunning spectacle in store for him on this chilly afternoon: two haggard and emaciated figures trundling a pair of beat-up safety bicycles toward the Hotel de Peking.

The pathetic duo promptly identified themselves as William Sachtleben of Alton, Illinois, and Thomas Allen Jr. of Ferguson, Missouri—the same names given in a recently published dispatch from Pao-ting-fu (now Baoding), about ninety miles south of Peking, announcing their approach to the imperial capital. The weary wheelmen claimed to have just accomplished what Denby would soon describe to the secretary of state as "nothing less than the crossing of Asia, from Constantinople to Peking."

Indeed, the men professed to have covered the entire distance— some seven thousand miles—on their sturdy steeds, save for one six-hundred-mile stretch in Turkestan, when they reluctantly rode the newly operational trans-Caspian railway. Denby could scarcely believe this mind-boggling claim, much less their harrowing tales of hardship and deprivation. In riveting detail, the cyclists described how they had overcome an unrelenting succession of extreme conditions and hostile encounters, including a twelve-day crossing of the Gobi Desert.

True, their wheels looked as though they had been thoroughly abused. Both frames were scraped and battered. The integrity of one top tube had been crudely restored by means of an iron bar inserted into both broken ends, which was held in place with twisted telegraph wire. But ultimately it was the cyclists' "tattered and travel-worn look" that compelled the seasoned diplomat to believe their wild assertions. Observed Denby with a hint of amusement: "They presented a most picturesque appearance in which Turkish, Chinese and European clothing had lost their identity in a uniformity of rags."

The cyclists had formulated their bold itinerary some twenty months earlier in Athens, after Allen had returned from London with two new Humber bicycles equipped with the latest cushion tires. Having failed to obtain more favorable terms from either the Iroquois Cycle Company or the *PIP*, he had ended both relationships. But with more robust bicycles in hand, and with no pressing editorial duties, the cyclists had a freer hand mapping out the most appealing route to the Pacific.

After considerable debate, the young men decided to start their Asiatic journey in Constantinople after all, despite all the dire warnings to avoid tumultuous Turkey. From there, they planned to spend the next two cycling seasons—roughly April to November—pedaling relentlessly eastward to the Pacific coast, though they were not quite sure how to get there. Their preference was to follow the ancient Silk Road through northern China, though this would necessitate crossing the vast Gobi. Should this plan prove impractical, for bureaucratic or physical reasons, their backup plan was to take a more northern route via Siberia. Either way, they would need Russian travel papers, so they resolved to head to Teheran, where they could apply for permission to enter the czar's domain. Based on the results, they would finalize their route. If the Russians refused to cooperate, they could always retrace Stevens's southern route through India.

Their grand yet flexible scheme in place, the tourists sailed away from Athens in early March 1891, headed for the capital of the Ottoman Empire. There they found lodgings with an Armenian doctor. They learned rudimentary Turkish, toured historic sites, and prepared for their thousand-mile trek across Turkey. The grand vizier, the sultan's chief consultant, kindly supplied a letter of introduction that the cyclists could present to local officials en route, requesting their goodwill and protection. William Peet, the treasurer of the American Bible House, allowed the young men to purchase drafts they could cash at various missions along the way, thus eliminating the need to carry large sums of currency.

Finally, in early April, the pair crossed the mile-wide Bosporus in a small steamer, accompanied by their host's twelve-year-old son, who had volunteered to point out the caravan road on the other side of the strait. As the Americans hopped on their wheels and began their first pedal strokes on Asian soil, the boy bade them an emotional farewell. Allen described the wrenching scene in their book *Across Asia on a Bicycle:* "He trotted for some distance by our side and then, pressing our hands in both of his, he said with childlike sincerity: 'I hope God will take care of you.'"

At first it seemed as though they were still in Europe, a land that had presented few cultural or linguistic barriers. As they skirted the Sea of Marmara and streaked toward the ancient city of Ismid (Izmit), they still had a familiar and reassuring lifeline at their side. Cutting through the lush fields was the sultan's new railroad, which German engineers were busily extending all the way to Baghdad. At Gevieh, one hundred miles south of Constantinople, they saw for themselves how this modern marvel was already changing ancient ways of life. There, dozens of men busily transferred piles of goods from camels' backs to freight cars. Only a few years earlier, the beasts would have continued all the way to the Bosporus.

As they turned their wheels east, however, toward the great plains of Anatolia, the harsh reality began to sink in. They knew they would not see another train until they had reached the other

end of Turkey. Large cities, where they might hope to find some
creature comforts, would be few and far between. The long, desolate tracts in between were said to harbor ruthless brigands poised
to pounce on any foreigner who exuded wealth. Only sporadically
could they count on the hospitality of missionaries and diplomats
stationed along the route. Fortunately, the lads, anticipating the
added hardships, had beefed up their provisions. They now carried
a tin with bicycle oil and two blankets. On the downside, their burden had ballooned to about forty pounds apiece.

They began each day at the inn dousing their bodies with water
from a large spouted can, the traditional "Turkish bath." They consumed regional staples such as coffee, yogurt, and raisins, though
they sometimes found the diet an "incongruous mixture of sweet
and sour." On rare occasions, they feasted on a roasted chicken.
They also consumed traditional bran flour paste, baked in a huge
disk. That peculiar form gave them a bright idea. They punched
gaping holes in the middle of the disks and wore the giant rings
around their necks, a setup that allowed them to snack all day long
without descending from their wheels.

A week into their Asian journey, sailing over gentle hills in
beautiful spring weather, the cyclists emerged on the Angora Pla-
teau, where King Midas and Alexander the Great once trod. There
they found nomadic tribesmen, dwelling in caves and mud huts
and tending to the shaggy indigenous sheep famous for their fine
fleece. At the city of Angora (now the capital city of Ankara), they
stopped to inspect the venerable fortress. A few nights later, they
were roused from their slumber by the sounds of cannon fire and
bagpipes announcing the start of Ramadan, the month-long ob-
servance that commemorates the revelation of the Koran to the
prophet Muhammad.

Already, a number of vexing routines had become painfully familiar. Whenever they arrived in a town in the evening to search
for an inn, they inevitably found themselves surrounded by animated mobs of men and boys hollering, "Bin, bin!" (Ride, ride!).
The cyclists quickly enriched their lexicon with the Turkish

equivalent for "impossible," but such protestations, however sincere, rarely staved off the mandatory demonstration.

The privileged few who gained admittance to the cyclists' inner sanctum, their rented room, found many more mysterious devices, such as Kodak cameras and fountain pens. But perhaps the travelers' most amazing possession was a giant map of Asia, which they obligingly spread out on the floor. As the crowd hovered over it, the cyclists pointed out where they had been and where they were going. Many simply could not fathom how the foreigners knew the names and locations of towns they had yet to visit. The concept of a global circuit was even more perplexing. The cyclists patiently explained how, if they kept going east, they would eventually return to their starting point. "Around the world!" the onlookers kept muttering, with mystified expressions.

Inevitably, the cyclists received a summons from the local authorities, notably the powerful civilian governors known as *valis*. Some had already received an official cable from the central government in Constantinople, known as the *porte*, alerting them to the approach of the "devil's carts." Ostensibly, these conferences allowed the officials to flaunt their authority as they inspected the cyclists' credentials. The Americans, meanwhile, were plied with tea, coffee, cigarettes, and at times even full meals. The officials usually asked for, and received, a cycling demonstration of their own.

The valis often imposed yet another tiresome bother: an escort service involving one or more *zaptiehs*, or armed guards on horseback, charged with seeing the tourists safely to their day's destination. The Americans were told that this was for their own good, but they strongly suspected that the alleged dangers lurking ahead were often contrived or exaggerated in order to give these men gainful employment. Even when the lads had made no arrangements to hire a guide, they would often find one come morning, patiently lurking outside their inn.

The cyclists naturally resented these unsolicited escorts, who they felt were, for the most part, foisted upon them. In addition to his daily wage, the zaptieh expected a sizable *baksheesh*, or tip, which the Americans were often reluctant to grant. Another frequent source of tension between the parties was the discordant gaits of their respective mounts. Whenever a poor stretch of road or steep ascent forced the cyclists to dismount, their guide would inevitably bring his horse to a halt, cast a look of disdain on his lowly charges, and roll up a cigarette. But when the road was favorable, or the horse tired, the wheels easily outraced the hooves. The desperate guide would either direct his horse off the road, in hopes of cutting the cyclists off at a pass, or yell at the top of his lungs for the tearing wheelmen to slow down.

Despite these aggravations and the obvious language barrier, the cyclists generally got along tolerably well with their guides, to the point of sharing meals and conversations. In truth, the guides sometimes performed useful services, such as securing a room at an inn or clearing a pathway through a mob. On occasion, they even carried the young men and their gear on horseback across swollen streams, saving them time and trouble. Still, the cyclists reserved the right to exploit their superior speed over the long haul whenever an irresistible opportunity arose. More than once, they left their poor zaptieh in the dust and callously carried on without him.

Another recurring agony was the miserable quality of the *khans*, or inns, in which they stayed. Invariably, their rooms were dirty and the cots unbearably hard. Worse, they frequently found themselves trying to sleep while unwanted company chatted, smoked, and gambled. On one occasion, they forcibly ejected a pesky young visitor, throwing him down the stairs. During his descent, he took a number of bystanders with him, prompting the irate owner to demand their own eviction. Hours later, the outcasts found themselves trudging into the cold, dark countryside. Mercifully, they came across a camp, where the astonished shepherds graciously offered them soup and makeshift beds for the night.

At Sivas, a major crossroad city and the highest one in central

Anatolia, Sachtleben suddenly came down with the telltale symptoms of typhoid fever, probably as a reaction to contaminated water imbibed at a roadside stream. For the first time in Asia, the travelers were compelled to make a prolonged stop. Fortunately, the American consul, Henry Jewett, provided comfortable quarters and saw to their needs. The missionary women, meanwhile, who were well accustomed to treating such an ailment, nursed Sachtleben back to health. Several weeks later, the young men were back on the road.

In late June 1891, the cyclists entered the valley of the Euphrates in eastern Turkey. Their travails continued. Sachtleben's bicycle had been compromised while parked in Sivas, after a mule kicked out a few spokes. The cyclists had yet to find a blacksmith who knew how to repair a wheel. Near Kara-Hissar, they had to cross a fierce mountain stream while holding their bicycles above their heads.

In Erzurum, they met with the vali to obtain papers authorizing their passage to Bayazid, the last city before the Persian border. The official was amazed by their progress and eager to interview them. He agreed to furnish the papers on two conditions. First, they had to stage a cycling demonstration for his benefit. Second, they had to take along a zaptieh to negotiate the treacherous Deli Baba Pass, which began fifty miles east of the city. The cyclists wisely agreed to both conditions. As the vali escorted them to the door, he cracked, "I shall be pleased to have your horses quartered and fed at government expense."

A few days later, the Americans rode out to the outskirts of the city to give the promised exhibition. The vali came along atop a dashing white charger, surrounded by his entourage. On hand were several British and American diplomats and missionaries, equally determined to see the renowned safety bicycle. Adding to the international ambience were the two small flags the cyclists had installed on either side of their handlebars, one with stars and stripes and the other with a star and crescent. After the performance, the vali expressed his complete satisfaction and rode off. Sachtleben and Allen, meanwhile, bade farewell to their audience and proceeded east with their guard.

Just before entering Persia, the cyclists indulged in a little diversion: climbing Mount Ararat, the towering landmark bordering the empires of the sultan, the czar, and the shah. No American had ever climbed that biblical peak, nor had anyone else in a good fifteen years. After spending a few excruciating days trudging through the snow, with a handful of hired guides and a bare minimum of supplies, they reached the seventeen-thousand-foot summit on July 4, 1891, exactly a year after they had arrived in Liverpool. They celebrated their feat, as well as the national holiday, by planting an American flag and firing four shots into the air.

Resuming their ride, the cyclists encountered yet another persistent nuisance: shepherd dogs that chased after them and nipped at their heels. At times, their owners seemed to egg them on. The cyclists occasionally fended off the beasts by blasting their revolvers into the air. They used the same tactic to deter rock-throwing villagers.

At last, the cyclists crossed into Persia. Spread out before them was a barren land with a few scattered trees and mountains looming on the horizon. Stopping at the first village, they met the local prince, known as a *khan*, who put them up for the night. They continued to clash with their imposed guides, called *ferashes* in the local vernacular. Other familiar bothers soon reestablished themselves, including the demanding mobs and miserable accommodations. They enjoyed, however, a richer diet of eggs, pomegranates, and pillao, a rice dish boiled in grease. Meanwhile, the temperature was rising, reaching as high as 120 degrees Fahrenheit in the noonday sun.

Five days after entering Persia, on July 12, the Americans rode into Tabriz, one of Persia's most important cities, located in the northwest corner of the country, just south of the Russian border. They took in its chief landmark, the Ark, an ancient fortified castle, and called on the crown prince who resided there. Although the city reputedly offered therapeutic air, Sachtleben came down with cholera, forcing yet another unplanned layover. Once again the local American missionaries provided him with aid and comfort.

William Whipple, an agent for the American Bible Society and a resident of Tabriz, gave his impression of the cyclists in a letter to a New York newspaper dated August 10:

> They are plucky fellows and thoroughly American. We have had them as our guests for three weeks and have enjoyed talking to them concerning their route from Liverpool to here. It seems marvelous how they can travel through Turkey and Persia without the languages or guides. But they have managed to do so, and with little difficulty; also very cheaply. They have had to ford rivers, carrying their wheels over high mountain passes, etc., and live nativelike in every place they stop.

Finally, in mid-August, the cyclists resumed their ride to Teheran. They closely followed the telegraph poles, spending one night in a German operator's room. One evening they were caught outdoors by the nightfall. They had to descend from their wheels and push them forward in pitch-blackness, as swarms of mosquitoes bit through their clothing. At last, they detected a passing caravan of camels and hastened toward the dimly lit lanterns. The drivers, shocked by the sudden appearance of the shadowy cyclists, drew their weapons and yelled. But the Americans managed to communicate their peaceful intentions and obtained permission to fall in line.

Allen would later describe the ordeal:

> Footsore and hungry, with an almost intolerable thirst, we trudged along till morning, to the ding-dong, ding-dong of the deep-toned camel bells. Finally, we reached a sluggish river, but did not dare to satisfy our thirst, except by washing out our mouths, and taking occasional swallows. We fell asleep from sheer exhaustion. When we awoke the midday sun was shining, and a party of Persian travelers was bending over us.

Reaching Teheran in late August, they tarried there while they awaited the Russian papers. Meanwhile, they socialized with the resident diplomats and missionaries. When fall arrived and they were still without papers, their anxiety began to rise as quickly as the temperature fell. Finally, the Russian minister persuaded them to continue east to Meshed (Mashhad), the holiest city of Islam after Mecca, where the Shiites buried their pious dead. When the papers arrived from St. Petersburg, the consul assured them, he would relay them by telegraph to his colleague in that holy city. The cyclists accepted the plan, and on October 4, 1891, they left the capital to embark on a six-hundred-mile pilgrimage.

Once again, the young men faced desertlike conditions. This time, however, they found frequent stations where they could purchase food and juicy melons to quench their thirst. Along the way, they clashed with yet another innkeeper, who demanded a sum far greater than what they had laid down. When the cyclists attempted to make a getaway, the owner and his son grabbed hold of their wheels. The four men promptly tumbled to the ground, and a fierce scuffle ensued. The women in the adjacent harem, driven out by the melee, quickly separated the men and imposed a compromise settlement.

As was often the case during their travels, the cyclists shifted effortlessly between hovel and palace from one day to the next. The following evening they called on the governor of Bostam, who had invited them to dinner. The servants rushed in benches to accommodate the foreigners, while the governor took his usual position on the carpet. Surrounded by an array of personal dishes piled high with delicacies, the attentive official looked after his guests even as he enjoyed his own meal. While the men conducted pleasant conversation, the official would occasionally fish out the choicest morsels of lamb kebob and stuffed grape leaves from his personal plates and pass them to his servants, who in turn delivered them to his guests.

Two weeks after they had left Teheran, the cyclists at last reached Meshed. But night had already fallen, and the ancient city gates were shut tight. Allen described the eerie scene: "We knocked and pounded, but a hollow echo was our only response. At last the light of a lantern illuminated the crevices in the weather-beaten doors. A weird looking face appeared in the mid-way opening." The flustered guard explained to his unexpected visitors that the key had already been sent to the governor's palace. No one, but no one, could enter the city at this late hour.

But the ever-resourceful Sachtleben would not take no for an answer. He hastily scrawled a note explaining their predicament, addressing it to the British consul residing behind the gate, who was expecting their arrival. He then folded the paper over a healthy *inam*—the Persian equivalent of baksheesh—and slipped the assemblage through the crack. The suddenly sympathetic guard dutifully delivered the message. The consul, in turn, quickly wrote a note of his own and had his servant run it over to the palace. Before long, the wheelmen could hear a squad of horsemen arriving behind the gate. After "a click of locks, a clanking of chains, and a creaking of rusty hinges," the massive doors swung open, revealing a large and wholly unexpected welcoming committee.

The next day the young men called on the Russian consul general. His servants ushered the cyclists into his elegant home, where the consul himself awaited them, alongside his English wife dressed in a flowing gown. While serving her guests tea, she revealed that the governor of Askabad in Turkistan had indeed granted them permission to proceed thither. "The news lifted a heavy load from our minds," Allen recorded. "Our desert journey, therefore, had not been made in vain, and the prospect brightened for a trip through the heart of Asia."

The wheelmen promptly took the military highway to Askabad, wending their way northwest. Although they were crossing a rugged mountain range, the road was so hard and smooth that they covered as many as seventy-five miles in a day, nearly double their average pace in Anatolia. In early November, after having logged some fourteen hundred miles in Persian territory, they finally reached the Russian border. There they blew past the bewildered officials. The bright city of Askabad, with some twenty thousand residents, offered the weary wheelmen a welcome dose of modern civilization.

The next day the governor, Aleksei N. Kuropatkin, held a dinner in honor of the American visitors. He assured his guests that they could continue on toward Siberia, but he implored them to take the new trans-Caspian railway as far as Samarkind, some six hundred miles distant, so as to avoid the interlying desert. Feeling pinched for time and in little mood for more scorching conditions, the cyclists gratefully accepted his proposition.

Along the way, the cyclists stopped in Bukhara, where the curious locals besieged them. At Samarkind, they found a delightfully exotic Oriental city filled with blue domes, minarets, and the ruins of ancient palaces and tombs. In the noisy and crowded native quarters, men with white turbans strolled about, socializing and bartering with street vendors. The newly constructed Russian quarter, in contrast, boasted broad and quiet boulevards lined with comfortable houses. After a pleasant week's stay, the cyclists remounted their bicycles and headed along the highway to Tashkent, 180 miles distant.

Four days later, at the end of November, they entered the capital of Turkistan, a major military base and a sprawling city of 100,000, including some of the czar's least-favored relatives. Digging in for the long winter, they secured lodging with a German-speaking Russian businessman. They quickly found themselves enjoying surprisingly pleasant circumstances. Their host pampered them with hearty meals and a steady flow of vodka. And thanks to his high standing, the cyclists joined the city's party circuit and impressed the local elites with their intellects and broad knowledge of world affairs.

Of course, the lads still had plenty of time on their hands. To make the most of it, they took Russian lessons and patronized the local theater and opera house. They occasionally visited the popular military halls, where their peers frequently gathered to drink, smoke, banter, and play cards. Allen observed with a strong hint of disapproval: "Drunkenness, gambling, and social laxity have followed upon the introduction of western morals and culture." Some standards, however, remained intact, as the young men unhappily discovered one spring morning while cycling in a park. A vigilant policeman stopped their progress and castigated them for exposing their kneecaps in public.

During their hiatus, Sachtleben somehow managed to squeeze in a round trip to London—spending a collective month on trains. While there, he ordered new parts for their bicycles, including seats, chains, and chain oil. Fearing that the supplies would not arrive in Tashkent before their departure, he had them shipped to Tomsk, a city in Siberia through which he expected to pass sometime in late spring. The cyclists' friends in Tashkent had all but persuaded them to abandon the mad idea of crossing China and to take instead a more northern route across Siberia, to Vladivostok, where they could board a steamer bound for America.

At last, May arrived, and the roads out of Tashkent were finally passable. The cyclists were ready to roll for a third season, and they were determined to reach the Pacific coast before the next winter set in. After bidding heartfelt goodbyes to their host and friends, they headed toward Vernoye (now Almaty), a remote outpost some 250 miles northeast of Tashkent and a gateway into Siberia.

The cyclists clipped along the barren and boundless road traversing a rugged steppe, averaging about seven miles an hour. "With the absence of landmarks," Allen lamented, "you never seem to be getting anywhere." They frequently encountered bemused horsemen, who invariably challenged them to a race. Once, Sachtleben crashed full speed into a horse. He vaulted over the handlebars and dislocated an arm. The sympathetic onlookers, after jerking his limb back into its socket, fashioned a sling to keep it in place. Not entirely satisfied with the remedy, the travelers stopped at the next village to consult the local physician. She turned out to be an old blind woman "of the faith-cure persuasion." After soothing Sachtleben's pain with her deft massaging, she served up slices of bread with prayers inscribed in the butter coating.

At Vernoye, a French engineer persuaded the cyclists that they could still cross China after all, if their papers proved to be in order. He suggested that they head east to Kuldja (Yining), a Chinese city just over the border. There they could ask the local Russian consul if their papers issued in London would admit them into China. At the same time, they could grill the local Catholic missionaries to determine the feasibility of a foray into the Gobi Desert. Should they decide against proceeding into China, they could easily make their way back to the Siberian highway and resume the northern route. The cyclists decided to follow that plan.

On June 4, 1892 (the same day Lenz left New York City), after having covered more than one thousand miles of Russian territory, the cyclists crossed the border river Ili. Approaching Kuldja, they were detained at the customhouse by the chief Chinese official. "Putting on his huge spectacles," Allen recalled,

> he read aloud the visa from the Chinese minister in London. His wonderment was increased when he read that such a journey was being made on the "foot-moved carriages," which were then being curiously fingered by the attendants. Our garments were also minutely scrutinized, especially the buttons. Meanwhile, our caps and dark-colored spectacles were taken from our heads and passed around for each to try on, amid much laughter.

Settling into the city's Russian quarter as guests of the Russian consul, the Americans braced themselves for a long lull. Regardless of where they went next, they would need to have their bicycle parts redirected to Kuldja at once, for their wheels were no longer functional without repairs. Indeed, they were in dire need of new tires, axles, ball bearings, rims, and spokes. The lads telegraphed the chief of police in Tomsk and asked him to forward their package to Kuldja. Still, they knew it would be some time before their goods arrived.

In the meantime, the young men resolved once more to make the most of their hiatus. They again took language lessons, but this time they studied up on Chinese to prepare for an eventual excursion through that country. At the same time, they initiated their inquiries to determine whether that was a practical plan that would meet with the approval of the Chinese authorities.

Not all was business, however. With the cooperation of local authorities, they staged their most memorable public performance yet: a bizarre two-mile race against four horsemen for the benefit of three thousand animated citizens. At the sound of the gun, the cyclists took off atop the ancient city walls. The horsemen, who were making comparable loops along the ring road at ground level, bolted ahead and had built a comfortable lead after the first mile. By the third lap, however, the charging cyclists had overtaken their rivals, and they sailed to victory amid deafening cheers.

As for their future travel plans, the cyclists got plenty of contradictory advice. Minister Denby would note in his report:

> Russian friends in Kuldja did what they could to dissuade the two adventurous wheelmen from their bold undertaking, pointing out not only the difficulties of Gobi, whose shifting sands afforded a most difficult and uncertain surface for their fragile vehicles, but also the danger of venturing alone into China in such an unusual fashion, amongst a people little acquainted with foreigners and never too friendly to them. Perseverance, they were told, would probably cost them their lives.

The local missionaries, however, were far less pessimistic. They not only believed that it was possible to traverse the Gobi but also outlined the best route to the desert. That was exactly what the cyclists wanted to hear. And when the Russian consul concluded that their papers from the Chinese minister in London did indeed authorize transit to Peking, their decision was made for them. They would follow the most adventurous route, across northern China.

When the bicycle parts arrived in early July, they readied their mounts with the help of a local blacksmith. To minimize the weight of their bicycles, they shortened their handlebars and seat-posts. At the same time, they took steps to reduce their own weight. They trimmed their clothing, removed buttons, and exchanged their shoes for flimsy Chinese sandals. They even shaved their heads and faces.

To limit their load to about twenty-four pounds apiece, they sold one of their cameras, ditched their leather bags, and replaced their blankets with two light sleeping bags. Their minimized cargo would include a tin of chain oil, two handguns, notebooks, a map, a shaving blade they used on each other, a small supply of medicines, including eye lotion and quinine tablets, and a stash of tea and sugar provided by the Russian consul. They also abandoned all surplus clothing, resolving to frequently wash their scant garb with soap bars in streams. They could always cycle bare-chested, after all, while their shirts, tied to their handlebars, dried in the sun.

For currency, they would carry a wad of Russian paper money and about five pounds of silver chips apiece, to be stored in their hollow handlebars—enough, they calculated, to last them to Peking. This clever arrangement not only eliminated the need for additional containers but also concealed their wealth from potential robbers.

Finally, in mid-July, after a seven-week lull, the cyclists set forth for the desert. Their initial experiences hardly underscored the wisdom of their decision. One evening, while ingesting sheep's fat at a Kirghiz campsite, the two young men explained their plans to the chief, who could only stare back at them in disbelief. The next morning he dispatched a band of horsemen to lead the travelers to the caravan road. Upon reaching it, the horsemen somberly dismounted and formed a circle around the cyclists. They proceeded to utter a prayer to Allah for the safety of their guests. As the horsemen bade farewell to the cyclists, a few of them silently drew their fingers across their throats, as a warning to look out for treacherous Chinese.

Indeed, the cyclists could not shake off a gnawing sense of impending doom. Reaching a desolate valley, they came across a gruesome reminder of their dangerous surroundings and their own fragile mortality. Mounted on a pole, in a cage, was the shaggy, severed head of an erstwhile brigand, staring blankly ahead. The local authorities had installed the spectacle to serve as a stark warning to all would-be marauders. Though it no doubt served its purpose, it gave the innocent passerby little comfort.

Four days out of Kuldja, Sachtleben's chainwheel suddenly broke in two, rendering his bicycle useless. The tourists decided to leave both their vehicles at a Kirghiz camp, while they headed back to Kuldja on horseback with the broken piece. Once it was repaired, they intended to travel back the same way to reclaim their wheels, fix the broken one, and carry on.

The locals were hardly surprised to see the cyclists back in Kuldja so soon after their departure. Naturally, they figured that the young Americans had finally come to their senses. Much to their amazement, however, the adventurers exhibited no intention of abandoning their mission. On the contrary, once the local blacksmith had successfully repaired the chainwheel, the pair promptly headed back to the campsite where their wheels awaited.

Over the next several weeks, the cyclists slowly made their way through a variety of terrains, ranging from arid valleys to lush mountains, passing through the cities of Manas and Urumtsi (now Urumqui). On occasion, when faced with a hill or a swamp, they had to dismount and walk. They continued to brave the usual Asian hardships, including hostile dogs, animated mobs, demanding officials, and grimy, insect-infested inns with hard mattresses and overcharging owners. Their rooms invariably lacked locks and at times even doors, exacerbating their vulnerability.

On the bright side, the Chinese diet was generally varied and satisfying. At the abundant teahouses, the cyclists gleefully sunk their chopsticks into piles of sliced meat and stewed vegetables, soaked in zesty sauces. Moreover, local officials were generally accommodating, and rarely did they foist guards upon the cyclists. Some even posted notices in the local villages warning citizens not to molest the foreigners.

Finally, on August 10, the wanderers reached the last oasis village on the western edge of the great Gobi Desert. Suddenly they found themselves, as Allen put it, "standing at the end of the world, looking out into the realm of nowhere." Stretched out before them, as far as the eye could see, was an ocean of red sand, rippled by the howling wind. The magnitude—and perhaps the folly—of their mission was beginning to sink in. Perhaps their Russian friends in Kuldja had been right after all. The young men spent a restless night in town, contemplating their precarious fate.

As they began their trek across the desert, however, they were pleasantly surprised by the tolerable conditions. They found the roads reasonably firm and conducive to bicycle riding. Nor did they lack for company. This was, after all, the only highway connecting western and eastern China, and the caravan traffic was heavy. To their great relief, they found a post station—a sparse cluster of mud huts encircling a well—every thirty miles or so. Every station offered a kitchen where weary travelers could prepare their own food. That is, if they had any. The cyclists soon discovered that the managers had little to offer in the way of provisions. "When we asked if they had an egg, or a piece of vegetable," Allen recalled, "they would shout 'Ma-you!' ('there is none!'), in a tone of rebuke, as much as to say, 'My conscience, man! What do you expect on the Gobi?'"

In fact, all they could procure at the stations was coarse flour. But by mixing in sugar, drawn from their personal stash, the clever cyclists were soon producing a sweet treat they dubbed "Gobi cakes," which they gratefully consumed with tea. They always baked a surplus so that they would have a ready supply to take with them on the road. Occasionally, they found supplementary food in Kirghiz camps along the roadside. Once, upon reaching the top of a rare hill, they were astonished to find a Mongolian monastery looming in the distance. The resident monks, however,

were even more surprised to see the cyclists at their doorstep. Recovering their composure, the priests graciously suspended their
prayers to serve the wheelmen tea.

The climate was also a great challenge. The sun was often impossibly oppressive, and the tourists took pains to avoid cycling
in the middle of the day, seeking instead a shady refuge. For the
most part, they could find no inns and had to sleep out in the open,
though mercifully the night air was comfortably cool.

The cyclists made surprisingly good progress in the Gobi, covering up to fifty miles a day. But just when it appeared that they
would enjoy relatively smooth sailing, Allen's health deteriorated.
He had developed, it seemed, a bad reaction to his intake of salty
water. Sachtleben stepped up his production of Gobi cakes for
added sustenance and nursed his companion back to health.

Twelve days after entering the desert, the cyclists finally
reached the other side. They were not only much relieved to enter
a genuine town but astonished at what they saw there. Looming
before their own eyes was the western extreme of the Great Wall,
"rising and falling in picturesque undulations as far as the Tibetan
ranges."

At that moment, it struck the pair that they were on the verge
of accomplishing something truly epic. Before they had entered
the Gobi, their ride, though remarkable, had largely mirrored that
of Thomas Stevens. That was obviously no longer the case. Moreover, once they reached Peking, only a few thousand miles away,
they could claim to have accomplished, as Denby would put it, an
"exceedingly original and remarkable" feat: the crossing of China
from west to east, a monumental achievement unheard of since the
distant days of Marco Polo.

The lads nonetheless wisely resolved not to let the jubilation of
the moment jeopardize a successful conclusion to their Asian adventure. Following the Great Wall for a good four hundred miles,
they reached Lanchou (now Lanzhou), the bustling capital city of
the Gansu province, alongside the Yellow River, in the dead center of China. There they gratefully accepted the thoughtful gifts

of a viceroy, who presented them with yellow cloth flags to fly
on their bicycles identifying them as "traveling scholars" not to
be disturbed. Over the next two months, they rolled relentlessly
through the provinces of Shensi, Shansi, and Chikli and, finally,
into Peking.

In his lengthy report, Denby declared that the young Americans' adventure "shows, if nothing else, that for traveling immense
distances over rough and mountainous roads, the bicycle is a swift
and reliable means of locomotion." He suggested that American officials take due note of the young men's singular accomplishment
and its profound implications for military maneuvers.

Denby also asserted that the cyclists' experience revealed
much about present-day China. He summarized their rude reception: "They excited the unbounded curiosity of the natives, who
had never seen a bicycle before. They encountered some hostility,
which manifested itself in showers of stones and abusive epithets."
Denby nonetheless praised the local officials who, "from the highest to the lowest, gave them every aid and attention." He attributed their cooperation to the "admiration and wonder" that the
lads' "remarkable exploit" commanded, though he also credited
"the excellence of the passport received from the Chinese minister
in London."

Denby freely acknowledged his own esteem for the intrepid
young men, even as he offered a fatherly reproach: "It would be
justly estimated a foolhardy undertaking for two young men, ignorant of the languages and customs of the countries through
which they were to pass, and unaccompanied by guide, servant, or
interpreter, to venture across the comparatively unknown lands of
Central Asia on bicycles." Still, the diplomat conceded, their courage, determination, and resourcefulness had somehow seen them
through. Quoting the seventeenth-century French poet Jean-
François Regnard, Denby concluded: "Qui parvient au succès n'a
jamais trop osé" (Whoever succeeds never risked too much).

At last, the cyclists' long ordeal was effectively over, and their
fame, if not yet their fortune, seemed assured. True, they still had

to get to Shanghai, where they would board a ship bound for the west coast of North America. Then they would face a third continent. Still, their worst travails were clearly behind them. For the time being, they were content to linger in Peking. Thanks to Denby's son, who kindly replenished their wardrobes, they miraculously reverted to elegant young men. Taking advantage of their newfound celebrity, they became the toast of numerous foreign legations.

The travelers wisely opted to proceed to the coastal city of Tientsin (Tianjin) by houseboat, given the woeful state of their vehicles and the swampy terrain they would have had to cross.

After a leisurely thirty-six-hour float down the Pei-ho River, they stepped off the vessel to meet the resident American consul, William Bowman. The aging southerner kindly hosted the cyclists at his comfortable residence. He delighted his young countrymen with a most unexpected proposition: a private audience with General Li-Hung-Chang, China's foremost statesman. Needless to say, they accepted wholeheartedly.

The next morning the young men made their way to the American consulate, where two ornate sedan chairs awaited, surrounded by a dozen "coolies," or lower-class laborers. The young men took their seats and were promptly carted off to the viceroy's residence, a sprawling, one-story structure built of wood and adobe brick. A servant at the doorway greeted the honored guests. He then led them through a maze of stark rooms and a dark narrow hallway leading to an airy courtyard. There they entered a lavish parlor reserved for foreign dignitaries.

As they waited for their host, they sat down beside a warm hearth and chatted amiably with the viceroy's nineteen-year-old son, who peppered them with questions about the United States in fluent English. Charles Tenney, Bowman's American secretary, soon joined the party to act as an interpreter.

At last, two body-servants briskly strode into the room, followed by the statuesque statesman himself, his colorful silk dress flowing behind him. The Americans rose as the general approached them with a faint smile and an outstretched hand. Barely breaking stride, he led them into an adjoining conference room. After filling an armchair at the head of the long table, he motioned for the wheelmen to sit in the two seats to his left, while his son and Tenney dutifully assumed opposite positions. Allen later recalled the awkward lull that ensued:

> For almost a minute, not a word was spoken on either side. The viceroy had fixed his gaze intently upon us. Like a good general perhaps, he was taking a thorough survey of the field before he opened up with a cannonade of questions.
> "Well gentlemen," he said at last, "you don't look any the worse for your long journey."
> "We are glad to hear Your Excellency say so," replied Sachtleben, adding with more tact than sincerity: "Our appearance speaks well for the treatment we have received in China."

The viceroy, however, showed little inclination to prolong the small talk. "What was your real object in undertaking such a peculiar journey?" he demanded minutes into the conversation. The startled cyclists promptly replied that they were seeking a greater understanding of the world and its peoples, and the bicycle was merely the most convenient means to get around.

The viceroy then asked them to name their favorite country. The lads responded without hesitation that it was the United States. If that was the case, the viceroy asked testily, what was the point of traveling elsewhere? They replied that they would not have known this for sure if they had not traveled so extensively.

Li-Hung-Chang seemed to doubt that their objectives were purely educational. Nor could he understand why sensible men of means would opt to travel under their own power when they could easily induce others to do the work for them. In any case, he wondered aloud, why had they not gone through India and southern China, an obviously easier and safer route?

While listening to their replies, the viceroy frequently paused to draw whiffs of tobacco from a long pipe held to his mouth by one of his servants. He continued to ask the lads about the lands they had seen and solicited their thoughts on various pressing diplomatic issues. Finally, he focused the conversation on his own country: What did they think of China's cuisine and her roads? What did his countrymen make of their strange vehicles, and what did they call them? Had they ever been robbed? How had the people and governors of the various provinces treated them?

The Americans, who likewise paused periodically to puff their cigarettes, responded freely, if tactfully. For the most part, they had enjoyed the cuisine and found the roads tolerable. Huge crowds had assembled to view their vehicles, which were called everything from foot-moving machines to self-moving carts. They had lost nothing en route, although they often felt threatened by the populace. The officials were helpful, though they frequently demanded that the cyclists demonstrate their wheels.

By now the men had grown quite comfortable with one another. They shared a bottle of champagne and exchanged toasts to their respective countries. The viceroy's questions suddenly became more personal and pointed. He asked the Americans how much they had spent during their travels and whether they expected to make a profit. How rich were their parents? What were their political allegiances, and would they ever run for office? Did they realize that they could easily have vanished deep in China, without their loved ones ever learning their fate?

The cyclists deftly deflected most of the viceroy's questions, revealing only that one of them was a Democrat while the other was a Republican. When asked how this could be so, Sachtleben offered a simple and succinct explanation: "You see, Your Majesty, we have different thinkers inside our heads."

Overall, the Americans were greatly impressed by the viceroy's insatiable curiosity. Back home, they had met a few aggressive reporters and dogged investigators, but those fellows were hopelessly lax compared to this distinguished gentleman. Several times the young men politely signaled their restlessness. But just when it appeared that the inquisition was at last winding down, the probing statesman opened up a new line of questioning.

Finally, Li-Hung-Chang began to rise slowly from his chair, prompting his servants to grasp him by the elbows and help him to his feet. The cyclists breathed a muted sigh of relief before cheerfully thanking the viceroy for the great honor he had bestowed upon them. He replied, with a gentle smile, that he had merely performed his duty. "Scholars," he declared, "must receive scholars." Walking slowly but deliberately, he led his guests back to the main entrance. He gave both wheelmen another vigorous handshake before gracefully bowing out.

Later that day Allen and Sachtleben sailed to Shanghai. There they spent the next few weeks hobnobbing with foreign dignitaries. At one point they heard that another globe girdler would soon arrive from San Francisco to begin his own trip across China, traveling in the opposite direction. His name was Frank Lenz, and he hailed from Pittsburgh. Hoping to meet him, the two young men dawdled a few weeks longer. But when Lenz failed to turn up on schedule, they reluctantly decided that they could wait no longer. On December 6, 1892, they boarded the *Empress of China*, a six-thousand-ton steamer owned by the Canadian Pacific Railway, for a two-week voyage to Vancouver, British Columbia.

Indeed, after two and a half years abroad, the young men were anxious to return to their homeland. In their haste, they even abandoned plans to tour Japan, satisfying themselves instead with brief port calls to Nagasaki, Kobe, and Osaka. As they pulled out to sea for the long haul across the Pacific, a deep sense of satisfaction and serenity pervaded their hearts. They were returning home with their heads high, well poised to reap the just rewards of their arduous adventure.

5

SHANGHAI, CHINA

December 15, 1892

J OHN O'SHEA, an Irish reporter with the *Celestial Empire*, an English-language daily, finally got the tip he had been awaiting all week long. The "other" round-the-world cyclist, Frank Lenz of Pittsburgh, had just registered at the Astor House. Only twelve days earlier, Allen and Sachtleben, his famous predecessors, had checked out of that very same hotel in the heart of the Bund, the city's vibrant foreign quarters.

Entering the posh lobby, O'Shea had little trouble spotting his subject, whom he described as "a pleasant faced, boyish looking fellow." Lenz beamed as the journalist approached. "I suppose you came to hear about my trip?" the cyclist inquired with a sly smile. When O'Shea confirmed the obvious, Lenz replied most hospitably: "Well, come right up to my room and I will tell you all you want to know."

After the two settled in Lenz's spacious quarters, the cyclist described his first six months on the road. During the first five, devoted to crossing North America, he had registered five thousand miles—the longest transcontinental ride on record. Over the past month, he had toured Japan, where he logged another one thousand miles. He was thus well on pace to cover twenty thousand miles within twenty-four months. "My pocket-book here has notes about every place I visited and every hotel I stayed at," Lenz explained, "as well as accounts of numerous little incidents."

O'Shea was doubly impressed—this chap was evidently as thorough as he was athletic. As the journalist leafed through Lenz's diary, the cyclist cautioned that while these "minute details" had been "of great interest to me at the time, enlivening my lonely way," they were "very similar to the experiences of other wheelmen who have covered the same ground." Added Lenz, almost apologetically, "So far I have met with only ordinary tribulations. But I look to China to provide me with something thrilling."

The journalist shot a quick glance at Lenz, unsure if his subject was jesting. "I expect it will oblige," O'Shea remarked at last. "And exactly how do you plan to cross China, Mr. Lenz?" Without hesitation, the cyclist replied: "I propose to leave here next week and, by the advice of the gentlemen in charge of the Chinese Telegraph department here, to follow the telegraph line along the Yangtse river, right up to Bhamo, in Burma, on the headwaters of the Irrawaddy. Along those banks I mean to proceed to Mandalay, thence through the mountain passes to Aracan. From there I intend to skirt the coast to Calcutta. The rest of the journey will be comparatively easy."

No doubt it would be, O'Shea thought to himself—should Lenz make it out of China alive. The mere thought of this sympathetic but naive young man heading off alone on his bicycle into the hostile heart of China, in the dead of winter no less, sent chills down O'Shea's spine. Only recently, in the summer of 1891, a wave of antiforeigner riots had broken out in that very valley, quickly spreading across the country. Hundreds of Chinese Christians were massacred, and dozens of stations were set on fire or looted. In Wusuch, an unruly mob killed an English customs official and a Methodist missionary. Nor was the hostility confined to the rabble. As one American journalist had recently remarked: "An intense dislike to foreigners prevails among China's literary and official classes. They look upon us as savages and boors."

Suppressing the urge to lecture Lenz, O'Shea calmly asked the wheelman to sketch out the balance of his global itinerary. Lenz explained that upon reaching Calcutta he intended to cross India, Persia, and Turkey without ever leaving terra firma—an unheard-of feat. Sometime in late 1893 or early 1894, he would enter Europe for the final leg of his tour, then take a steamer back to New York.

Later that afternoon, O'Shea headed to the office to write up his story. He could not suppress his anxiety for the wheelman's well-being, declaring: "We fear that Mr. Lenz, plucky and determined though he is, has a very slight acquaintance with the difficulties of overland travel in China. We do not see how he is going to accomplish the great journey he has mapped out for himself, through the most hostile provinces of the interior."

Clearly, Lenz was heading for trouble—and relishing his growing notoriety. The next day he cycled over to the offices of the *North China Daily News*, the city's other English-language daily. The startled editor gloated: "It is not often that a subject so openly enters the net of the interviewer." The resulting article, entitled "Another Bicyclist in China," outlined Lenz's audacious plans for "a holiday likely to afford a little adventure." It concluded: "If determination can surmount obstacles, Mr. Lenz seems well equipped for the undertaking."

Lenz's supreme self-confidence was not entirely unjustified, for he was holding up remarkably well. His weight had barely fluctuated, and his health was excellent. Only once or twice had he fallen ill, and only for brief spells. His machine was also working admirably, including the pneumatic tires. He had suffered only a handful of flats, despite the abysmal state of American roads. And contrary to his modest assertions, he had already overcome an impressive array of hardships and close calls.

Admittedly, he had done "the easiest part first." His first leg, a ride up the lush Hudson Valley to Albany, was little more than a carefree romp punctuated by brief visits to Washington Irving's Sleepy Hollow and Vassar College in Poughkeepsie, though regrettably he had resisted the temptation to tarry with the "girls."

Whenever the roads became intolerably muddy and a railroad passed nearby, Lenz regained the hard cinder path within the tracks, keeping a constant lookout for broken bottles and approaching trains. "It's dangerous and I don't like to do it," Lenz maintained, though he would continue the practice throughout his transcontinental journey.

At Albany, Lenz turned his wheel west to follow the Erie Canal, alternating between the towpath and the turnpike. He crossed the scenic Mohawk Valley and then rode past thriving farmlands to Ilion, home of the famous Remington typewriters and bicycles. He reached Syracuse just in time to lead a parade. He paused in Rochester, home of the celebrated Kodak and the Rochester Optical Company, makers of his own camera. In bicycle-mad Buffalo, he spent a full three days, basking in the limelight.

Lenz soon found himself in Canada, gazing at the thundering Niagara Falls. An alert but insensitive customs official spoiled the majesty of the moment by demanding a 30 percent duty on the wheel. Lenz, flustered and indignant, produced his letter from the American secretary of state. The official looked it over and apologized for the intrusion. Lenz was allowed to proceed into Ontario without further molestation.

During his week in the Queen's Dominion, Lenz weathered oppressive heat, frequent rain showers, and his first dog attack. He sailed by endless fields of strawberries and grain as well as large flocks of grazing sheep, frequently enjoying the spontaneous company of other wheelmen. In Hamilton, Toronto, and London, he met scores of Canadian cyclists, including prominent pioneers from the early days of high-wheeling.

At Windsor, Lenz took a ferry to Detroit, site of the most recent LAW national meet and "one of the largest manufacturing cities in the United States." Indeed, a generation later the Ford plant in Highland Park would pump out scores of Model Ts after adopting mass-production techniques already under development by the thriving bicycle industry.

Lenz headed to Ann Arbor, home of the University of Michigan, the largest campus in the country with an enrollment of three thousand students. At Jackson, he was again feted by the local wheelmen, and his bicycle was put on display in a store window. On July 4, Lenz left South Bend, Indiana, at five in the morning so as to reach Chicago in time to celebrate the national holiday.

To avoid the flooded roads, Lenz again rolled between the railroad tracks. Entering Illinois, he passed by the enormous Pullman plant, maker of the world's finest sleeper cars. Just ahead were the looming structures of the upcoming Columbian Exposition, the world's fair in Chicago. Lenz correctly predicted that it would "eclipse any exposition ever held." Little did he know, however, that it would owe much of its future success to a fellow Pittsburgher. George Ferris in fact had just proposed a massive, upright wheel calculated to whip screaming passengers through the air. Ferris had been inspired by an earlier invention dear to Lenz's heart: the high-wheel bicycle.

That evening Lenz cut through Chicago's flowery Washington Park to Michigan Avenue. He reached the Grand Pacific Hotel covered in mud but satisfied with his progress. After one month on the road, he had registered his first thousand miles, averaging nearly sixty miles every riding day. He dawdled for a few days in the big city, touring bicycle clubhouses and catching up with correspondence. With the help of Robert Bruce, his shadowy escort, Lenz wrote his first reports and developed his first batch of photographs.

Although Lenz left Chicago with a hearty band of escorts, one man stood out: William A. Amory, a mute. Observed Lenz: "He was rather quiet company, riding side by side with me for mile after mile without saying a word. But sometimes we would rest by the roadside, and he would bring forth pen and paper and we would hold written conversation." To Lenz's great surprise, Amory pulled to a halt just after the Wisconsin line. He somehow managed to utter an intelligible word: "Dead!" Lenz immediately understood that his buddy was spent and ready to turn back.

Lenz stopped at a malted milk factory in Racine and pronounced the product "the most invigorating and refreshing drink I have ever tasted." James Horlick, the inventor, promised to "forward the gentleman quantities during his trip around the globe." Although the English-born pharmacist failed to keep that promise, he was soon supplying his calorie-laden, nonperishable drink to other famous adventurers, notably Arctic explorers. At Milwaukee, the capital of beer, and Madison, the charming capital city, Lenz was again the center of attention. Passing through Baraboo, the winter home of the Ringling Brothers circus, Lenz took in bewitching Devil's Lake.

But his budding affection for Wisconsin soon waned. While crossing a railroad bridge spanning a steep ravine, an express train suddenly lurched around the bend. Instead of beating a hasty retreat, Lenz suspended himself and his vehicle off one side of the trestle. With one hand he clung to the underside of a tie, and with the other he dangled his bicycle by its front wheel. The train promptly flew by within two feet of his upper hand, while the bridge "trembled and groaned." A few days later, he found himself trudging and cursing along the impossibly mucky road to Lacrosse.

At last, he came to the Mississippi. Passing over six or seven bridges connecting a string of islands, he entered Minnesota. At Winona, he observed a great lumber center. Heading toward St. Paul in poor weather, Lenz stuck to the railroad beds. "I bumped along rather jubilantly," he reported. Workmen and farmers interrupted their chores to marvel at his remarkable ability to ride the ties. Passing through Merrimac Island, Lenz reached the capital city, where some fifty wheelmen promptly treated him to a theater party and banquet. A few days later, at historic Fort Snelling, Lenz bade a hasty goodbye to Bruce, who was unexpectedly called away on personal business.

Lenz lingered a few days in Minneapolis, cavorting with local wheelmen. One, Thomas Bird, escorted the tourist out of town and stayed with him for a few days, insisting on carrying his camera case. After a quick sail around Lake Minnetonka, a fashionable resort, the pair headed west. They passed through small prairie towns populated mostly by Scandinavian immigrants. One evening Lenz admired, for the first time, the northern lights.

Meanwhile, newspaper reporters along the route scrambled to intercept the roving king of the wheel. In Granite Falls, one fortunate journalist got to spend two hours with Lenz, whom he pronounced "the greatest adventurer in his line of this century." The writer concluded his article with a heartfelt "Good luck to you, Frank." A journalist in Montevideo, however, took a dimmer view of the cyclist, remarking, perhaps with literal intent, "In our estimation he has more sand than sense."

Passing alone into South Dakota, Lenz spotted tepees for the first time. Enjoying smooth roads and a cool breeze, he sailed on to Aberdeen, the largest city on his route since Minneapolis. It boasted eighty wheelmen and twenty lady riders. When Lenz arrived at the Sherman Hotel, he found a large crowd awaiting him, including a reporter who judged Lenz "full of life and fun." After a bath and dinner, the obliging cyclist "cheerfully showed the local wheelmen his outfit, answering a multitude of questions."

Lenz decided to wheel north along the James River to Jamestown, North Dakota, where he turned west to follow the Northern Pacific line. A reporter in Bismarck described the cyclist's dramatic arrival:

> He came into the city amid a cloud of dust, and at a surprising rate of speed. To the casual observer his outfit was a queer one. Valises galore were strapped all over the wheel. He finally rode up to the Sheridan and took his wheel inside, removing his baggage. He registered as "F. G. Lenz, World's Tour Awheel" and immediately it was known that he was the young fellow employed by *Outing*. A crowd soon gathered to inspect his wheel and baggage, casting furtive glances at Lenz himself, who stood removing the stains of travel from his face.

The next morning, however, the alert reporter noticed that Lenz was "not by any means well." The journalist theorized that the cyclist was "unused to the water from the muddy Missouri." Lenz nevertheless made good use of his extended stay. Receiving a new tire and chain by the morning express, he spent most of the day repairing his wheel. The cyclist's unflagging spirits deeply impressed the reporter. "Lenz seemed not one whit discouraged, saying he will make the trip with flying colors."

Heading west into the Badlands, Lenz met a host of colorful and sympathetic characters. A cowboy presented him with a hunting knife, while an Indian gave him a drinking horn. The crewmen aboard passing trains repeatedly implored him "to get on and ride a stretch," though he refused to do so. Near the Montana line, he met the Eaton brothers, former Pittsburghers who operated the Custer Trail Ranch, so named because General George A. Custer had camped nearby on his way to his Last Stand. While staying at their lodge, which was popular with eastern tourists, Lenz was surprised and elated when in marched three of his buddies from back home, clad as cowboys.

Passing into Montana in mid-August, Lenz regained the prairie but suffered from stifling heat as temperatures soared to over 100 degrees Fahrenheit. Reaching Miles City, he was struck by its evident prosperity. Although it had recently lost its lucrative buffalo trade with the virtual extinction of that once-ubiquitous beast, the city had risen "phoenix-like" thanks to its imported livestock. In fact, it was fast becoming "the greatest cattle center in the world."

Faced with the need to cross the Yellowstone River, Lenz engineered yet another brush with disaster. Spotting an abandoned skiff on the opposite bank, he decided to swim over to it so that he could return with the means to transport his goods to the other side of the Yellowstone. "I didn't know anything about that river," Lenz later confessed. "If I had, I would have left it alone. The minute I struck the water I was swept down with the current like a leaf, and it was about all I could do to get out."

The western wilderness imposed many more challenges. Stray needles from cactuses proved as "stiff as steel" and flatted both tires before Lenz appreciated the need for vigilance. Many times he found himself parched with no water in sight. Once he was immobilized for an entire day after drinking contaminated water. He blamed himself for not having purified it beforehand with his ginger tablets. Several times he carelessly fell off steep hills, narrowly escaping serious injury. In Yellowstone Park, a pristine land "snatched from the hand of the Creator," he camped under a rock for a day and a half while a snowstorm raged.

Still, the going was smoother than Lenz had expected. "Back East they had tried to frighten the young rider with stories of the wild and wooly West," a San Francisco paper recounted. "They said that Indians would wear his scalp and cowboys would make him dance at the muzzle of a gun." But as Lenz would later confess: "I had no trouble with anything except dogs." He passed by many reservations and met plenty of Indians, but they were "civil enough." Seeking only to "handle his wheel," they generally concluded: "Good horse, no eat!" He saw many cowboys too, but they wanted nothing more than to ride beside him and chat—until their horses tired of the chase. "The fact is," Lenz concluded, "people are all alike in this country. And if a man minds his own business he won't get into trouble."

Reaching Bozeman, at the foot of pine-forested mountains, Lenz found a "picture of Western enterprise." Its electric lights, among other telltale signs of progress, proved that "the westward march of the empire has already passed this point." And of course, with prosperity came vice. "As is customary in all far Western towns," Lenz observed, "the saloon and gambling dive can be found without the assistance of a detective. And while I neither drink nor play, I saw some folks who evidently do plenty of both."

In early September, Lenz landed in the state capital, which was born forty years earlier amid the area's still-productive gold mines. "I tarried for five days in hospitable Helena," the wheelman reported, "and was kept very busy scribbling notes, developing negatives, and inspecting the place." He felt "quite at home" with the city's wheelmen, thirty "kindly fellows." They put on "one of those dinners which make life pleasant and enable a wheelman to laugh

at the next mountain range." Lenz nevertheless took a few practical steps to prepare for the precipitous roads ahead. He flipped
his rear wheel to engage his low gear, and he shifted his one brake
from the front to the rear wheel to increase his stopping power.

And then he began his long ascent, walking much of the way.
"The approach to the Rockies, that huge backbone to the continent,
is indescribably impressive," Lenz effused. "A mountain range was
never better named—with its soaring heights, monstrous cliffs,
and its grim, shadow-laden gorges stretching as far as the eye can
see." Three days later, Lenz emerged on the other side, regain-
ing civilization at Missoula, a major military outpost and trading
center. Its ten wheelmen, only one of whom rode pneumatic tires,
begged Lenz to stay for a few days, to no avail.

In mid-September, Lenz reached Pend d'Oreille, Idaho. A reporter described the scene: "His arrival excited quite a little curiosity as a bicycle is not seen here every day. And when it became known that he had come from New York in three months on
his machine, and that he was on his way around the world, he attracted as much attention as a circus." Once again Lenz was unfazed by all the attention. "He changed his apparel and appeared
very neatly dressed. He strolled around the streets asking numerous questions about the place. He sent the magazine he represents
a fifteen page letter." When Lenz left town the next day, he went
over "the long trestle at a high rate of speed, and was watched by
quite a crowd of wondering people till he was out of sight."

While he was in Idaho, Lenz reported, "forest fires were raging,
and I had trouble with fallen timbers. Often my pedals would strike
a stump, and I would go one way and my machine the other." But
after passing through Spokane, Washington—"a city that seemed
to have been transplanted from the east"—Lenz faced even worse
conditions. In fact, traversing Oregon's Columbia River Gorge
proved "the hardest part of the journey." Recounted Lenz: "The
desert between Walla Walla and the Dalles—that was tough. I was
enveloped in a sand storm and had to walk 100 miles in five days. I

had a canteen of coffee and some hardtack [biscuit], but they were gone long before I could find a settler to stock up from."

As consolation for his sufferings, however, Lenz enjoyed a steady stream of spectacular scenery that seemed to change "at every bend in the river." He gushed to a reporter: "What a grand gorge that Columbia is! What a magnificent river! It is worth coming clear across the continent to see it. In all my journey, I have seen nothing to compare with it." Told that he would find similar scenes when he crossed the Siskiyou Mountains in southern Oregon, Lenz snapped: "I don't want to see anything grander. I don't think the Columbia can be beaten."

By the end of September, Lenz had reached the bustling city of Portland on the banks of the Willamette River. His first evening at the Hotel Portland proved a memorable one. "I went into the toilet room and commenced washing," Lenz recalled. "The janitor eyed me suspiciously. I confess that I did not present a very creditable appearance." Seconds later, the employee ordered the intruder off the premises. But Lenz issued a terse "Guess not" and calmly carried on with his chore. Infuriated, the janitor yelled: "Be gone or I'll throw you out. We don't allow tramps around here!" Lenz at last turned to his antagonist and stated matter-of-factly, "Well, my friend, I am a guest here." Lenz would never forget the man's horrified reaction. "I never saw an Irishman so astonished in all my life. He had to go upstairs and satisfy himself from the clerks. After that, there wasn't a darky in the hotel more attentive to me."

The next evening Lenz attended a reception in his honor. He explained the finer points of his wheel and camera to a rapt audience of some 150 wheelmen. After one day of much-needed rest, he joined some 65 cyclists for a Sunday excursion to Vancouver, Washington, site of the famous fort. He tarried one more day in Portland, so reluctant was he to leave his adoring friends. At the same time, however, he was anxious to reach the Pacific coast. Finally, on the morning of October 3, he prepared to resume his ride.

Before leaving the hotel, Lenz dashed off a letter to his step-uncle, Fred Lenz, back in Pittsburgh. It alluded to the darker motives behind his long journey. "Dear Sir," he began in his beautiful cursive.

> At the request of my mother I write you so you will rest assured that I have no ill-feeling against you. Having had nothing but a miserable existence at home under my step-father, I at last decided to travel the world awheel, for my own learning and pleasure. So far I am well pleased with my trip, every foot I am making on this wheel, 4,028 [miles] so far. From here I go to San Francisco, then sail for Asia. I may return maybe fifteen months again. Of course, I make some money writing for the N.Y. magazine *Outing*. With kind regards to your wife, I remain, Yours Truly, Frank Lenz.

A few days later, at Grants Pass on the Rogue River, an enterprising journalist used a novel, if taxing, technique to gain an interview. "Sunday being our day of rest," he explained to his readers, "we mounted our flying Dutchman and accompanied the tourist as far as Gold Hill, returning on the evening express. We made the eighteen miles in 2:30." The grueling workout, however, destroyed the writer's romantic notions about long-distance cycling. "From a common standpoint," he opined, "it seems very easy to ride a bicycle. But it gets very monotonous and tiresome after a few thousand miles."

At Ashland, the local wheelmen warned Lenz that the five-mile road to the first summit was a sheer "terror." He began his ascent on foot and was soon panting. Behind him, he heard a faint rumbling. Turning around, he spotted an oncoming wagon. The driver, a farmer, was furiously whipping his horses, in an apparent effort to catch up to him. Lenz, anxious to save his breath and avoid a round of inane questioning, picked up his pace. But the determined driver leapt from his vehicle and managed to catch up to the cyclist on foot. "He sheepishly asked me, by way of starting a conversation, if I was really going to the top of the mountain,"

Lenz recalled. "I gruffly answered in the affirmative and spoke no further. He wisely troubled me no more."

As Lenz sauntered on, a light rain began to fall. It had turned into freezing sleet by the time he reached the snowy summit. Still, he concluded that the climb "was not as bad as I had been led to believe." He paused to take in the spectacular view from 4,300 feet above sea level. To the south, in California, he could see the stage road wind its way over "ridge after ridge of mountains." He climbed on his bicycle and quickly reached a breakneck speed as his rear wheel skipped over the wet pebbles. He applied his brake spoon, but soon desisted when he realized that its leather casing had worn off. Mercifully, he reached Edgewood intact and retired for the night in the shadow of Mount Shasta.

Over the next two days, Lenz negotiated even steeper grades. Except for a few packhorses and wagons carrying prospectors and migrant families, he had little company. The only reminders of civilization were the wagon road itself and the rails of the Southern Pacific, which occasionally came into view. At last, he reached Redding and the fertile Sacramento Valley. Passing through beautiful Chico on a graveled, tree-lined road, he entered the capital city, whose prominent dome reminded him of the national Capitol building. The local cyclists took charge of him, and a number escorted him to Stockton the next day, including one "splendid lady rider."

Leaving the valley at Livermore, a mere forty miles from the Golden Gate, Lenz made a final push for the coastline. Reaching a prominent hilltop, he looked down on the "welcome expanse of San Francisco Bay, glimmering in the bright sunlight." He gleefully coasted downhill on smooth, shaded streets lined with elegant houses. That evening Lenz boarded a ferry in Oakland. Passing Goat Island, the vessel at last docked at the Golden Gate, his home for the next five days.

Lenz loved the "witchingly beautiful" landscape of San Francisco: its steep hills, foggy beaches, and coastal rocks filled with barking seals. He admired its bustling port, the wild and expansive Golden Gate Park, and the neat rows of "artistically built" homes. He lamented, however, that the preponderance of wooden constructions invited "a great conflagration at some future day." (Indeed, some fourteen years later fires ignited by the great earthquake would destroy much of the city.) Despite its inclines, Lenz enjoyed riding about town, taking advantage of the cable car slots on the major avenues.

Lenz found one square mile of the old city center especially intriguing: dirty, jam-packed Chinatown, where some thirteen thousand souls—over half the city's Chinese population—"huddled together in terrible conditions." It made him think nervously ahead to his date with the native Chinese, for he felt as though he had just walked into "China proper." Pungent restaurants serving Asian fare abounded. Countless shops sold everything from junk to jewelry, while a host of artisans busily practiced their trades. The inquisitive Lenz even took in an afternoon of Chinese opera.

Lenz readily discovered that this beehive had its sordid and shocking underside. True, the gambling houses were not unlike the dives he had seen in Montana. But the smoky opium dens were something else entirely. There he saw "sickly wrecks of men," slaves to the dreadful drug that poisoned their brains with "wondrous visions" while robbing them of any hope. The filthy lodging houses, where each room held two or three wretches crammed together, were no less disturbing.

Still, Lenz felt little sympathy for Chinese Americans. He found the "bitter hatred" harbored by his western compatriots toward them "hardly surprising." Declared Lenz: "The Chinese, with their great cunning, oust American labor. They work at what would be starving wages to a white man, then leave for home a few years later with their hoarded earnings." Lenz decried their resistance to American culture. "Their mode of dress they never change, showing no affinity to the United States whatever."

Fortunately, the city's vibrant cycling community kept Lenz from dwelling on the negative. Two days before his departure, on October 23, he joined fifty members of the Bay City Wheelmen for a sixty-six-mile bayside run to Palo Alto and back. The group enjoyed a hearty lunch in leafy Redwood City and a tour of the nearby Stanford campus. Lenz was reportedly "much impressed by the buildings of the university."

The next evening, the same club held a lavish banquet at a downtown hotel. The guest of honor spoke about his transcontinental journey, showing photographs he had taken en route—before getting himself into a fix. "After the last cup of black coffee had been drained," the *Chronicle* reported, "Lenz and his new-found friends started up Market street, filling the air with joyful adieus. The young men were seven abreast, and everybody else had to clear the way for this imposing front." Suddenly the lads noticed a bar across the street and made a beeline for it. Lenz, the self-professed teetotaler, imbibed a few too many beers and wound up spending the night in jail.

The next morning the groggy wheelman appeared in police court. "Lenz was disturbing the peace," Officer John Green explained to the judge, "and no one could sleep on the same block." The officer asserted that he had advised the young man to go home, "but Lenz declared he would not, until he had traversed the Tartar desert and conquered Africa's sands, or something to that effect."

Then it was Lenz's turn to march to the stand. "It was just this way," he began in a firm voice. "I have been in many cities but I never saw such a policeman as this one," he declared, thrusting an accusative finger in the direction of the arresting officer. "I was standing quietly with my friends, and he rushed in furiously. He saw I was the smallest, so he grabbed me."

After Lenz concluded his statement, the judge sat expressionless for a few moments. Suddenly he "smiled peacefully." Without further ado, he announced his decision. He could not fault the officer for his course of action, but he would nonetheless dismiss the case so that the overzealous but earnest wheelman would not miss his boat, scheduled to depart that very afternoon for Honolulu.

Returning to his hotel to collect his gear, a still-somber Lenz was struck by a sudden and sobering realization: "to wheel around a world is no trifling task." Up to that moment, he had "retained the privilege" to turn his wheel around and reverse his course, even if he had never seriously considered such a humiliating retreat. Once aboard the *Oceanic*, however, there could be no turning back. As he mounted his loaded bicycle and headed toward the pier, he tried valiantly to rally his flagging spirits.

As he prepared to board his vessel along with five hundred fellow passengers—mostly Asians who would be crammed into steerage—Lenz paused to shake hands with his small entourage. In the background, he could hear the missionary ladies singing sacred songs to their departing brethren. As he clutched his bicycle and approached the plank, it occurred to him that he was about to take his last step on American soil for "many a day." Minutes later he stood on the deck watching as the steamship pulled away and a flock of seagulls followed in its wake.

A week later, on the morning of November 1, the *Oceanic* approached the mountainous Hawaiian Islands. After entering the bay of Honolulu, it anchored just outside the coral reef. Several long boats, paddled by enterprising oarsmen, suddenly appeared at the ship's side. Lenz boarded one with his bicycle and soon landed on the island of Oahu. Spinning his way along narrow streets, he took stock of the locals. "Some were as black as negroes, others of a brown color; all have black, straight hair, and many boast beautiful and intellectual countenances." Lenz especially admired the "picturesque" police, "clad in their white linen trousers and blue coats." He soon deduced that "nearly all the natives speak English, and are very polite."

Lenz called on George Paris, a former resident of San Francisco and the local agent of Columbia wheels. The two wheeled up Punchbowl Hill, taking in a magnificent panoramic view of the surrounding islands. In the distance, Lenz spotted his vessel, bobbing like a toy in a tub. In the city center, Lenz photographed himself and his bicycle before the Iolani Palace, the official residence of the Hawaiian monarch. He then reluctantly retreated to the port to board the *Oceanic*. That same evening, as it departed for Yokohama, Lenz bid a fond farewell to this picturesque "one horse kingdom."

Back on the high seas, Lenz battled seasickness and his persistent "blue funk." During the day, while the officers and other cabin passengers played cricket and other spirited games on the deck, he stood idly by, staring blankly at the endless sea. Every evening he returned to the same spot to ponder the stunningly beautiful sunsets. "Sometimes I vaguely wondered what might await me in lands overseas," he confessed in his first report since leaving shore, "and if I was to face any serious perils."

Still, Lenz found a few pleasant diversions aboard. He would often descend to the engine room to admire the great furnace, "fired by Chinese stokers stripped to the waist." He conversed regularly with his fellow cabin passengers, some forty in all, including two American missionaries returning to Kobe, Japan, whom he promised to visit shortly. He also spent much time in his cozy cabin, attacking the pile of mail he had collected in San Francisco. For the most part, he enjoyed writing his friends to tell them of his progress. A reply to his step-uncle Fred in Pittsburgh, however, was painful to write. It ended with an earnest plea reflecting his growing anxiety. "If you see my mother, always try to drive the fear from her, as I will no doubt get through everywhere without trouble."

On November 14, the *Oceanic* anchored in the harbor of Yokohama at dawn. Hundreds of sampans, small scows propelled by oars, quickly surrounded the steamer. A swarm of Japanese merchants invaded the vessel. They spread out their wares on its main deck to entice the captive Chinese passengers, who were not allowed to debark. Three of them could not have descended anyway, having died in transit. Their bodies were being embalmed for the final leg of their voyage back to their homeland.

Lenz was eager to explore Japan, having read up on its history and culture, including this passage from Thomas Stevens: "Artificial lakes, islands, waterfalls, bridges, temples, and groves abound. Occasionally, a large figure of the Buddha squats serenely on a pedestal, smiling in happy contemplation of the peace, prosperity, and beauty of everything and everybody. Happy people! Happy country!" The Japanese, in turn, had thought highly of the peculiar ordinary rider. Wrote one journalist: "Stevens is a tough fellow, fit and well dressed; said to eat noodles as he travels." Another was struck by Stevens's willingness to sleep in tents or even outdoors, gushing: "It's hard to believe he comes from an advanced nation where luxury is the norm."

With the majestic Fuji, a snowcapped volcano, already visible in the distance, Lenz was certain that Japan would live up to its billing as an "Earthly Eden." He looked forward to spectacular scenery, even if he knew he was in for a few rough climbs. He was not quite sure how he would cope with the strange language, diet, and customs, but he sensed that he would get along well with Japan's "clever and industrious" citizens.

First, however, he had to get past the pesky customs officials, who demanded a 5 percent duty on his bicycle and camera. Lenz grudgingly forked over the $5 they had stipulated. He later appealed to the American consul but was told that, to get a refund, he would have to exit from the same port. Lenz took some consolation in the fact that the clueless officials had undervalued his gear.

Lenz spent two days in Yokohama, a bustling city of 115,000. He toured its curio shops, stores, and temples replete with splendid wooden carvings. Spinning around the city on his wheel, he admired its charming canals and strange watercraft. The narrow streets were crowded with rickshaws and pedestrians carrying babies tied to their backs and goods suspended on poles. He attended a theater and found the production refreshingly different from the Chinese performance he had seen in San Francisco. He relished his first visit to a teahouse, where "beautiful Japanese girls smile and bow." Lenz mused: "How different from America," where a man was lucky just to get "ordinary politeness" from café employees.

Although, by treaty, foreigners did not need special papers to visit or reside in six Japanese ports, including Yokohama and Tokyo, Lenz would need special papers from the Japanese government to enter the interior. He thus made his way to the American embassy in Tokyo to procure a passport. The eighteen-mile ride was popular with the wheelmen in both cities, a sparse but enthusiastic lot.

Reaching the capital, Lenz was impressed by its horse-drawn streetcars and other signs of modernity. He also appreciated its many captivating shrines and temples, but was taken aback by the city's huge red light district, with its "large and spacious buildings." At night from ten to twenty "beautiful girls" sat in plain view at the street level, "like so many wax figures." Lenz elaborated: "The windows have no glass, simply bars of wood, enabling passers-by to converse at will with the inmates. Their costumes are magnificent and their toilets and hair-dressings are carefully attended to. So runs house after house for entire blocks, all brilliantly illuminated and without the slightest concealment."

Lenz explained to his readers that "in the Flowery Land it is considered no disgrace to be a prostitute." He added that Japanese parents were prone to sell their daughters to these houses of ill repute to raise money for acquisitions or to pay off debts. "And so self-sacrificing are Japanese girls," he asserted, "they obey their elders without question." Just as shocking, Lenz observed, was the fact that Japanese men often plucked their brides from this "degraded sisterhood," although they retained the right to divorce their wives "on the smallest pretext."

Lenz returned to Yokohoma on November 18 to make final preparations for his ride through Japan. By the time he left the city the next morning, at least ten local newspapers had announced his presence and his intention to cycle to Nagasaki. Wrote one: "Lenz claims that at high speed, the bicycle he rides can run 15 miles an hour, a rate of 70 miles per day." Added another: "Lenz is a talented photographer and is carrying with him a light-weight camera. He takes fine scenic photographs of the locations he passes through."

Starting down the eastern coast of Honshu, Japan's central island, Lenz sailed past endless rice paddies, where men and women were wading up to their waists to cut the ubiquitous grain. He soon reached Kamakura, home of the famous giant bronze Buddha cast around the year 1250. Its face alone measured eight and a half feet in height. As Lenz pushed on, he was struck by the friendliness of the locals, who yelled to him "ohayo" (good morning) and "sayonara" (goodbye). He soon made his way to his first beach and the picturesque island of Enoshima, where he explored a cave.

Meanwhile, Lenz was rapidly adjusting to Japanese life. He feasted on rice, eggs, and fish, though he preferred to use his own utensils rather than the supplied chopsticks. He learned to remove his shoes indoors and to kneel on the floor while socializing. At inns, he even partook in coed bathing—that is, once he got over the initial shock. The first time he naively headed toward a tub, clad only in a bathrobe, he was flabbergasted to discover that he was about to join six naked Japanese ladies and gentlemen. "Recovering my breath," Lenz recounted, "I thought it best not to appear surprised. So I disrobed nonchalantly and joined the group as if I had been doing this for years."

Halfway to Nagasaki, Lenz came across a formidable mountain range and wisely hired a coolie to help him haul his machine over the summit. "Together we struggled for two and a half hours," Lenz recalled, "stepping from stone to stone. Sometimes the coolie gave out and sometimes I did." Still, the work was not entirely unpleasant. From his lofty vantage point, Lenz took in pristine forests, sparkling mountain lakes, and spectacular ocean views.

Suddenly, daunting China seemed a world away. Lenz felt nothing but joy traversing the enchanting land of the rising sun. He found the cost of living quite reasonable. Hotels were basic but clean and comfortable. The food was good and plentiful. Three or four times a day he would stop at roadside stands for nourishment. The roads were generally tolerable as well. Sailing along the Tokaido, a tree-lined, graveled road paralleling the Imperial Railway, he found level stretches as long as sixty miles. The land was stunningly beautiful, and the countryside was dotted with captivating relics, notably ancient pagodas and graceful wooden bridges.

Most intriguing of all were the denizens. Lenz met no end of interesting characters. Once, he spotted three gentlemen teetering along on old-fashioned boneshakers, making a frightful racket. "When they saw me they dismounted," Lenz recalled, "and gazed with envy at my pneumatic tire, rolling easily and silently along." Another time he knelt down with a local police chief and his daughter to hold conversation in English. When his legs cramped, he stretched them out, only to learn from the daughter that he was showing bad form, whereupon he reluctantly resumed his painful posture. Another time a blind masseur, hearing that Lenz had just cycled sixty miles, offered his services. Lenz could hardly refuse, though he would later lament: "The man proceeded to finger, push and bore every muscle in my body until I feared he would spend all night at it."

The onset of winter, however, tempered his bliss. One morning he awoke to find a Japanese attendant at the foot of his bed pointing out the window while uttering "Yuki." Lenz had a look for himself, and sure enough, he beheld a mantle of snow cloaking the city's rooftops and surrounding hills. Undeterred, he bought a pair of gloves and glided through the slush toward Kyoto, where the emperor had resided until the advent of the current Meiji era twenty-five years earlier.

After a brief stay in the former capital city filled with smoking factories, Lenz reached Kobe and its busy harbor reminiscent of Yokohama, jammed with vessels from all over the world. On the overlooking hills loomed "the beautiful homes of the foreigners." Checking into the Oriental Hotel, he was happy to be among white people again after nine days in Japan. He called on the two missionaries he had met aboard the *Oceanic*. He also met Robert Hughes, a middle-aged English businessman, who invited the wheelman to stop by his residence, eight miles west, on his way to Nagasaki.

A few days later, heading out from Kobe, Lenz hit a smooth stretch. To his great surprise, he came across a huge American flag draped from a bamboo arch spanning the width of the road. He suddenly remembered Hughes's invitation. His host had thoughtfully installed this prominent reminder near the entrance to his residence. Lenz sheepishly descended from his wheel and received a warm reception from Hughes and his large staff of Japanese servants.

On his final stretch in Honshu, Lenz suffered his biggest setback in Japan when a sly chambermaid lifted a $20 bill from his wallet. After persistent protest, he managed to recover it, but the affair left him embittered. Fortunately, his mood brightened a few days later when he came across a flock of laughing school children lined along the road to watch him pass. Partaking in a shrimp feast in Hiroshima also helped to restore his faith in Japan. At Iwakuni, he took in "one of the oldest and most peculiar bridges I ever saw. It consisted of five arches, each describing part of a circle from pier to pier, independent of one another. Crossing over it was like climbing over five immense casks."

To reach Kiusiu Island across the strait, at the base of Japan, Lenz boarded a small steamboat. He soon found himself negotiating one last Japanese mountain range, this time unassisted. At last, on December 10, the stunning harbor of Nagasaki loomed into view. He admired its beautiful setting, surrounded by "tier after tier of forested hills." The *Rising Sun* recapped his visit:

> Frank Lenz arrived here at 11:00 am on Saturday last from Yoko-hama, having traversed the intervening distance, some 960 miles, in seventeen and a half riding days. From the very limited acquaintance he has had with the people during his flying visit he has formed a very favourable impression of them, and considers the country a very interesting and pleasant one to travel through.

A popular Japanese magazine for youth, *Shonen-En*, also made note of Lenz's successful arrival in Nagasaki, though it deemed Allen and Sachtleben's recent arrival in Peking "even more incredible." The paper praised both parties and drew a parallel with a homegrown hero: "Although horseback riding and cycling have certain distinctions, these cyclists can be compared to our nation's own adventurer, Major Yasumasa Fukushima." Indeed, the military leader had left Berlin on his horse the previous February for Vladivostok, some nine thousand miles distant. He was making steady progress, compiling copious notes.

After a two-day sail, Lenz reached Shanghai. Its densely populated, walled-in center reminded him of San Francisco's congested Chinatown, on a much larger scale. He noted that some 200,000 unfortunates lived there in filthy and cramped quarters, amid "fearful" odors. Along the narrow streets, which were barely ten feet wide, lay scores of beggars and cripples pleading for alms. Outside the ancient walls, Lenz observed how the other half lived. There, too, conditions were often deplorable. But at least the populace seemed gainfully employed. Countless numbers toiled in dingy little shops, while scores of coolies scurried about hauling wheelbarrows and rickshaws. Others toiled at construction projects, belting out soulful tunes to lighten their load.

Lenz quickly detected numerous Chinese foibles: they wrote backwards, kept their hats on during social calls, shook their own hands, and wore white when mourning. One habit was downright repulsive: the propensity of wealthy women to bind their feet to make themselves more attractive to men. "Some have feet not more than three inches long," Lenz observed, "and upon these poor, wee, concentrated tootsies they manage to stump awkwardly, as though they were upon pegs."

In San Francisco, Lenz had pondered American attitudes toward the Chinese. In Shanghai, he contemplated the reverse sentiment, wondering in particular what sort of treatment the populace would "mete out to a prowling American wheelman." He was certain that "the Chinese hate all whites." After all, the vast majority of China's 400 million citizens "struggle hard for an existence." It was only natural that they would resent Western prosperity and might.

Indeed, Lenz conceded, "John Chinaman" had a legitimate grudge against the "foreign devil" who routinely abused him abroad and imposed unspeakable evils at home, such as the deadly opium and senseless imperial wars. Lenz saw for himself how British officials routinely manhandled the poor coolies and generally abused the locals. He reasoned: "I fail to see how Europeans can expect anything but bitter hatred from the Chinese in return for their policies."

During his week in Shanghai, Lenz busily prepared for his trek to Burma. He sought advice from missionaries, diplomats, and telegraph operators. Invariably, they implored him to abandon his dangerous scheme. Of course, he entertained no such thought. He did, however, agree to change his course. Originally, he planned to follow a more southern route to Bhamo, similar to the one taken by Augustus Margary (a British diplomat who was murdered in 1874 on the way back to Shanghai). But the telegraph operators persuaded Lenz to follow their poles instead. Although this route would add about one thousand miles, it was better marked, and it followed a river for most of the way. Lenz could present his letter of introduction and stay overnight at the stations along the way.

For currency, he assembled a bagful of silver and brass coins. Warned to expect bitter cold and meager bedding at inns, he purchased an overcoat and a blanket, even though they added twenty pounds to his already considerable load. At last, two days before Christmas, he bade goodbye to the Astor House staff and began to pedal with "a feeling closely akin to dread."

6

VANCOUVER, CANADA

December 20, 1892

AFTER DEBARKING FROM the *Empress of India,* Thomas Allen and William Sachtleben headed straight to the Manor House, a comfortable lodge in downtown Vancouver. There they granted their first interview in North America, to an enterprising journalist. They spent the next two days canvassing the port town, which only a few years earlier, before the arrival of a train line, had been a non-entity. Since then, it had blossomed into a thriving trade center of some thirteen thousand citizens, and it now boasted impressive landmarks like an elegant opera house.

The travelers were tempted to cycle down the coast, but the weather was cold and rainy. Besides, they reckoned, if they took the coastal train, they could arrive in San Francisco in time for a Christmas feast. So they booked berths in a sleeper car and climbed aboard. The ride was quite pleasant, offering panoramic views of forests, Mount St. Helens, and the Columbia River Gorge.

The relentless rain slowed the train to a crawl, and as Christmas unfolded Sachtleben and Allen were still riding it. Unfazed, they made do with the meager offerings of the buffet car. "After two and a half years on bicycles, running through the wildest parts of the world," Sachtleben reflected, "we could easily put up with a little inconvenience." Indeed, they were thrilled simply to be back in their homeland. After finally arriving in the city in the wee hours of December 26, they made a dash to the fashionable Occidental Hotel on Montgomery Street, where they enjoyed a sound sleep.

The next day they received a stream of reporters in their hotel room. They managed, nonetheless, to take a long lunch break featuring "the biggest porterhouse steak in the city." At last, Americans were about to learn the full details of their extraordinary adventure. The next morning the *Call* reproduced their likenesses from photographs and devoted an entire page to what it described as "the most remarkable journey of the century, and perhaps of any century."

The travelers had a few things to catch up on themselves. Democrat Grover Cleveland, backing the gold standard, was about to return to the White House after a four-year hiatus. During the cyclists' absence, the Union had admitted two more states, Idaho and Wyoming, raising the total to forty-four. The West had been effectively won, at long last, following the massacre of the Lakotas at Wounded Knee, South Dakota. Thomas Edison was rumored to have invented a cabinet through which one could view a moving picture, called the kinetoscope.

One of the most extraordinary—and for the cyclists, fortuitous—developments was the continued success of the safety bicycle. In 1890, when Sachtleben and Allen left for England, a mere seventeen American bicycle makers were producing a modest forty thousand wheels a year, while English firms supplied much of the growing domestic demand for hard-tired safeties. Dozens of manufacturers across the United States were now catering to the astonishing demand for pneumatic safeties, having produced nearly one quarter of a million units in the season just passed.

True, the typical price for a well-made bicycle remained about $100, a significant sum to the average citizen, who was lucky to make $20 a week. Still, the safety wheels of 1892 not only sported inflatable tires, but they were also significantly lighter and better built than their immediate forerunners. All signs indicated that the American cycle industry would enjoy an even greater bonanza in the coming season.

Clearly, the globe girdlers were well poised to capitalize on their fame, which seemed to grow by the day. Shortly after their arrival in San Francisco, they shared the limelight with no less a celebrity than Albert A. Pope, the bicycle magnate himself, at a banquet hosted by the San Francisco Bicycle Club. They knew they could count on other bicycle clubs to extend royal treatment as they made their way back to the East Coast. There they would shop their book proposal to major publishers. With twenty-two diaries between them, all crammed with meticulous notes, they were not short on material. No doubt a lecture tour featuring their numerous snapshots was also in the offing.

Before they could resume cycling, however, they would need a new pair of wheels to replace their battered Humbers. They sent the relics home by rail and accepted two brand-new Victors from the firm's San Francisco agent, their fourth pair of cycles in three years. These were by far their best mounts, and now they, too, could enjoy the benefits of the pneumatic tire.

The tourists were inclined to make a beeline to St. Louis, where their families anxiously awaited their return. Hearing reports of wintry weather in the Midwest, however, they decided to head south instead, passing through Los Angeles. From there, they could head east along the main line of the Southern Pacific, all the way to New Orleans. At the Crescent City, they could swing up to New York City just in time for spring weather. Once they had taken care of business there, they could return to their homes by rail.

Their plans secure, the cyclists left San Francisco on January 11, 1893. That very evening the Garden City Cyclers of San Jose entertained them with music and humorous songs. They enjoyed smooth sailing in California, reaching the southern city of Santa Barbara within a week. There they assured a local reporter that "they had seen no finer scenery than that here." In Los Angeles, they made a day tour with the local wheelmen through Pasadena, Santa Anita, and Monrovia, where they had lunch. In Riverside, hundreds lined the main street to welcome the globe girdlers.

Meanwhile, the local wheelmen led the pair to their new club-house. At the center of the table rested a huge basket filled with oranges and a pile of cigars, courtesy of the local druggist.

For five days, the cyclists made their way across the Colorado Desert, sleeping in the open air two of those nights. Making liberal use of the railroad beds, they averaged over fifty miles a day. Compared to the Gobi, they found these arid environs downright pleasant. At the end of January, they emerged in the frontier town of Yuma, Arizona. The editor of the *Sentinel* judged them "intelligent, educated and refined young men," while noting approvingly that they were "greatly interested in Yuma and her future."

At Maricopa, five cyclists from the Valley Cycle Club of Phoenix persuaded the lads to spend the night in their city. The group took off under a full moon, arriving at three in the morning. Later that day, according to a local reporter, the tourists were "lionized" by adoring wheelmen. That afternoon they visited a photographic studio and had their picture taken with club members. In the evening, a prominent citizen held a music-filled reception in their honor, complete with oysters.

Passing through Tucson—where they consumed a hearty breakfast courtesy of the University of Arizona—the tourists reached Deming, New Mexico, near the Mexican border. The local newspaper editor was impressed by their modesty, having detected "nothing of that petty conceit which so often marks those who have won fame by means of some extraordinary feat." For their part, the cyclists were surprised to find that even this small city, barely a decade old, boasted an active cycling club with a dozen members.

Approaching El Paso, Texas, the lads were again met by local cyclists and escorted to the big city. The next day their hosts, eager to extend "the courtesies of the town," put on a lavish program. The lantern parade had to be scuttled owing to strong winds, but the banquet went off without a hitch. The globe girdlers sat down with fifty fellow wheelmen at a "richly laden table" to enjoy a six-

course meal and a "flow of soul." Vice President Payne, addressing the topic of "The Progress of the Bicycle," recapped the glorious transformation "from the treacherous old ordinary, which had
landed so many riders on picket fences, to the modern Safety."

Riding the railroad tracks out of town, past sandy stretches devoid of vegetation, the wheelmen made good time. One day they
even set a new personal record, covering ninety miles. Finally, in
early March, they reached Dallas. This time it was not only the cyclists who greeted them but also Sachtleben's resident relatives,
including his brother Charles, sister Emma, and brother-in-law
James Wilkinson. Feeling increasingly homesick, the pair decided
to head straight to St. Louis after all, the snow be damned. All
they had to do was to follow the Missouri-Kansas-Texas railroad
for about seven hundred miles. After a suitable rest, they could resume their ride to New York City in the spring.

The tourists headed to Sherman, where they enjoyed yet another banquet. They entered the Indian Territories (now Oklahoma) and made their way to the southeast corner of Kansas. At
Fort Scott, Harry E. Harris, the president of the Kansas division
of the LAW, escorted the cyclists across the state line to Sedalia,
Missouri. A reporter in Tipton, in the dead center of the state,
noted their arrival: "About 5:30 in the afternoon, a young man on
a bicycle was seen speeding down Moniteau street. He pulled up at
the City Hotel. A few moments later a second young man appeared
and headed for the same destination." The reporter tracked the
visitors down and discovered their identities.

In late March, the pair toured Jefferson City and met with the
newly elected governor, William J. Stone. Continuing along the
tracks, through heavy snow, they finally reached Kirkwood, a suburb of St. Louis. The next morning they were greeted by dozens
of St. Louis cyclists who had come to escort the heroes back to the
city they had left almost three years earlier. A large crowd awaited
their arrival there, including Sachtleben's father, who had taken
the morning train from Alton. News of their dramatic return was

cabled around the world. That evening the jubilant pair continued on to Ferguson, where they settled into the home of Thomas
Allen Sr.

The following week the cyclists declined numerous invitations
to attend events in St. Louis so that they could attend a long-
planned banquet in Alton instead. The *Sentinel Democrat* described
their rousing reception in Sachtleben's hometown:

> It was just 6:15 pm Monday, April 3, when Messrs. Sachtleben and
> Allen dashed down Second street hill to the store of Joestling &
> Sachtleben. They dismounted from their wheels and received a
> most flattering welcome. They were not expected so early, but as
> soon as they were recognized a shout went up all along the line
> and in five minutes the store was filled with a crowd of old friends
> eager to congratulate the boys on their arrival home. After fifteen
> minutes they escaped from the throng and went to the home of
> Mr. Sachtleben on Langdon street. Throughout the evening and
> next day the boys held an impromptu reception and received the
> handshakes of hundreds of old friends.

The next evening the cyclists were the stars of the "happiest
and most largely attended banquet ever given in the city of Alton."
Reported the *Telegraph:*

> The World Cyclists were banqueted in grand style last night. At
> 8:30 a stylish closed carriage drove up to the entrance of the Ho-
> tel Madison and Messrs. Sachtleben and Allen stepped out. Upon
> ascending the stairway an orchestra of string music announced
> their arrival and they were immediately surrounded by an inter-
> ested audience and escorted to the parlors. Here they related to
> the attentive listeners anecdotes of their great journey. At nine
> o'clock supper was announced, and seventy-six guests entered
> the brilliantly lighted dining room to take seats at tables covered
> with snow white linen. The tables were arranged in the form of
> an "H." Stands of fruit and table palms added to the attractiveness
> of a well-set board. Toastmaster McMillen then called upon Hon.

F. W. Joestling, and the mayor welcomed the visitors cordially to the Bluff City. Next came the supper of six courses.

The first speaker that evening was Colonel John J. Brenholt, a local attorney. He defined a hero as someone who successfully accomplishes "a great undertaking." Noting that Sachtleben and Allen were about to achieve the "stupendous work of traveling with the sun around the globe," he pronounced them heroes, to deafening cheers. (Ironically, four years later, Brenholt himself would be widely regarded as a hero, at least by Alton's black residents, after he led the fight to overturn the city's decision to segregate its grade schools.)

In response, Allen arose, "not the least bit ruffled by the resounding applause." Speaking

> in clear tones, he delighted the audience with an impromptu speech. Mr. Allen has a very attractive manner. He thanked the citizens for their excellent banquet and drew a parallel to the menu they were subjected to in the heart of China. He paid a warm tribute to his companion Mr. Sachtleben, proclaiming him a true friend upon whom he could depend in any emergency.

Several more prominent citizens spoke on a variety of topics before Sachtleben got the last word. He described numerous travails, starting with their struggle to get Robert Lincoln to write a letter of introduction and going on to describe their hardships in the Gobi as well as their clashes with hostile Chinese. On a humorous note, he recounted an anecdote about Allen. One morning his companion, fresh from the Gobi Desert, "fancied eggs for breakfast." He tried "every known method" to explain what he wanted to the befuddled innkeeper, to no avail. A dejected Allen started to walk away, when suddenly he wheeled around and began to jump up and down, flapping his arms like a rooster's wings. "The Chinaman was much amused," Sachtleben related, "and got the eggs."

Finally, just after one in the morning, the banquet broke up. Allen and Sachtleben remounted their carriage and headed for Langdon Street, feeling quite content. They had a busy schedule ahead, including a lecture at the Academy of Sciences in St. Louis. They planned to leave for New York City on their bicycles sometime in early May, though that task was beginning to feel like a frivolous formality.

7

KIUKIANG, CHINA

January 27, 1893

P EN IN HAND, Frank Lenz gazed out his bedroom window, watching wistfully as the heavy snow blanketed the Yangtse Valley, obscuring his view of the river itself. Although he was quite comfortable in the cozy and cheerful bungalow of the Reverend and Mrs. John R. Hykes, nestled in Kiukiang's foreign settlement, he was worried about his slow progress. Just then he heard the collective laughter of the Hykeses' four children, aged three to eleven. For a moment, his somber mood brightened, until he resumed his letter to Charlie Petticord.

Here he was, a month after leaving Shanghai, barely five hundred miles upstream. And he still had nearly two thousand miles to go in China, mostly over mountain passes "where a bicycle would seldom be of use, and often a great hindrance." He had fallen months behind schedule, and with all this snow it might be weeks before he could start moving again. Indeed, he noted to his friend, "it has been the severest winter here in twenty years." Confessed Lenz: "It may be three or four months before I reach Calcutta. But I am determined to cross China on wheel or on foot, no matter what the consequences."

As Lenz began to recount his travails in China, his spirits sank even lower. "The cry of 'foreign devil' greets me everywhere," he complained to Charlie.

Twice I have used my revolver to frighten off Chinese who stoned me. The roads here are fearful, the tires of my wheel stand alright, but the frame and rim I have had to patch. I put up with chopsticks among the Chinese and subsist mostly on rice and greens. Although I expected beastly accommodations, words cannot describe the filth that abounds here. The Chinese have stolen my tripod, tool bag and tools, opera glasses and spool of film. I am compelled to watch my wheel and camera like a hawk.

Trying hard to strike a more positive note, Lenz continued: "Occasionally, I reach missionaries who kindly welcome me to their homes. Foreign food and beds are indeed luxuries." He noted with pride that Thomas Stevens had also come to this city, six years earlier, and that the locals still talked about him. Stevens had marched into town with a band of soldiers, leaning an arm on his saddle, prompting the locals to construe the wheel as an elaborate walking aid. "The weather will soon get warmer," closed Lenz, "and I may make better time through this heathenish and God-forsaken country. I am exceedingly happy in getting this far, as everyone who heard of my intention to wheel through China thought it impossible. Of course I will be glad to see the hills of old Pennsylvania again."

Lenz's frustration with China was understandable. He had barely pushed off from Shanghai when his troubles began. The telegraph line, which was supposed to lead him all the way to Burma, quickly stranded him at a canal with no side path. Then came the huge crowds. He had expected attention, of course, having attracted an animated following from time to time in Japan. But nothing like this. "The curiosity of the Chinese is something fearful," he reported. When he pulled over for his first roadside meal in China, he had hoped that the restaurant at least would provide a temporary refuge from the rabble. He even gamely employed chopsticks in an effort to blend in with the clientele. But to no avail: "The eating house was jammed with pushing and squirming Chinese," Lenz lamented, "eager to see the foreigner."

Thirty-eight miles from Shanghai, with no inn in sight, darkness fell on poor Lenz. He spotted a vacant shed by a rice field and settled there for the night. He retained his overcoat and wrapped himself in his blanket in a fruitless effort to stay warm. All night long he heard the barking of dogs and the muffled voices of oarsmen as they glided along the nearby canal. "My first night out of Shanghai was surely discouraging," Lenz conceded in a gross understatement.

At Soochow (Suzhou), a silk center famous for its enchanting stone bridges and elaborate gardens, Lenz descended from his bicycle to walk the crowded, narrow streets. Evading a mob, he hustled over to the home of Alvin P. Parker, a Southern Methodist missionary, who kindly took in the weary wheelman. After summarizing Lenz's trip in his diary that evening, the reverend added tersely, "He has a hard trip before him between here and Calcutta." The next day Lenz and the minister devoured a hearty Christmas dinner. Before leaving town, Lenz stopped at Parker's school to demonstrate his bicycle to the howling children.

Paralleling the Grand Canal, Lenz rattled thousands of honking ducks. He also caught the attention of the men in the boats. "Loud yells and laughter arose everywhere," he noted, "and there was much craning of necks." Reaching Wusih, Lenz delivered a letter from Parker to an English-speaking Chinese doctor, who took in Lenz for the night. His host candidly discussed his people's aversion to Westerners and their medicine. Lenz soberly surmised that a real devil on the loose in these parts might be less conspicuous than he.

From this point on, Lenz had little choice but to lodge at inhospitable inns. To claim his miserable cot, he quickly established a modus operandi: "On arriving at a Chinese inn, I never ask any questions, but simply roll the wheel right in. I then sit down among the Chinamen, and order my rice as unconcernedly as a native." Some inns, however, offered only communal dining. The guests helped themselves to bowls of rice, fish, and greens placed in the center of a long table. Lenz typically devoured between two and four bowls at every sitting, easily besting the competition.

At Tanyang, where rioters had recently burned down a Jesuit mission, Lenz narrowly escaped a disaster of his own as he strolled down the main street with his bicycle in tow. A crowd quickly enveloped and jostled him, and he accidentally knocked over a table. As the irate merchant vented his anger, Lenz nimbly picked up a stray stone and hammered the detached leg back into place. He then handed over a fistful of coins and was allowed to proceed. He later realized, however, that during the hubbub someone had deftly lifted his handkerchief and field-glass from his coat pocket.

Working his way along the river, heading ever deeper into China, Lenz stopped in Chinkiang, Nanking, and Wuhu, all major cities with large foreign enclaves where he happily took refuge. By the time New Year's Day 1893 dawned, however, he was beginning to feel more at ease with the Chinese. "My distrust of the natives had partially vanished," Lenz affirmed. "I rubbed shoulders with them in their towns and inns as though they were the friendly Japanese."

Still, the near-disasters kept coming. One morning, while getting dressed, Lenz heard a loud bang at the rear of the inn. "I rushed out to find a crowd of scared Chinamen surrounding my bicycle," Lenz related. "One of them had pulled out the revolver from my luggage, which I had forgotten to remove before retiring, and pulled the trigger, luckily without damage. It might have fared hard with me had he accidentally shot a bystander."

Two weeks earlier, when the snow began to fall, Lenz had found himself stranded in a freezing country inn. He passed his time planted in front of a fireplace, trying desperately to stay warm. Meanwhile, the locals, old and young, male and female, streamed in on a daily basis to pay their respects. The conversations were limited, but his uninvited guests seemed particularly amused by his tools, especially the small monkey wrench, which they kept screwing and unscrewing.

Despite the blizzard, Lenz resolved to push on to Kiukiang, preferring to wait out the winter with the Hykeses. He hired two coolies with a wheelbarrow, and for twelve days the trio marched through "cold, ice, snow and mud." Along the way, they bickered over wages and got lost, extending their ordeal by four days and 165 miles. Finally, Lenz reached Kiukiang, where he stopped at the telegraph office to inquire about the way to the Hykeses' home. The couple was overjoyed to see him at long last at their front door.

Lenz felt a strange attraction to the walled city of Kiukiang, population 100,000, with its ruined pagoda and temple, though its charm faded the longer February progressed. He passed much of his time at the customhouse, fraternizing with the British officers. He also became quite friendly with Reverend Hykes, a forty-year-old missionary and fellow Pennsylvanian who had spent half his life in this remote outpost, serving the Central China Mission of the Methodist Episcopal Church. Hykes had just returned from his first furlough in sixteen years, and Lenz pumped him for news of home.

Lenz was deeply impressed with the reverend's dedication to his work, a subject Hykes himself had recently addressed in an article entitled "The Importance of Winning China for Christ," published in the *Missionary Review of the World.* "China is unquestionably the greatest and most important field for missionary operations on the planet," Hykes declared, "especially when one considers her vast territory and population, her abundance of natural resources, ancient culture, and the character and possibilities of her people."

To be sure, Hykes readily conceded, converting the Chinese was "an extremely difficult task." He even acknowledged the argument against the practice: "Some would have us believe that the evangelization of the Chinese is an unnecessary and presumptuous task. They say: 'The Chinese are good enough. They are vastly superior in civilization and morality to many heathen nations; they are perhaps even better off in their beliefs than we are in ours. So let them alone. Keep your meddlesome and fanatical missionaries at home and give them work among the slums of New York.'"

Hykes countered, however, that none of China's major religions
—Confucianism, Buddhism, and Taoism—were adequate substi-
tutes for Christianity. "Confucianism contains many beautiful sentiments and is a splendid system of ethics," he conceded, "but it
contains no hope for ordinary mortals either in life or in death. After forty centuries of trial, it has failed to elevate the nation morally
and spiritually." Buddhism, too, he maintained, "after more than
1,800 years of trial, has failed to elevate the Chinese to a higher life
and nobler purpose." Taoism, he insisted, was not even a true religion but rather a school of philosophy.

Summing up the case for conversions to Christianity, Hykes asserted: "God has great plans for the Chinese race. China is destined
to become one of the great factors in the future development of the
world." Although he did not agree with those who predicted that
China would become "the great military power of the future, con-
quering Russia and India, and crossing swords with England and
the United States," he closed with the sobering thought: "What
might not an awakened, civilized China do with forty million soldiers? I repeat: the evangelization of China is the most important
work in this age. Self preservation alone demands as much."

On the sixteenth of February, Lenz was pleasantly surprised
by the clamorous arrival of the Chinese New Year. "All the shops,
stores, and houses are lit up with lanterns," the cyclist reported,
"and paper picture charms are pasted on the doors and overheads.
At midnight, there was a terrific banging, crackling and rushing
of crackers and rockets. At daybreak, every Chinaman dresses in
his best hat and clothes, silks and satins and white soled shoes, to
make his New Year's calls."

Lenz soon discovered, however, that this was no passing holiday. "Two, three and four weeks are idled away," he surmised,

until empty purses compel the revelers to work again. The business streets on New Year's Day are as deserted as Broadway on an
early Sunday morning. Some owners of the poorer shops open up
within a week, but the wealthier ones do not renew their business

until the fifteenth of the following month, on which the dragon celebration is held.

At last, in late February, a month after his arrival in Kiukiang, the winter thawed. Lenz bid a fond farewell to his gracious hosts and resumed his journey. One week and 170 miles later, after enjoying a relatively smooth ride and the hospitality of several agents of the London-based China Inland Mission, he reached Hankow.

Still, his situation had hardly improved. Lamented Lenz in a letter home: "the roads continue to be bad. From ten to forty-five miles a day has been my record, sometimes walking mile after mile." He had had to patch up his frame with the help of a blacksmith. The locals continued to hurl mud, stones, and sandals in his path. Added Lenz: "When I come along they yell like so many demons out of hell. Day after day I run the gauntlet and only by tremendous will power can I control my temper. If I ever strike one of them I would no doubt get killed on the spot." Lenz wisely resolved to "never show fear and to try to satisfy their curiosity." At least, he noted, "the tires hold out wonderfully," and he had collected many "splendid pictures."

In mid-March, Lenz lodged at the telegraph station at Shashe in Hubei Province, near Hunan, the province where Mao Tse-tung would be born nine months later. The Chinese clerk implored the cyclist to take a riverboat at least as far as Ichang (Yichang), eighty-six miles distant, warning that he was about to enter the most hostile part of the Yangste Valley. But the stubborn wheelman refused, declaring: "I had traveled too far in China by overland to shrink from any seeming danger." He reluctantly agreed, however, to hire an escort, a young soldier named Cheng Hong Yuen, who wore a bright orange coat with red borders.

Unfortunately, Cheng quickly proved something of a liability. Lenz frequently had to pull up and wait for his sluggish escort. Even when Cheng resurfaced, the people he was supposed to deter exhibited "no respect whatever" for his authority. In fact, Lenz himself had little regard for his escort, whom he proclaimed to be "as lousy as any other coolie," citing Cheng's constant consumption of rice wine and opium. Still, he was glad to have Cheng's company when the attacks occurred, for moral support if nothing else.

The pair barely made it to Ichang after all. When spring bloomed, a correspondent with the *North China Daily News* found Lenz languishing in that port city, thankful just to be alive after a near-fatal clash in the countryside beyond Shashe. In riveting detail, the journalist related Lenz's ordeal:

Mr. Lenz, after a sharp spin over a bit of flat country, pulled up to await a telegraph soldier who was traveling with him. He was immediately surrounded by a dozen or so agricultural laborers. They began to yell and hoot at him. One of their number bared his breast and arms, and made motions challenging the cyclist to fight. Mr. Lenz simply smiled good-naturedly and signaled he had no desire for pugilistic honours.

Their attitude then became so threatening, and the cyclist and his machine were being so badly mauled, that Mr. Lenz reluctantly drew his revolver and fired three shots over their heads in quick succession. The fast increasing crowd drew off a bit. Mr. Lenz was on his machine in an instant, and rushed off at breakneck speed along the narrow path that led across the plain, amid a peal of diabolical yells.

Meanwhile, labourers were at work in their fields on either side of the path. "Strike! Strike! Kill! Kill!" was the cry taken up from the mob in the rear, and passed along from field to field far quicker than the rider could cover the distance, riding for dear life though he was. The labourers suddenly looking up, beheld a sight well calculated to rouse their worst superstitions: a foreign devil literally flying over their country on a hellish contrivance of glittering wheels and pumping legs. It was as if the thing had dropped straight out of the sky. With inflamed passions and uplifted hoes they darted towards the path.

Mr. Lenz pressed on, thinking it more prudent to run this murderous gauntlet than to find himself surrounded by a howling crowd, eager for his blood. He dodged this blow, charged that man, and besides a knock or two on the knapsack and some bad bruises on his machine, was doing wonderfully well—until he was suddenly confronted with an embankment, about forty feet high, whose crest was crowned with about one hundred and fifty excited Chinamen, awaiting his arrival with hoe and bamboo. He was now encircled.

In a letter home, Lenz himself described what happened next:

I got off and walked right toward them, to meet my fate then and there. For a moment it was touch and go. Two score of hoes and clubs were many times more than a match for my revolver and I knew it. To fight was useless; to pray seemed equally vain, for it appeared as if the Lord had overlooked his lonely Yankee wanderer. But for some unknown reason, Providence interfered, I firmly believe. The mob held their hands. It was a dramatic pause—like the paws of a grizzly bear. One may need experience it but once in his life. The scene is burnt into my memory and will never be forgotten. I was calm, for in truth I could hear the rippling of the dark river. There was no need to think of struggle any more—I realized that I had probably enjoyed my last outing.

Then one old gentleman leveled a blow at my head with a hoe that, had I not dodged it, would have cleft my skull and finished the business right away. As it was I got a bad bruise on my ear. Fortunately, my camera saved my shoulder, but was smashed by the blow. What happened then for a few moments I cannot tell. "Vic" and I somehow got parted. I presently found myself on the edge of the crowd, while one of the better-class Chinamen bid it to desist.

When he had succeeded in this, I picked up my machine. Instinct told me I must make these people laugh. So I began to explain by gesticulation, for I only know two words of their language, food and bed. I began fooling around and falling off the bicycle. I mounted one of their number and dexterously gave him a header. The wrath disappeared from their faces like magic. Stolidity gave way to smiles, and smiles to peals of laughter. Meanwhile, the crowds who had been chasing me came up in rear, and soon joined in the chorus. I thus turned men thirsting for my blood into an admiring audience, and presently begged, and was allowed, to proceed unmolested.

During his four-day layover in Ichang, a suddenly somber Lenz gave another introspective interview, this time to Thomas Holman, a British sailor writing for the *Pall Mall Budget*, a popular illustrated London weekly. The transcript, published three months later, read as follows:

"How do you like the Chinese, Mr. Lenz?" I asked.

"Oh, they're a plaguey bad lot," he answered, with an American accent.

"Do you expect to get through the country after your recent experience?"

"Guess I shall give it a try. Everyone tells me I shan't. From the United States consuls to the oldest foreign inhabitants."

"Yet you expect to?"

"Certainly. I may not get the machine through, though. Still, the worst, most hostile, and thickly populated part of the journey is now accomplished. I was told I should not get two hundred miles from Shanghai. Yet here I am, sound in wind and limb, at over a thousand miles from that city. Old 'Vic,' though, got a few broken ribs in that last scrum," said Lenz smiling, as [he] looked down complacently upon his wheel.

"Did you have a narrow squeak yourself, Mr. Lenz?"

"Very narrow, and in the country too. All the trouble before has been in the cities and big towns. There they have stoned me, pulled my hair, forced me to ride in narrow and crowded streets, upset me, and knocked me about generally. But always in a town or city or its suburbs. The countryfolk and I had gotten along wonderfully before this. I have always arranged my journeys so as to put up at a village or hamlet for the night, so as to avoid hostile crowds in the cities."

"What brought about the last attack?"

"Well I can hardly tell. I was in a bad district—I can tell that. The day before, I got through a city in darkness, but not without a good deal of mud, stones, and old sandals being thrown at me before I put up for the night. The next morning, I was about early and had already ridden for about three or four hours, passing my only coolie, a telegraph employee, who was to show me the way, as I had to leave my only chart, i.e., the telegraph poles, for a while. I stopped and dismounted to await for him in the middle of a plain and was instantly surrounded."

Lenz explained once again how he had mollified the crowd by doing stunts on his bicycle.

"That was very cleverly done, Mr. Lenz."

"Yes, you see I am alone and too weak to fight a mob, so must hold parley and fool with them. My object is to get through the country, and the end justifies the means."

"Why are you traveling alone?"

"I know I can command my own temper. A companion might be hasty, and lead us both into trouble."

"Are not the officials bound to protect you?"

"Oh yes, but I never go near them if I can help it. They create no end of a pother, and hinder me in the morning when I like to be away early."

"And how do you get on at the inns?"

"Ah, there I do capitally. I eat and sleep exactly the same as an ordinary Chinaman, and frequently pitch into a meal with, or sleep beside my own coolie, if I happen to have one, which only occurs in hilly districts. When I arrive in the evening I order my supper and bed, and allow the crowd to satisfy their curiosity about me and the machine to their hearts' content. If they get too troublesome, I produce this puzzle key and set them to work on it. A mechanical puzzle is, as you know, a powerful attraction to the natural curiosity of the Celestial. They squabble and quarrel about the solution of the puzzle and entirely forget me, and I eat my meal and write up my notes. When all have failed, I show them the solution, and each man despises his neighbor for not having discovered so simple a trick, and there is a hearty roar of laughter. Then I produce this mouth organ, and after running down the scales as a preliminary, get to business thus."

Lenz then interrupted himself, playing several popular and lively airs.

"Then I get tired, and as we are by that time on the best of terms, I say good night, make my kowtow with a bland smile, and retire to bed. But they insist on accompanying me to my room, and make what further investigations they choose while I am undressing—it would be simple madness to resist or resent. Then, when I am in bed, the landlord takes away the candle and I am left without further molestation. In the morning, I am up and off with the notes of the first chanticleer. That is the way to fool them."

"But they seem to have had the last innings with you, haven't they, Mr. Lenz?"

"Oh, yes! But I shall be even with them yet. Here is my camera, for instance. I get pictures of them when they have no idea what I am about. It never comes out of its leather case. I simply uncover the lens and rest it on a wall or mound, and get the picture by my 'Finder.' Then I set the clockwork arrangement of mine in motion and mingle with the crowd, arrest their attention on some particular object until I hear a click. Then I know the clockwork has done its work and I have got a shot with the exposure I adjusted for, while the Chinamen have been taken willy-nilly."

"But how did you come through the worst districts?"

"Simply traveled by night, when their superstitious nature keeps most of them within doors. Then I can pass through their cities and towns in spite of them."

"How about the soldiers at the gates?"

"These Chinese documents are sufficient to open the tightest gates in China, when only officials are present. It is the uncontrollable mobs that yell at my heels all through the country that are the greatest nuisance."

"And what is the object of your tour? What does it prove if you succeed?"

"It is chiefly educational. I have always had a strong desire to travel and my trip before I got to China, and I hope after I get out of it, will go to prove that there is a fraternal feeling among the human race, besides the natural love of self; that with civilization comes toleration, and a more sympathetic appreciation of fellow men among all nations. It will certainly bring this home to young Americans, if it does no more."

"Is China the worst part of your journey?"

"Yes, I am doing the worst part first. Afghanistan, Persia, and Asia Minor, each have formidable difficulties. But they are not of so dangerous a nature as those who entertain the superstitious belief that a man on a bicycle is a flying devil from the clouds. They will, at least, give me the credit of being human, however badly they may use me for other reasons."

"Your camera, you say, is broken?"

"Broken, but not useless. Mr. Edwards, of her Majesty's ship *Esk*, himself an enthusiastic amateur photographer—will help me repair it, and he has kindly promised to doctor my old friend 'Vic' for me."

"When do you expect to be in the United Kingdom, Mr. Lenz?"

"All being well I should get there by midsummer, or early autumn, 1894."

And no doubt the cycle clubs throughout the kingdom will see to it that so valorous a champion of their favourite pastime will receive such a welcome as he will richly deserve, should he succeed in accomplishing the task he has set himself to do.

Lenz, in fact, was desperately looking ahead to his arrival in fair Europe, when he would have Petticord at his side. The *Daily News* Ichang correspondent, however, openly doubted that Lenz would get that far, even as he paid tribute to the wheelman's sterling courage and character:

Whether this plucky gentleman will ever succeed in accomplishing the task he has set for himself remains to be seen—even whether he will ever get out of China alive. But one thing is certain. Any man who can keep his head and extricate himself from such a dangerous position by such coolness, tact, and judgment deserves to succeed. He obviously knows more about human nature than the ordinary crank.

8

ARDMORE, PENNSYLVANIA

May 31, 1893

D
ECORATION DAY 1893 found Allen and Sachtleben sailing along Pennsylvania's Lancaster Pike, the oldest paved
road in the United States. After nearly three years on the road,
their world tour was at last nearing completion. Approaching the
leafy suburb of Ardmore, they broke into wide smiles. In the distance, they could make out about fifty cyclists waiting in the shade
by the roadside. The travelers knew instantly that these were
members of the West Philadelphia Cyclers. The welcoming committee soon erupted into cheers as it set off fireworks.

The Cyclers had offered to host a banquet that evening at their
clubhouse, but the tourists had regretfully declined, explaining
that they were bound for Haddonfield, New Jersey, where Allen's
sister lived. The wheelmen had nonetheless insisted on meeting
the tourists about ten miles out on the pike, to escort them to Philadelphia's City Hall. There another fifty cyclists from New Jersey
awaited, ready to accompany the globe girdlers the rest of the way.
Among that group was Allen's sister Elizabeth, who had ridden
there on a tandem with her husband George H. Clement, a prominent merchant.

Later that afternoon, after Allen and Sachtleben met the New
Jersey–bound contingent, they took the Market Street ferry across
the Delaware River to Camden. From that point, the group cy-

cled another ten miles to Haddonfield. The prosperous town gave
the globe girdlers a hearty welcome. Recounted the *Philadelphia
Item:* "The military company honored the pageant with a salute
from their cannons. The fire company drew out their engines to
the roadside and rang every available bell. Meanwhile, the streets
were thronged with people anxious to catch a glimpse of the far-
famed travelers." The cyclists proceeded to the Clement estate on
West End Avenue, where they were "sumptuously entertained."

It had been only three weeks since Allen and Sachtleben left St.
Louis for the final push to New York City. Returning to the rails,
they followed the Vandalia track for three days to Terre Haute,
Indiana. From there, they took the rugged National Road to its
terminus in Cumberland, Maryland. They then headed north into
eastern Pennsylvania, stopping for a day in Gettysburg to survey
the famous battlefield. Along the way, several bicycle clubs had
given them receptions, as well as a fresh pile of medals.

At every stop they attracted curious crowds and inquisitive reporters. In the larger cities, like Columbus and Indianapolis, they
were instantly recognized and glowingly written up in the local
papers. Declared the *Wheeling Daily Intelligencer:* "Their trip will
pass into history as the greatest bicycle journey so far attempted
knocking out the record of Thomas Stevens." Some of the small-
town reporters, however, were just catching on. "They told a great
story of their travels," wrote one journalist in St. Clairsville, Ohio,
"and the tale is doubtless true."

Indeed, the cyclists projected an aura of importance befitting
globe girdlers. They dressed in "neat bicycle suits of light cordu-
roy, with knee breeches, blue velvet jackets, and bicycle caps." With
their tan faces, they radiated "that hardy wholesome and healthy
look which is the natural result of an active outdoor life." And their
rambling discourse was thoroughly convincing. "Both are ready
and bright talkers," observed a reporter in Washington, Pennsylvania, "overflowing with a fund of reminiscence which would take
them months to tell."

And now here they were, in Haddonfield, New Jersey, just

ninety miles from New York City. As eager as they were to get to
the metropolis, they decided to linger the next day at the Clem-
ents' home. Early on the morning of June 2, they left that town
for one final push. With the help of a friend who served as a pacer,
they made fast time to the ferry in Jersey City. At five in the afternoon, they rolled up to the Astor House, widely considered one
of the finest hotels in the country, located on Broadway between
Vessey and Barclay, by City Hall Park. Their spirited finale put, in
effect, an exclamation point on a trip that had itself been designed
to serve as a "finishing touch."

On hand at the hotel to greet them were a handful of reporters
and a small group of wheelmen who had seen to their hotel expenses for the next few days while they lingered in town to tend to
their business. After all their adventures and banquets, they found
the low-key reception a touch anticlimactic. Still, they were just as
glad to forgo further fanfare. They had had their fill of adulation,
at least for the time being. It was time to secure a publishing deal
and get on with their lives.

By their own calculations, they had logged a total of 15,044
miles in 344 days of riding. "A mathematical genius," reported the
Wheel, "has figured out that their wheels revolved 5,327,857 times."
The lads had indeed eclipsed Thomas Stevens. Having crossed the
entire landmass of Asia, they could claim the "longest continuous
land journey" on record. They were now, in sum, the greatest travelers since Marco Polo and Christopher Columbus.

Still, they were well aware that their fame might prove fleet-
ing. With so many people taking up the wheel and heading off on
long tours, it was perhaps only a matter of time before someone
eclipsed their performance. They confessed to one reporter that,
under ideal conditions, a similar journey "could be done in half the
time." They even professed some doubt as to the wisdom of their
course of action. "They say they have wasted three valuable years,"
noted the *Wheel*, "but that it will repay them eventually, as they
have a stock of health and vitality."

Of course, they were also counting on a healthy return from a book and lectures, if only to offset the $5,000 each had invested in the tour. And they were eager to seal a deal while their feat was still fresh. To make themselves more appealing to the public and to a prospective publisher, they stressed that they were not athletic freaks or publicity seekers, but merely two disinterested gentlemen who had set forth "to see a bit of the world before settling down for life." They added that they had traveled without the financial support of any newspaper, conveniently overlooking their falling-out with *PIP* and their fruitless efforts to enlist a new sponsor.

Their apparent lack of an ulterior motive smacking of crass commercialism placed them a cut above similar adventurers in the employ of a journal, such as Thomas Stevens or *Outing*'s current representative, Frank Lenz, now languishing somewhere in China. Wrote the *Wheel* about Allen and Sachtleben: "They are not showmen, nor is there anything sensational about them. In a word, they are gentlemen." The paper noted that they even had a "graceful way of giving in to each other when recounting their experience."

Indeed, speaking to reporters, the pair often decried the ugly mercantile instinct that afflicts the human race. "The first thing we learned," Sachtleben asserted to the *Wheel* reporter, "is that the people of every nation are out for the almighty dollar. They overcharged us for everything at every place." Their forthcoming book and lectures would, of course, serve to fulfill their educational duties to humanity, not to line their own pockets.

After settling in New York City, the cyclists spent a week making the rounds with publishers. They then retreated to Haddonfield to enjoy a leisurely summer while they mulled over a number of "flattering" offers. By August, they had come to terms with the Century Publishing Company. The wheelmen agreed to produce a series of eight articles detailing the Asiatic portion of their trip, leaving out their less sensational rides across Europe and the United States. For its part, Century would publish each article in

its monthly magazine, using the cyclists' own photographs for illustrations. By Christmas 1894, the articles would be bundled into
a volume and sold as a book.

In mid-August, Sachtleben and Allen finally headed back to the
Midwest by train. Before they retreated to their respective homes,
they shared one last adventure: a week in Chicago to tour the magnificent Columbian Exposition. There they were widely recognized and cheered. The program, after all, reflected the bicycle's
enormous popularity. It included the inaugural world champion-
ships for track cycling and a large collection of historic bicycles on
display in the Transportation Building.

By fall, Sachtleben was back in his father's house in Alton de-
compressing from his long journey. Lacking the patience to devote long hours to book writing, the cyclist all but delegated that
task to Allen. Sachtleben, meanwhile, occasionally lectured the locals about his trip, but at the publisher's request, pending the release of the book, he refrained from going on tour. To help pass the
time, he took up acting. In December, he played a leading role in a
play entitled *A Dream of Ancient Greece*, put on at Alton's Temple
Theater.

The following spring, in 1894, just as his first *Century* articles
appeared, Sachtleben again turned to the bicycle for amusement
and reward. Along with Homer A. Canfield, a prominent local cyclist, Sachtleben opened a three-story bicycle store in downtown
St. Louis that specialized in Victor bicycles. He also helped launch
the Victor Cycling Club and frequently led its excursions. He even
dabbled in racing, easily taking a ten-mile road race in St. Charles
that summer before some fifteen hundred adoring fans.

Yet as much as Sachtleben relished the role of cycling celebrity,
he craved something more. He was not content to confine his wanderings to a salesroom floor, busy as it was. After having experienced one harrowing adventure after another the world over for
three straight years, he desperately needed some new challenge to
absorb his considerable energies. But what could he possibly do for
an encore?

Suddenly he had a wild idea: why not be the first to cycle across the breadth of Africa? After all, the Dark Continent was one of the last partially uncharted territories. Only a generation earlier, Dr. David Livingstone had famously, if unsuccessfully, sought the source of the Nile. Sachtleben's bold proposition caused a buzz in the press, much of it disparaging. "In spite of his achievement in China," observed the *Wheelmen's Gazette*, "the critics generally agree that he cannot cross Africa in the manner proposed."

The paper suggested that Sachtleben follow footpaths instead. "Africa is a perfect network of paths from one end of the continent to the other," it asserted, "and every village is connected to every other village. It is true the natives are not engineers. The paths are narrow and winding, turning aside to avoid every obstacle like a tree or rock, which is easier to go around than remove. But they are beaten hard and smooth by the tread of countless feet for centuries, and are perfectly feasible for bicycles."

Still, the paper cautioned, "haste will mean disaster," adding,

> If Sachtleben is content to take it easy he has many chances in his favor. But he will need to be a man of resources and nerve, as he will meet with wild animals and wilder men. A rifle, revolver and knife will be as necessary as a tent and provisions. Doubtless Mr. Sachtleben is aware of the obstacles and is prepared to meet them. Certainly, he is not going to be deterred by the reflection that no man has been able to perform the feat before. There has to be a beginning to everything, even to crossing Africa on a bicycle, and there is no time better than the present.

Sachtleben reluctantly abandoned the idea, however, after failing to enlist a sponsor. That fall, to occupy his time, the globe girdler immersed himself in the affairs of his cycling club. He was soon quoted in the newspapers denouncing his own Victors as a "drinking club," angering certain club mates. In a special meeting called to consider his expulsion, which he failed to attend, a critic read aloud Sachtleben's offending remarks. An irate Louis Meidner went up to the podium next and demanded to know: "What has the accused member ever done for the club?" Meidner then sarcastically answered his own question, thanking the absent wheelman "for the watch he had donated for the Victor meet and won himself." After the howls of laughter had subsided, the orator declared that Sachtleben had to be expelled "or the club will go to ruin." He might well have been, then and there, had not Canfield come to his defense and succeeded in staving off a final decision until the next meeting, when Sachtleben would presumably defend himself.

Several weeks later, in mid-October, Sachtleben got his say. Speaking over hoots and howls, the defendant maintained that he had been misquoted in the papers. He had not meant to denounce the entire club—only "certain members who get drunk and are far from respectable." He singled out the absent Meidner as a case in point. Indeed, Sachtleben declared that he would no longer associate with certain members, "owing to their beer-swilling propensities and general rowdyism." He urged the club to purge itself immediately of its "tough element."

In light of Sachtleben's deft posturing, the club dropped all charges against the globe girdler. But rather than beat a discreet retreat, Sachtleben took the floor once again to deliver what one paper described as "an unmerciful tirade against Meidner's character" filled with "drastic and violent language." The club agreed to defer the matter of Meidner's expulsion. Eventually, his membership was upheld.

Many found Sachtleben's petty and vengeful outburst entirely unbecoming of a gentleman of his stature. Indeed, Sachtleben himself recognized that his harsh words and poor judgment had badly tarnished his carefully cultivated image of culture and refinement. He knew it was time to embark on a new adventure that would take him, once again, to some distant and exotic destination.

9

CALCUTTA, INDIA

September 17, 1893

I'M A BICYCLIST by choice," chirped Frank Lenz to a reporter representing the *Englishman*, a Calcutta daily, a day after reaching that city by steamer from Rangoon (now Yangon), Burma. "I am fond of it, even after thousands of miles of varied and wearying riding. And I'm fairly strong through it all, though I am none too big, am I?" The journalist, startled by Lenz's folksy manner, dutifully sized up his subject before conceding that the celebrated cyclist was in fact not "unusually stalwart." Beaming, Lenz continued his discourse: "I hold that, weight for energy, small men are better than big ones. Not that I profess to be overly energetic, mind you. On the contrary, I rarely ride above eight miles an hour. That's probably due to laziness."

Lenz had good reason to be in a playful mood. He had finally arrived in India's major port, the sprawling and captivating "City of Palaces" by the Hooghly River. True, his last six months had been excruciating. He had practically trudged across western China, and the arrival of the rainy season had forced him to renounce cycling across Burma. His bicycle was "done," and he had fallen a good six months behind schedule. He even had to scramble to recover his trunk, which had been sold by the shipping agent as unclaimed merchandise. Still, there he was in Calcutta, safe and sound. The worst was behind him, and the end was in sight.

As news of his progress filtered back to the United States, his fame was already eclipsing that of Allen and Sachtleben. "However foolhardy his tour may be," remarked the Chicago *Interocean*,

> Lenz must be given great credit for the hardihood he displayed in his dangerous trip across China. While the stories of his narrow escapes and terrible hardships may have been exaggerated, it is nevertheless a fact that he has traversed a country totally unknown to white men. He has, moreover, gone through it all alone. Lenz has been absent now something over a year and a half, but the pleasantest part of his journey is before him. All through Europe he will undoubtedly receive the plaudits of every wheelman he meets.

Lenz had indeed come a long way. At the start of the past spring, he was still entrenched in Ichang, tending to his damaged wheel and camera. Fortunately, he soon managed to restore both instruments to working order, with the help of two British machinists aboard the gunboat *Esk*. He vowed to exercise greater caution the rest of the way, painting his wheel black to make it less conspicuous. To be sure, he had lost a bit of his swagger. Still, he remained determined to complete his mission. Indeed, to his mind, it had grown in meaning and importance.

On March 24, Lenz finally left Ichang to face what he called a "maze of mountains" stretching to the Burmese border. Recognizing that he would be unable to cycle most of that distance, Lenz began a routine he would continue throughout his long trek. He hired a "line walker," an employee of the telegraph company who knew the layout of the poles, and two coolies, who often sang heartily as they carried his bicycle suspended between two bamboo poles, one end to each shoulder.

Every day the party logged between twenty and thirty miles. "Sometimes we welcomed a restful downgrade," Lenz recounted, "but climbing was the rule, frequently along narrow ledges with steep dropoffs, where one misstep meant the destruction of bicycle and coolies." In the descent, Lenz led the way. He often glanced back nervously at his plodding entourage, praying that they did not "lose their foothold and come clattering down on me."

The spectacular scenery, reminiscent of the Rockies and the Columbia River Gorge, proved a healthy distraction. At times Lenz could even see the Yangtse, running some three thousand feet below. "The valley was so narrow and quiet," he recalled, "a loud voice would echo and re-echo from one mountain to another." Occasionally he came across striking reminders of an ancient civilization in the form of graveyards, pagodas, and gigantic Buddhas carved in the rocks.

Whenever possible, Lenz lodged at telegraph stations. There he would draw from his supply of brass coins to pay off his men, who would return to their starting point by sampan, sailing along the Yangtse. Lenz, meanwhile, would spend a restful night at the station, which was invariably well equipped with cots and a kitchen to accommodate its small staff. His hosts were generally Chinese but occasionally European. After a day or two of rest, Lenz would resume his trek with a freshly hired crew.

On occasion, the coolies would convince Lenz that they could not possibly proceed in the wilds with the suspended bicycle. He would allow them to take the wheel and go by sampan to the next major town, where they would all reunite by nightfall. Lenz and his lineman, meanwhile, would gamely push on by foot. At times the ledges were so narrow that they had to crawl on all fours. "How the linemen stretched their cables over these fearful chasms is a mystery to me," Lenz marveled. "Some of the poles are on the edges of the highest cliffs, where only a man of iron nerve could have climbed to string wires."

On April 1, Lenz and his men found themselves alongside fearsome rapids, stepping from stone to stone. They reached the walled town of Wusan, the first telegraph station in the Szechwan province. "The sun shone warmly," Lenz recalled, "and the fields in the valley were all green." Among the many crops Lenz spotted were beans, wheat, vegetables, tea leaves, and opium. The cyclist's spirits were on the rise. He and his men were making slow but steady progress, having become quite adept at negotiating mountain passes and coping with the occasional thundershower or wild goat.

The relatively few villagers Lenz met along the way were, for the most part, "pleasant and agreeable." He no longer felt threatened by the populace and had even learned to enjoy their attention. They often asked him where he had come from and where he was headed. In response, the wheelman would give only "the last city I had left and the next one ahead." He knew well that they would find the answer unsatisfying, but he was determined to keep the conversation short. Besides, he deduced, "America and India are hardly known to the lower classes, and then only as barbarous countries."

The locals, it seemed, were thoroughly convinced that "every foreigner is a doctor of sure cure." During the evenings when he stopped at inns, Lenz was often approached for medical advice. Once, an anxious innkeeper introduced his ailing son and lifted up the boy's garments to reveal "ugly running sores on his hips." Another time the wheelman was shown an old man "in the last stages of consumption." The best Lenz could do in these hopeless situations was to shake his head in silent sympathy.

The townsfolk, of course, were anxious to see Lenz's strange vehicle in action. At Wusan, with the help of the telegraph clerk, Lenz staged a memorable exhibition along the river beach. One eager and confident pupil, a young man who "prided himself on being a good horseman," gamely mounted the wheel. Lenz began to push it along, but he soon noticed that the novice was having great difficulty keeping his feet on the pedals, which were battering his ankles. To end his agony, as well as to discourage any more onlookers from tempting fate, Lenz unceremoniously "dumped him in the sand," to the great amusement of the spectators.

One evening at a village inn, a mandarin's son gave Lenz a good look-over before asking how far he could see with those blue-gray eyes. He took Lenz at once to his *yamen*, "a large building containing much handsome furniture and surrounded by an artistic garden." There Lenz staged another demonstration "for the benefit of the ladies of the household." He circled the courtyard while servants held up hand-lamps and lanterns. Lenz then rolled around his host, who became so enthralled with the bicycle that he wanted to buy it on the spot. After tea, Lenz took in a musical performance featuring a two-string violin and an elaborate whistle. He shared in the meal but declined to participate in the post-feast card games and opium sessions.

Another colorful character Lenz encountered was a dapper lineman who briefly joined the wheelman's entourage. "He was quite a dude," Lenz recalled. The man's elaborate costume included a "black silk coat, blue silk sash and white trousers." His most impressive accoutrement was a "large, ancient sword swung across his back." Ostensibly, it served to cut through brush, but it also came in handy controlling crowds, as he demonstrated one evening at an inn. To protect the privacy of Lenz and his men as they dined in the garden, the thoughtful innkeeper had hastily erected a bamboo screen. The crowd, however, continued to encroach, fighting for a view through the slats. From time to time, the lineman coolly thrust his blade between the poles, eliciting a collective gasp on both sides of the barrier and forcing the crowd to maintain a respectful distance.

Also helping to break the routine were the occasional ceremonies Lenz stumbled upon. In one town, he watched a peculiar procession featuring "ragged men and small boys carrying brass gongs, banners, and silver paper images of some gods." Coolies followed, carrying a dressed pig spread out on two poles. Underneath that carcass walked a sacrificial goat, followed by several men seated in carrying chairs. Lenz learned that the villagers were staging the elaborate rite as a tribute to ancestral spirits.

At Wanshien, Lenz found another walled town, this one with 6,000 residents, including hundreds of women who spun cotton all day long on looms. For the first time since leaving Ichang, 325 miles back, Lenz met a missionary: the Reverend W. Hope-Gill of the China Inland Mission. The cleric had heard nothing about

Lenz's journey and was astonished to come across a wheelman in those parts. As Lenz prepared for his departure, the missionary warned him that the two-hundred-mile road to Chungking, though billed as paved, was impassable by bicycle since it rose and fell by means of steep stone steps.

In fact, it took Lenz a week to trudge to Chungking, a bustling city of 300,000. Among its thirty resident foreigners was the English-born W. Nelson Lovatt. To Lenz, the businessman's cozy home "seemed like an earthly Eden after my long walk over the mountains." Lenz stayed there for three days, spending much of his time in the city's vibrant center filled with "well dressed and intelligent natives" and shops selling "silks, satins, and embroideries." To his mind, the colorful scene evoked the "flourishing times of Marco Polo's visit, six hundred years ago."

It was now mid-April, and Lenz had covered 539 miles since Ichang—all but 34 on foot. At least he was having little trouble with the locals. Often they "strung themselves along the road" to watch him pass, yelling out their approval. Once, Lenz amazed everyone, himself included, when he and his wheel gracefully sailed over a pig slumbering on the road. The occasional indignities he shrugged off. At one point, several "mischievous rascals" crept behind the moving bicycle and pushed it into a pond. "I went in up to my knees and the wheel disappeared entirely," Lenz recalled. "There was nothing to do but to take it good naturedly and go on."

At Sweifu, Lenz again took refuge among the missionaries and demonstrated his wheel at the local yamen. The grateful ruler "served an excellent dinner and tea." He advised Lenz to cover his wheel thereafter, lest the sight of the strange vehicle overexcite the citizenry. Lenz, however, feared that they might react even worse to "a large, mysterious bundle," which could conceivably contain a body or perhaps "a choice bunch of kidnapped youngsters." He thus preferred to expose the wheel and take his chances. At least the bicycle served to deflect attention away from himself.

At the end of April, Lenz at last peeled away from the river and passed into Yunnan, the southwestern-most province in China and the last one before Burma. "This is the heart of the famine district," he explained to his friends back home, "and the suffering of the people is beyond description." He was particularly struck by the lowly status of the native woman. "She is of little value," he concluded, "save as a worker. Young girls are seldom educated, and those of the lower classes are not infrequently sold as slaves. As in Japan, go-betweens arrange marriages. Even the wife in high class circles leads a life of seclusion, never going anywhere and doing her husband's every bidding without question."

On the morning of May 14, a year minus a day after Lenz had left Pittsburgh, he was in for a rare treat: a smooth, eighty-mile road to the city of Yunnanfu. He gleefully sprinted off and left his coolies behind. That evening, stopping at a teahouse to await them, he sipped his tea and reflected on his first year of travel. "The continual change of people, scenery and excitement aided the flight of time," he mused, "and I could hardly realize that twelve months had already slipped away."

A few days later, Lenz reached Yunnanfu. With a population of 150,000, it was the last large city before Burma, now just 400 miles away. He again stayed with the missionaries of the China Inland Mission, three men and three women. "The work here is beset by many difficulties," the secretary had conceded in the last annual report, adding that "many additional workers are needed." Despite frequent preaching tours and heavy distribution of religious literature, the missionaries at this remote station had registered only two baptisms in each of the past two years. The natives seemed more interested in remedies for opium poisoning than a Christian education.

Before leaving Yunnanfu, Lenz hired two coolies to accompany him on the 272-mile trek to Talifu along the great highway connecting Bhamo and Peking. He left with a certain trepidation: he knew that he would soon face the toughest mountains yet. Worse, the inhabitants along the way reportedly despised foreigners and frequently robbed caravans. Lenz was nevertheless determined "to fight my way to Bhamo at any cost."

Indeed, the stretch proved trying in the extreme, starting with the grisly sight of three executed criminals, their "naked trunks and severed heads" cast by the roadside. A coolie stumbled and fell, taking down his colleague and the bicycle. Lenz, however, was thankful that the accident did not produce "two dead coolies and one smashed up bicycle."

At last, the party reached Talifu, a picturesque city nestled in the mountains that was famous for its marble quarries. Lenz stayed at the home of the Reverend John Smith, another missionary who was astounded to come across a wheelman. Once again, Lenz demonstrated his wheel at the local yamen. "I circled about for the old man," Lenz reported, though "he never changed the expression of his face. But I knew he was pleased when he presented me with pressed tea and sweets."

Lenz gamely pushed on, crossing a long chain bridge spanning the Mekong River. On the anniversary of his departure from New York, he found himself once again "drearily tramping over the seemingly endless mountain ranges of western China, lost to the world." Finally, in the middle of June, the wheelman reached Tengyau.

Here Lenz found refuge in a telegraph station, the last one before the Burmese border. Chatting with the friendly Chinese staff, Lenz learned that Danish engineers had overseen the recent extension of the line, which had required three long years to complete. The delay was due partly to the rugged state of the terrain and partly to the resistance of the locals, who feared that the wires would "disturb the graves of the Fingshin, the spirit of wind and water."

When Lenz fell seriously ill for the first time during his trip, afflicted by severe stomachaches, he was forced to prolong his interminable sojourn in China. "My strong constitution broke down," he explained in a letter home. "For two weeks I lay ill in bed in the telegraph office, and only by the aid of quinine and camphor pills which I carried in my medicine pouch, was I able to keep off a severe fever." To pass the time, he taught English to the staff. They, in turn, "were very good Samaritans to me."

Finally, at the close of June, Lenz, a guide, and several soldiers set off for the Burmese border, 128 miles away. They made slow progress, slogging through rice fields and crossing swollen streams. One day out, Lenza called on a sympathetic Chinese official he had met during his recent convalescence. Assigning him a "splendid room," the man persuaded Lenz to resume his rest for a few days. Writing home to his mother, Lenz accentuated the positive, noting that he had already been as far as he would get from home and was thus on his way back.

When Lenz was ready to resume his journey, his host furnished six soldiers to escort him to the Burmese frontier. Finally, in early July, Lenz reached the banks of the Nampangho River, which divided China from Burma. In the six long months since he had left Shanghai, he had logged a staggering 2,884 miles, a good majority of them on foot. Leaving China, he felt nothing but relief. "God help the unfortunate cycler or traveler who crosses China," he wrote home. "I could never do it again."

Still, the Celestial Empire had left Lenz with a deep impression. He admired its elaborate network of rivers and canals, stunning natural beauty, storied past, and vast cultural treasures. And despite his many run-ins with the locals, he shared Hykes's conviction that the Chinese, for all their flaws, were hard workers with vast possibilities. At the same time, however, he was appalled by the widespread poverty and blamed the Chinese government for oppressing its people, deliberately shielding them from Western culture and values.

Lenz credited above all his missionary hosts for his salvation. They, in turn, were amazed by his remarkable pluck. Five months later, George Ernest Morrison, an Australian medical student, would set off from Ichang to retrace Lenz's route to Burma. "I often heard of Lenz," the explorer revealed. "All the missionar-

ies praised his courage, endurance, and admirable good humour."
Morrison pronounced Lenz's feat "the most remarkable journey
of all," adding that Lenz had surmounted "hardships and dangers
that few men would venture to face."

Along the way, Morrison heard but one complaint about Lenz.
An exacting missionary lamented that the wheelman "did not pos-
sess a close acquaintance with the Bible." Explained Morrison:
"During family prayers, poor Lenz was discovered feverishly seeking the Epistle to the Galatians in the Old Testament. When his
host gently pointed out his mistake, he was not discouraged, far
from it. To the missionary's great dismay, the wheelman declared
that, in the United States, this Epistle is always reckoned a part of
the Pentateuch."

Across the river in Burma lay a British army encampment.
Spotting Lenz and his party, the soldiers, all Sikh Sepoys from
India, cheerfully blared their trumpets. The clatter brought out
their commander, Lieutenant J. H. Whitehead. "The English officer hailed me with delight," Lenz recounted, "and asked me to
come over at once. The stream was shoulder deep, and rushing
down the canyon at a tremendous rate. But with the assistance of
three native savages, all holding a pole, I forded the strong current
successfully. Grasping the officer's friendly hand, I at last stood on
Burma's soil."

For nearly seventy years, the British had maintained a strong
military presence in this predominantly Buddhist country. Forty
years earlier, following its victory over King Mindon in the first
Anglo-Burmese War, Britain had annexed all of Lower Burma.
Mindon's son and successor, King Thibaw, in his aspiration to reunite the country, forged an alliance with the French. Fearful of
his chances, the British had invaded Upper Burma seven years earlier and exiled Thibaw to India. All of Burma had thus become a
British colony.

"After a bath and a change of clothes," Lenz reported, "I felt the
happiest man on earth." He was now the third white man in the

camp, along with Whitehead and the telegraph operator. The native soldiers nevertheless dressed in the typical British manner, save for their thick black turbans. Lenz spent the next few days recuperating at Whitehead's residence and recounting his adventures in China. The official, in turn, briefed Lenz on what to expect in Burma.

The cyclist quickly realized his predicament. Although the monsoons generally started in mid-August, the rains had been unusually heavy, and the rivers were already overflowing. In addition, the temperature hovered around 100 degrees Fahrenheit. Not only would Lenz have little opportunity to ride, he also stood a good chance of contracting malaria. He vowed nonetheless to push on with the help of two hired coolies. Whitehead kindly provided four Sikhs to escort the party as far as Bhamo.

The men trudged deep into a forest filled with tigers, leopards, and elephants. They slowly made their way to the top of a mountain, taking in a panoramic view of the flooded Taiping and Irrawaddy Valleys. In the opposite direction, looking east, Lenz observed the last peaks he had climbed in China, "towering at a tremendous height." He could hardly believe that he had managed to get this far under his own speed.

In Miyothit, the first Burmese village along the Taiping River, Lenz observed the typical bamboo houses with roofs of woven palm leaves, standing on stilts several feet above the ground to protect against "high water and malarial fevers." The locals were "deep brown in color." The men wore little more than loincloths and were "well built and athletic." Many sported tattoos on their thighs, though the British regime frowned on the practice. Concluded Lenz: "The men take life very easily. The women are far more industrious, but neither sex are likely to kill themselves with hard work."

Beyond the village, the roads were flooded. Lenz sent his coolies and two of his soldiers ahead by boat, while he and the other two soldiers plodded through the jungle on foot, toting his bicycle. To his delight, Lenz found several stretches that were smooth and dry enough for cycling. Most of the time, however, he, like his party, had to trudge over flooded roads and ford deep streams.

Seven miles from Bhamo, at the banks of a stream, the entire group reunited, plus a newcomer the coolies had hired to lighten their load. After they had all crossed the stream, Lenz hopped on his bicycle and sped off. Four miles later, however, he had to halt before another stream. "I stepped into the water to test its depth," Lenz recalled, "and was immediately over head deep. Fortunately, I am a good swimmer, and was soon fast to a tree about one hundred yards away."

When the coolies arrived, fearing for their safety, Lenz ordered them to retreat with his bicycle to the last major town and to proceed to Bhamo by boat. The Chinese newcomer, however, insisted on testing the water for himself, despite Lenz's warnings. "He soon found out his mistake," Lenz reported, "and began struggling back. But he became exhausted. I heard a choking gulp, turned and saw he was drowning. His companions stood on the bank but twenty feet away and yelled advice. They finally pushed a log to him, which he failed to grasp. By the time I reached the spot he had gone down for the last time."

"It was a fearful death," Lenz wrote, "and all of us who had started out so cheerful were now gloomy at the terrible and quick fate of the poor fellow." The coolies implored Lenz to retrieve their companion's body. "With the aid of the log I floated nearly a half-hour," Lenz related, "and at last touched it with my feet. I raised it to the surface and brought it to the shore. We tried to roll him on a log, but life was extinct." Lenz flagged a passing boat manned by two Burmese oarsmen, who rowed his party, including the corpse, to the opposite bank. Lenz paid the men two rupees to bury the body.

A badly shaken Lenz managed to cycle into Bhamo, a city of some eight thousand. The wheelman soon found himself lodged at the comfortable residence of a British official. Lenz immediately took a bath, donned dry clothes, and devoured a fine meal while engaging in animated conversation, trying to forget the morning's tragedy. During his five-day stay, Lenz got a taste of colonial leisure life as he watched British officers hunt, fish, and play polo. He also encountered his first elephant, albeit a captive one.

Lenz continued southwest toward Mandalay, the king's fallen city some three hundred miles distant in the center of Upper Burma. From there, he planned to turn westward and cross the rugged interior to the Indian border, five hundred miles farther. Should those roads prove impassable, he was prepared to head due south to Rangoon, where he could catch a steamer to Calcutta. Of course, he was still hoping to reach India by the overland route, if at all possible.

Meanwhile, to get through the flooded countryside, Lenz reluctantly took a cargo boat to the next riverbank city to the west, Katha. He had hoped to resume cycling at that point, but he soon discovered that the roads were flooded there as well. Rather than continue by vessel down the Irrawaddy to Mandalay, or travel there by elephant, Lenz decided to forward his bicycle to that city by boat while he himself proceeded on foot along the partially completed railroad.

As he trudged along the railroad bed, Lenz observed hundreds of Madras Indians hard at work building the line, seemingly as oblivious to the scorching sun as they were to the pounding rain. He passed through numerous villages, finding lodging at telegraph stations and government-built bungalows. On occasion, he strayed from the railroad, only to find his way blocked by yet another stream. At Wuntho, the train to Mandalay was operational, but Lenz refused to take it. He nevertheless regretted not having his bicycle, so he telegraphed the flotilla company to have it sent by rail as far as Tantabin, a town halfway to his destination. A few days later, when he reclaimed his wheel, he promptly reeled off thirty-five miles, blissfully ignoring the light rain.

Finally, in late July, Lenz rode into Mandalay, where he found lodging at the home of Captain John E. Harvey. The wheelman took a liking to the large, ethnically diverse city where the cheer-

ful residents strolled about wrapped in colorful silk cloths. No
less conspicuous were the legions of Buddhist priests, with shaved
heads, dressed in "dull yellow" robes. Soldiers, too, were everywhere, some two thousand in all, three-quarters being of Indian or
Burmese extraction.

Within a week, Lenz came down with malarial fever. He moved
to the home of Thomas P. Purdie, a young Scotsman who managed
the Irrawaddy Flotilla Company. In mid-August, as the rainy season raged in full force, the cyclist was still bedridden. By the time
he resumed his trip, he realized that the roads to India were hopelessly flooded. He decided to head to Rangoon instead, 430 miles
south. He dashed off a letter to the Burma Bicycle Club, informing
them that he would be visiting the capital city after all, and he expressed his hope to meet with the members in about two or three
weeks. Meanwhile, he wrote another letter to Charlie, noting that
"the heat is terrible here, and the greatest care is necessary to escape sunstroke."

On August 22, Lenz left Mandalay, after nearly a month-long
stay. Once again he chose to follow the railroad tracks, on foot or
wheel but never by train. Along the way, he passed by lush banana
groves and rice paddies. To avoid the scorching midday sun, he
rested for two hours at train stations. Owing to a threadbare rear
tire, Lenz suffered a flat for the first time in eight months. He replaced the inner tube and taped the tire, knowing that he only had
to get as far as Rangoon. From there, he would sail to Calcutta,
where his trunk awaited with spare parts, including a frame. At
that point, he would completely overhaul his battered bicycle.

Lenz rode into Lower Burma, under steady rain, as the natives looked on incredulously. "The little Burmese boys immediately took a fancy to the wheel," Lenz reported, "and with giggling
laughs they raced after me." About forty miles north of Rangoon,
Lenz came upon hundreds of beasts being driven along the road.
"The cows and oxen were easily scared off," Lenz observed, "but
the buffalo were quite fierce looking, and only by bearing slowly
down on them would they stampede out of the way."

Nearing the city, Lenz came across two Europeans who were hunting in the nearby woods. They insisted that he join them for a lunch featuring fresh quail and snipe. Farther on, in the midst of a shower, Lenz ran into six cyclists from the Burma Bicycle Club who had gone out to intercept him. This was the first time abroad that he had run into fellow cyclists, and he was overjoyed to see them. They led him to the British India Hotel in central Rangoon, where he put up for a restful night.

Over the next two days, the club treated Lenz royally. "They took me in charge," he wrote to his friends. "Their clubhouse was thrown open to me, and all my wants were anticipated." They showed him the city's landmarks, including the six-hundred-year-old Shway Dagon, Burma's largest and grandest pagoda. On his final night, the club held a banquet in his honor and insisted on paying his hotel bills. For Lenz, it was further proof that better days had begun.

On September 11, just before he boarded his ship to Calcutta, Lenz sent "Charley and friends" a cheerful progress report:

> I have now wheeled and traveled almost 10,000 miles. Burma is a mass of water; nowhere is there passable country to India by the west coast. I had to travel 694 miles to get roundabout to India. I now ship to Calcutta, north from here, [where I will] repair broken parts of old "Vic," then really cycle in earnest again. I am happy, well, and in the best of spirits, the hardest part of the globe being now accomplished. What news? What tidings do the papers give of me? I never hear from America; it's all Asiatic and English news here. Regards to all the friends. We meet in '94. Yours Truly, F. G. Lenz.

As Lenz steamed into the vast and bustling harbor of Calcutta, he spotted a trio of monuments attesting to the decades-old British rule: the Government House, the Mint, and the Customs House. Indeed, this diverse metropolis of some 700,000 was the second-greatest city of the British Empire, after London itself. Strategically located midway between Europe and the Far East, at the mouth of two great rivers, the Ganges and the Brahmaputra, it was the "largest emporium in all Asia." In fact, Calcutta itself had become a major manufacturing center.

After reclaiming his trunk from an English resident who had acquired it, Lenz revamped his worn-out vehicle. "I had taken the precaution to ship ahead a new frame and bicycle parts," Lenz explained. "These enabled me to build up an almost new mount." In fact, the shiny nickel-plated frame was nearly identical to the original one, and just as obsolete. It was a far cry from the latest lightweight bicycles flooding the American market.

Lenz planned to stay in Calcutta for several weeks, waiting out the last of the monsoon season. In the meantime, he got to know the city well. He admired its thriving university, European-style buildings, and macadamized roads. He found expansive parks and gardens filled with monuments and an enormous zoo packed with a vast variety of indigenous creatures, including lions, tigers, leopards, hyenas, jackals, monkeys, and apes of all species. He gawked at the deadly cobra, boa constrictor, and python. He judged the collection of snakes, alligators, and lizards "the best the world over."

Still, Lenz was not entirely enthralled with the teeming city. He was repulsed by its dirty and overcrowded conditions and found many of the cultural conventions curious, if not abhorrent. Cows, sacred to the Hindu majority, were allowed to roam the streets freely, a sore point with the many Muslim residents who, for their part, were inclined to spare pigs. Lenz wondered how the Hindus could stand bathing in the filthy Hooghly every morning, however holy its water.

Especially disturbing to Lenz was the rigid Hindu system of castes, or hereditary social classes that "do not associate with one another, as if each were of a different race." Individuals, the cyclist noted, are grouped into five castes and identified by the "blots of different colored paint on their arms, bodies and faces." Elaborated Lenz: "The Brahmins are the first or highest caste. The second are descendants of the royal and military families. The third are merchants and cultivators, while the fourth consists of laborers and artificers." On the lowest rung were the "banished" ones "who have violated the principles of the other four."

Lenz marveled at how the raj managed to preside peacefully over nearly three hundred million mostly illiterate Indians, the world's largest population after China, and five times that of the United States, living in half the space. In his view, British rule had brought about great social and technological progress, while somehow holding together numerous "antagonistic elements, divided by seemingly impassible barriers of religion, languages, and creed." He chided India's relatively small but vocal "educated class," who, far from showing gratitude to their British rulers, saw themselves as "downtrodden and even persecuted."

Indeed, Lenz empathized strongly with the colonialists, with whom he constantly socialized. Contrary to the popular image, he asserted, they did not lead lives of decadence or endless leisure. On the contrary, they often had to sacrifice the comforts of home, while putting up with intense heat, not to mention the resentment and even hostility of the people. Observed Lenz: "I, for one, should not care to spend much of my life in India, no matter how comfortable things may seem."

Once again, the local colonial cyclists—two hundred strong and growing—showered Lenz with hospitality, holding a banquet in his honor. On the morning of October 8, a large contingent escorted him to the ancient Grand Trunk Road, where he was to begin a 1,300-mile trek across northern India. Upon reaching the endpoint at Lahore, Lenz planned to continue west into Afghanistan. If that route proved impractical, he would descend the Indus Valley to the coastal city of Kurrachee (now Karachi, Pakistan).

Leaving Calcutta along a smooth road shaded by palm trees, Lenz enjoyed excellent cycling for the first time in over a year. Apart from an occasional shower, the only hindrance was heavy traffic, the road being "dotted with white cows and oxen drawing the native carts." Lenz even met his first camel. The locals, though friendly, "proved exasperatingly awkward in their efforts to get out of the way." Still, Lenz sailed along in high spirits, past half-naked children, many of whom showed off their schooling as they yelled out a crisp "Good morning, sahib!"

He averaged about fifty miles a day before retiring to basic but comfortable government bungalows. Ten days out of Calcutta, he reached the first major inland city, Benares (now Varnasi). With the help of a Hindu guide, Lenz toured its palaces and temples. He took in its spectacular waterfront along the Ganges, where pilgrims from all across India congregated.

In nearby Allahabab, Lenz met William Dick, the editor of the English-language newspaper *The Pioneer.* At a city park, the two men watched the conclusion to the Hindu festival of Dussehra, whose nine days were dedicated to the nine forms of the Mother Goddess, or Shakti. From all parts of the city, colorfully dressed men and women rode in on cows and other sacred animals.

Reaching the beautiful city of Cawnpore (now Kanpur), Lenz toured the site of the bloody Indian Mutiny of 1857, comprising a well, a memorial church, and the famous marble "mournful seraph" commemorating the heavy loss of British life. There the notorious rebel Nana Sahib had ordered the slaughter of some 120 captives, including women and children. "He succeeded in escaping into Nepal, in the Himalayas," Lenz noted, "where nothing has been heard from him since, whether dead or alive."

In Agra, Lenz toured the majestic Taj Mahal and its lush gardens, built some 250 years earlier by Shah Jahan as a lavish tribute to his wife. It had taken seventeen years, hundreds of workers, and untold riches to complete. Lenz was so bewitched by its beauty that he paid a second visit by nightfall. "The silvery moonbeams fell softly on the white marble cheeks of this fairest of India's monuments," he waxed. "I stood for a moment in silent wonder. It seemed like a dream or a glimpse into fairyland."

In early November, Lenz reached Delhi, once the capital city of the vanquished Mogul Empire. He lingered there for four days, scouring the ruins of old battlegrounds. Pushing along the Grand Trunk, Lenz toured many more cities of historic interest. Finally, a month after leaving Calcutta, he reached Lahore, the capital of

Punjab. He visited the old fort, mosques, the city wall, and the ancient armory, pausing on occasion to admire the acts put on by snake charmers and street magicians.

With cold weather fast approaching, Lenz decided he would bypass Afghanistan. Instead, he headed down the Indus Valley toward the Arabian Sea. "The entire distance was uninteresting, and almost all a barren desert," Lenz reported. The roads were rough and sandy, the government bungalows few, and the food poor. Only along the railway did he find "good filtered water and, occasionally, good food." At the close of November, Lenz happily reentered civilization at Kurrachee, a cosmopolitan city of some 120,000. Recognizing the strategic importance of its port, which shipped tons of wheat and cotton to Europe, the raj had invested heavily to modernize the city.

In mid-December, Lenz, heading west along the coast, crossed into Balochistan. He soon found himself mired in the Makran Desert without food, water, or shelter. Fortunately, a camel caravan came to his rescue. He wisely retained a camel and driver to help him traverse the remaining four hundred miles of desert, though the service cost him a whopping $1.25 a day. New Year's Day 1894 found the cyclist in Gwadur, and a few days later he crossed into Persia, a large, sparsely settled country of five million. Braving strong winds, Lenz reached Jask in mid-January. At last he was out of the desert, where he had spent sixteen out of twenty-eight nights sleeping in the open air.

By the onset of February, Lenz had reached Bander Abbas, in the middle of the Strait of Hormoz, the gateway to the Persian Gulf. But he was wilting under the oppressive heat. So as not to fall further behind schedule, he grudgingly took a ship to Bushire, a dirty little port where a small British enclave looked after imperial interests. Like the rusting gunboat in its harbor, the pride of the shah's navy, Bushire struck Lenz as little more than a hollow shell. There he planned the balance of his Asian sojourn. Opting to bypass Baghdad and Palestine, he decided instead to head north twelve hundred miles through Persia, then west along the

ancient caravan road to Constantinople, where he had forwarded
his trunk.

From Bushire to Tabriz, Lenz planned to follow the telegraph
poles of the Indo-European Telegraph Company, founded in 1868
and financed largely by the Siemens family of Germany. For over
twenty years, its advanced network of land lines and underwater
cables had allowed London and Calcutta to exchange messages in
under an hour. Lenz planned to sleep as often as possible at the
stations, spaced from fifty to eighty miles apart. He knew he could
count on the hospitality of resident inspectors and clerks, most of
whom were Europeans.

On February 13, Lenz set forth for the interior. He quickly encountered extreme heat, dust, and swarms of flies and mosquitoes.
The roads were sandy, and the going slow. Lenz again observed
filthy living conditions, but at least the people were friendly. He
was pleasantly surprised by their relatively high standard of living, which included ample food produced from the country's "pro-
lific soil." For breakfast, he typically enjoyed boiled milk, eggs, and
thin bread; for lunch the fare was tea, raisins, and nuts, and for
supper chicken and rice. To quench his thirst, he consumed "sher-
berts and fruit." The innkeepers, who prided themselves on their
cooking, took up to three hours to prepare supper. Lenz often fell
asleep in his chair while awaiting his meal.

Setting off to Shiraz, Lenz entered a steep mountain range.
Gamely flinging his bicycle over his shoulder, he followed a series
of narrow mule paths, praying all the while that no such creatures
would appear. Midway through a second range, Lenz stopped at
a telegraph station. That evening he and his host, an English operator, sat at a table listening to the "Indian and Australian news
ticking through to London." During lulls, the operator would indulge in "chatting and gossiping" with his far-flung peers. Lenz
spent a peaceful night in his cot, only to awaken at six in the morning to a terrifying and seemingly interminable rumbling. "We have
earthquakes every day," the clerk placidly explained over breakfast. "One gets used to them."

Lenz pedaled past fields of tobacco and maize on his way to Kazerun, a small city filled with white stone buildings and small clusters of date palms and orange trees. On its outskirts, he came across the campsite of a nomadic tribe. "I wheeled straight into the midst of their goats' hair tents pitched under the cliff," Lenz recounted. "The children ran with fright, and the women, who were unveiled, stopped their work in wonder. In answer to my request for a drink they brought some very acceptable milk. The honey I tasted was excellent."

Approaching Shiraz from a vast plain, Lenz enjoyed a vista of "cypress spires, scattered gardens, and cupolas." Finding lodging once again with a telegraph operator, he toured this "Paris of Persia" celebrated as much for its native poets as for its beautiful gardens, lively bazaars, and ancient monuments. Indeed, much of the city lay in ruins, in part a testament to the frequent earthquakes. He found the climate "delicious but dangerous," noting the prevalence of the deadly "Shiraz fever."

Lenz soon reached Ispahan (now Esfahān), a thriving capital in antiquity largely reduced to rubble, though it still boasted its famous minarets. Farther on, he stayed at the home of a hospitable Persian who spoke English. "He suggested that we drink to the success of the remainder of my journey," Lenz recalled. "But I expressed doubt that wine could be had in a country where the precepts of the Koran are so strictly opposed to its use. He smiled at this indirect reflection on himself, and said he thought he knew where he could get some. In half an hour he returned with a couple of bottles of so-called Shiraz wine under his coat."

Passing long caravans of mules, Lenz entered Koom, a walled city with "picturesque white houses" featuring "colored domes, gayly-striped awnings and carved wooden balconies." Less appealing were the local scorpions, known for their unusual "size and venom." This was the second-holiest city in Persia, after Meshed, and one of the country's "favorite burial grounds." Explained the cyclist: "All Persians like their bones to lie near those of some saintly personage, in hope of gaining easy admittance into Paradise under the influence of his sanctity." The cyclist himself, however, felt uncomfortable there, noting: "The mere presence of 'infidels' in this holy place is viewed with disapprobation."

Heading north toward Teheran, Lenz passed through "sunlit fields of wheat and barley interspersed with bars of red and white poppies." Before long, the scenery turned dreary and the land "utterly devoid of vegetation." His mood sank even lower when, crossing the desert by moonlight, he ran into a caravan of mules, "each laden with two or three black boxes balanced like panniers across its back." Recalled Lenz: "Suddenly it dawned upon me that I was riding in the midst of a moving cemetery, for these boxes—pah! Another sense besides that of sight informed me—were all coffins. A sickness came over me that made me reel in my saddle."

Mercifully, Lenz enjoyed an easy run the next day to the capital, the "city of the shah." He admired its picturesque backdrop featuring snowcapped mountains and slender white towers that pierced the bright blue sky. He soon felt at home with the hospitable American missionaries and English telegraph officials, one being "the only wheelman I had the pleasure of meeting in the Shah's dominions." Unfortunately, however, Lenz came down with "Persian fever" and had to spend yet another week in bed.

Finally, in mid-April, Lenz left Teheran for Tabriz, via the ancient city of Kasveen. At the end of that month, he reached Tabriz. Thanks to General Waldo Wagner, a resident Austrian military adviser, Lenz visited the royal palace, where he met the crown prince himself, Mozaffar al-Din Shah. For most of his forty years, the future shah had been pursuing his pleasure in Tabriz, waiting for the day when he would replace his father in Teheran. A technology buff, he grilled Lenz about his gear and took copious notes. As a solid line of royal hangers-on watched in the wings, the prince himself took a photo of Lenz in the royal courtyard, mounted on his bicycle.

During his five-day stay, Lenz met numerous foreigners. Mary Whipple, wife of the missionary, recalled that the cyclist was in high spirits: "Lenz told us of a letter he had received from his mother, telling him how glad she was that he was so near the outside world where he would be safe. He, too, felt that he was nearing home." Concerned nonetheless for his safety, several Westerners in Teheran, including the English physician Hugh Adcock and W. H. Bright of the telegraph company, implored the wheelman to head to Europe via Russia rather than Turkey. Lenz, however, was determined to take the shortest route possible.

Lenz was happy indeed, knowing that he would soon have Charlie at his side. He was especially eager to visit Germany, the land of his forefathers. Karl Lenz, the younger brother of stepfather William, was already planning a grand reception in Karlsruhe to include local cyclists. Lenz was well on his way to meeting his goal of traveling twenty thousand miles overland, even though it would take him a bit longer than the two years he had originally allocated.

Just before he left Tabriz, Lenz dashed off a pensive letter to Charlie: "It has been a long while since I've tasted pie and ice cream. Nothing but sour cream and black bread most of the time now. But I'm only 900 miles from Constantinople." And to his old club mates he wrote: "Maybe you fellows think that I am tired of this kind of life. Well, I am not. I enjoy it hugely." He conceded, however, that "it has been rather rough for a year or over." To Worman, he was even more forthcoming. "I must confess to a feeling of homesickness. I am tired, very tired, of being a 'stranger.' I long for the day which will see me again on my native hearthstone and my wanderings at an end."

II
The Search

10

EAST LIVERPOOL, OHIO

October 12, 1894

F RANK LENZ IS LOST," blared the *Evening News Review*, stunning the residents of East Liverpool, Ohio, a prosperous pottery center on the banks of the Ohio River forty miles west of Pittsburgh. To the locals, the famous wheelman was the unassuming nephew of Mrs. Catherine Walper of Sixth Street. According to the paper, he had visited her frequently, "spending weeks at a time from boyhood days up." In fact, Mrs. Walper's son-in-law, John J. Purinton, a lawyer and a confidant of Lenz's distraught mother, was the source of the disturbing revelation. A few days earlier, the attorney had written the State Department to report Lenz's disappearance and to request an immediate investigation for the sake of Mrs. Lenz, "who already mourns her only son as lost to her forever."

To be sure, Anna had already feared for his life twice before. After word of Lenz's initial travails in China reached home, in early 1893, he fell terrifyingly silent. Letters sent to Calcutta, where he was expected that March, had been returned. By July, she was convinced that he had vanished in western China, until at last she received a letter from Frank announcing his arrival in Yunnan. Just a month earlier, in September 1894, Mrs. Lenz had suffered yet another scare when Frank fell silent once again after leaving Kurrachee. Happily, William Amory, Lenz's mute friend in Chicago, announced that Lenz had written him from Teheran on April 14, putting an end to the rumors that Lenz had perished in the scorching sand of Baluchistan.

This time, however, the situation seemed truly ominous. Explained the *News Review:* "Late last April, the young man wrote to his mother from Tabriz, Persia, stating that he would remain there a few days and then take the road for Erzeroum [*sic*], Turkey, which he expected to make in ten days. Since that time not a word has been heard of him. Week after week has passed and his friends have been growing more anxious." Compounding their worries were the sensational reports just reaching American newspapers of widespread massacres of Armenians in the very region where Lenz was bound.

Even under ideal circumstances, the three-hundred-mile stretch between Tabriz and Erzurum—filled with narrow mountainous passes and daunting rivers at their highest levels that time of year—was exceptionally dangerous. Worse, the inhabitants, especially the Kurds, were known to attack vulnerable travelers, often leaving them for dead. Worse still, much of the region on the Turkish side was sliding into a fiery chaos as Turks and Kurds mercilessly massacred Armenians in the wake of an ill-fated tax revolt begun in the town of Sassun. Conceivably, if Lenz had dawdled after Tabriz and bent his way southward after crossing into Turkey, he could have unwittingly drifted into the maelstrom.

What on earth had befallen the wayward wheelman? Some initially brushed off concerns, asserting that Lenz, as in the previous scares, was simply muddling through a tough stretch without access to modern communications, or perhaps keeping a low profile until the surrounding turmoil had passed. A few even suggested that his silence was part of an elaborate hoax staged to boost magazine sales. Charlie Petticord, however, would have none of that. "Oh, tut, tut, nonsense," he told a reporter. "Frank would never enter into such a scheme. He knows such silence would almost kill his mother. No amount of money could hire him to hide himself."

"Where is Lenz?" pressed *Cycling* of London as word of his

mysterious disappearance spread far and wide. The paper noted with alarm that the all-consuming question had been asked "half-humourously at first, when many believed that the round-the-world cycling tourist was merely laying low, but seriously enough now that his prolonged silence has given rise to the greatest fears."

Indeed, the rosy notion that Lenz was somehow still in charge of his destiny seemed increasingly implausible with each passing day. A more somber—but still hopeful—theory was that he had been temporarily waylaid by some unforeseen impediment. A less attractive prospect was that he was being held hostage. Darker still was the distinct possibility that he had succumbed to an illness, injury, or accident. The ugliest theory of all, of course, was that he had met with a violent end. Conceivably, he could have been targeted on account of his valuables, a perceived offense, or even his Christian faith.

Whatever his fate, if there was any hope of finding him alive, or indeed of recovering his remains, it was of paramount importance to determine just how far he had gotten along his proposed route—in particular, whether he had crossed the Turkish border about one-third of the way between Tabriz and Constantinople. Not only would that vital piece of information dictate which set of officials to engage in the search, but it might also shed light on the nature of Lenz's mysterious disappearance.

The Persian portion seemed the most likely territory for a kidnapping. After Khoi, as Sachtleben described it, "rose a wild and lonely mountain pass leading up to the highlands of Armenia." Every spring Kurds residing just over the border in Turkey were said to raid that territory to attack travelers and steal sheep. A foreigner on a shiny bicycle loaded with baggage might have been an especially tempting target. Lenz could easily have been ambushed in such rugged environs.

If, instead, Lenz had managed to cross the border, he would have entered the vast Alashgerd Plain. There, he was presumably less vulnerable to a surprise attack. Still, he would have faced several treacherous river crossings along the way. Perhaps the most dangerous obstacle of all was the Deli Baba Pass, about eighty miles east of Erzurum. Named after the town at the midpoint of the range, it was a notorious robbing ground. In this wild setting, the murder of a lone foreigner was an all-too-chilling possibility.

Mrs. Lenz had been worried sick about her son since mid-July, when she received an ominous telegram from Thomas Cook & Son, a worldwide travel agency based in London. The message from the Constantinople office tersely informed her that Frank's trunk remained unclaimed, along with a pile of mail. In desperation, she turned to her brother-in-law, Fred Lenz, who wrote to *Outing* to find out what it knew about Lenz's progress. Worman's secretary confessed that they were uncertain about his precise location, but insisted that they were not at all troubled by his long silence given that he was in a country with few mail facilities.

Privately, however, Worman himself was starting to worry about his long-silent correspondent, even though the July issue of *Outing* had falsely reported Lenz's safe arrival in Constantinople. In fact, the editor had received nothing from Lenz since the first of June, when his packet from Tabriz arrived. Moreover, Worman's subsequent letters to Constantinople had all been returned, including a $200 draft payable to Lenz. In mid-August, Worman wrote the American ministers in Constantinople and Teheran, asking them to quiz the locals for any news about his man.

Worman knew it would be about a month before he heard back from the diplomats, or twice that long if they posted rather than cabled their replies. In any case, by then, he fervently hoped to have already received happy tidings from Lenz. Still, as a precaution, he deemed it prudent to open correspondence with these officials. After all, he might need their help down the road, especially if, as he had begun to fear, Lenz had been taken prisoner.

When fall commenced, Worman had yet to receive any word from abroad. He had nonetheless convinced himself that Lenz's prolonged silence all but confirmed his captivity. Fearing, however, that publicizing that theory would only embolden the captors and prompt them to escalate their demands, Worman resolved to handle the matter as discreetly as possible. He reassured Lenz's loved ones that the lost traveler would soon re-emerge from the wilderness, even as he quietly continued to probe Lenz's fate. The magazine, meanwhile, after falsely reporting in July Lenz's arrival in Constantinople, imposed its own strange silence and offered no update on the wheelman's whereabouts.

Mrs. Lenz was now utterly distraught. She tried telling herself that Frank had fallen silent before, but she was now convinced that something had gone terribly wrong. At nights she lay awake in bed tossing and weeping, overcome by anxiety. Frank's friend Theodore Langhans tried his best to soothe her in her native language, and in a desperate drive to uncover Frank's whereabouts, he wrote letters on her behalf to missionaries and diplomats along Lenz's route. Petticord also sent out letters and met regularly with Mrs. Lenz at Pratt's sporting goods store to discuss the latest developments in the hunt for clues. Scores of other local wheelmen voiced their concern for Lenz's safety.

Lenz's sympathizers, in fact, were getting increasingly frustrated with Worman. Huffed the *Press:* "If they [*Outing*] know anything about Lenz they should make it public. The mere statement that he is alright is comforting, but it should be backed up with facts and some explanation for his long silence." The *Press* editor himself wrote Worman, demanding that he reveal exactly what he knew about Lenz's whereabouts.

Calls for a search party, meanwhile, intensified. The *Press* broached the subject, while expressing its disdain for *Outing:* "The company would do itself more credit if instead of saying it hopes the wheelman is alright, it would send out an expedition to see whether he is or not. This should have been done long ago." Petticord, for one, agreed wholeheartedly. He declared that he would have left months before for Asia Minor to search for his lost companion had it not been for his injured leg. Many urged Worman to dispatch immediately a dynamic rescuer in the mold of Henry Morton Stanley, Livingston's discoverer a generation earlier, to get to the bottom of the matter.

Others, however, questioned the wisdom of sending any more adventurers to that troubled region, at least until the State Department had completed an investigation. While conceding that its position might appear callous, a Philadelphia paper argued: "Is it not also inhumane to send out more individual riders who will in all probability meet with the same fate?"

By revealing Lenz's plight to his local newspaper, Purinton hoped to thrust the matter into the national spotlight and force swift and decisive action. The attorney succeeded on both counts. Within hours, dozens of newspapers across the country picked up the cable dispatch, much to Worman's dismay. Acting Secretary of State Edwin Uhl instructed the American ministers in Teheran and Constantinople to launch immediate investigations.

Even the sluggish Worman was spurred to action. He quietly dashed off a second round of letters to the same ministers, though he had yet to hear from either one. He also opened correspondence with several missionaries along Lenz's route—who had already heard from Purinton and Langhans—and sent a letter to Cook & Son in London requesting that its Constantinople office send a native guide to the area where Lenz had disappeared.

Publicly, however, Worman continued to feign complete confidence in Lenz's well-being. To one reporter he declared: "The sensational reports of his long silence are altogether unwarranted." Reassured the editor: "We have no serious apprehensions regarding his safety." He wrote Mrs. Lenz himself to assert that her son was fine and would soon resurface, though he offered no supporting evidence. He simply pointed out that Stevens had likewise fallen silent some years earlier while traversing the same remote region.

Worman nonetheless acknowledged that he was investigating the matter. Shortly after Purinton's story broke, he cabled the *Pittsburg Times:* "*Outing* wishes to advise the friends and relatives of Frank Lenz that all necessary steps have been taken to ascertain his whereabouts." But the editor steadfastly refused to reveal his course of action, citing the need for secrecy.

Soon, however, Worman gave in to the mounting pressure to come clean. In the November issue of *Outing*, he finally revealed the dates and places of Lenz's last communications. He also noted that he had engaged Cook & Son and he expected its report imminently. He even conceded that something was evidently amiss, though he continued to offer an upbeat theory: that Lenz had voluntarily gone into hiding.

At first, the press ran with that intriguing hypothesis. Among the possible refuges cited were Russian oil fields and the Holy Land. *Cycling* of London described the fanciful scenario worthy of a Sherlock Holmes adventure: "In some Eastern disguise, Lenz is visiting towns and temples where no European would knowingly be allowed to enter, but he is unable to speak to the outer world for fear of betraying his disguise."

Hope, however, continued to fade. In particular, the notion that Lenz, renowned for his dash and daring, had deftly maneuvered himself out of harm's way seemed increasingly untenable. Surely he would not voluntarily hold his silence indefinitely, knowing the pain it would cause his anxious mother.

Many were already convinced that Lenz had paid the "forfeit of his daring." William Sachtleben, who had ridden the same route between Erzurum and Tabriz, instantly suspected murder at the hands of the "lawless Kurds." His partner, Thomas Allen, shared that view, adding that a critical lapse of discretion on Lenz's part might have cost him his life. Allen noted that he and Sachtleben had spent "considerable time" in that hostile region familiarizing themselves with the "customs of the people" before daring to proceed. He surmised that Lenz had "omitted this precaution, and possibly quarreled with them, in which case he would have been very roughly dealt with."

Others preferred to think that Lenz, despite his athleticism and sound constitution, had succumbed to natural causes. He had been afflicted, after all, with the dreaded "Persian fever" while in Teheran, and that ordeal might have left him in a weakened state or in dire need of medical attention unavailable in the region. Certainly, a fatal accident could not be ruled out either. Robert Bruce, for one, strongly suspected that Lenz had drowned while trying to ford a turbulent river alone with all his gear—losing out, at last, to his "very rashness."

Only one faint hope remained: that Lenz had been taken captive. Worman had secretly suspected as much from the start and was now convinced that it was the most likely scenario, even if ransom demands had yet to be made. John Tyler, the American vice consul in Teheran, gave credence to the kidnapping theory in his belated reply to Worman. "Most of Lenz's acquaintances here," the diplomat confided, "hint that he may have fallen into the hands of brigands."

Nor was Worman the only one grasping at straws. "Depend on it, Lenz is living," Petticord insisted to a reporter. "I cannot think otherwise." Confided Purinton in his opening letter to the State Department: "Our fears are that he may be in the hands of the Kurds." The *Bulletin* even suggested that Lenz might be a political prisoner. "By too free use of his camera," the paper hypothesized, "Lenz aroused the suspicions of Kurds and was arrested as a spy."

Suddenly, startling news broke that seemed to vindicate the optimists. The Reverend Samuel G. Wilson, a missionary based in Tabriz who had just returned to his home in Indiana, Pennsylvania, on furlough, had reportedly hosted a healthy Lenz at his mission house that past July, two months after Lenz was thought to have left that city. Perhaps the wheelman had indeed recognized the danger ahead and stopped in his tracks after all. Alas, Wilson quickly clarified that the two had crossed paths in May, not July.

By November, with no word from Lenz, the public had grown distrustful of the State Department's ability to resolve the matter. The *Press*, asserting that governmental investigations always get bogged down in red tape, insisted that "Pittsburghers ought not to wait for anything of that sort." Nor was there widespread confidence in Worman's purported initiative. One cycling paper suggested that it was little more than a "Cheap John" sham calculated to save face and limit expenses.

The call for an independent search party quickly gained support. James P. Barr, the secretary of the Keystone Bicycle Club,
who had written both Worman and Overman to ask testily "if they
intended to do anything in the Lenz matter," started a public con-
scription with Pratt, the sporting goods dealer. The men asked
concerned wheelmen to contribute between one and five dollars
so that they could dispatch at once "a party of four to look for the
plucky wheelman."

The *Press* praised their initiative: "They have waited as long as
patience will hold out for the firm that sent Lenz on his trip around
the world awheel to do something in the line of rescuing him, or
at least finding out what has become of him." It predicted that the
men would have "no trouble" finding support, given that "no one
in all Pittsburg is more popular with the riders of the bicycle than
Frank Lenz."

In fact, contributions quickly flowed in. Nor was there any
shortage of volunteers. A. C. Moeckel, a friend of Lenz who had
left the jewelry business to join the booming cycle trade, offered to
quit his post at once to head to Turkey. Darwin McIlrath, who was
about to embark with his wife on a world cycling tour on behalf
of a Chicago daily, expressed his willingness to "hunt Lenz down."
Many others across the country wrote to offer their services.

The vibrant campaign was soon taken over by a committee
headed by Langhans and Purinton. They immediately appealed
to Congressman John Dalzell and Governor William J. Stone for
governmental support. They recognized, however, the pressing
need to identify Lenz's last known location. At the suggestion of
Reverend Wilson, they wired Dr. William S. Vanneman, a missionary in Tabriz, asking: "Where is Bicyclist Lenz? Ask Khoi and
Bayazid." Langhans also wrote to Sachtleben to ask for the names
of any people he knew along the caravan road who might be in a
position to assist the search.

In early December, Purinton received two replies from Erzurum
in the same post, both confirming, for the first time, that Lenz had
reached Turkey. The British consul, Robert Wyndham Graves,

wrote: "From private inquiries I have made I learn that a traveler answering in all respects to Mr. Lenz, passed the Turkish frontier at Kizil Dizeh, near Bayazid, sometime in May last. He continued his journey after a short halt, and from that moment nothing more has been heard of him. I have requested the Governor General of the province to make careful inquiries." The missionary William Chambers reported that the cyclist was seen on May 7 in Dyaden, Turkey, about 150 miles west from Tabriz, placing Lenz a good twenty miles past the border, in the Alashgerd Plain.

Over the next few weeks, information trickled in from Persia confirming that Lenz had made it safely out of that country. John C. Mechlin, an American missionary based in Salmas, reported that he had seen Lenz in that city in early May and had endeavored to dissuade the young adventurer from heading into Turkey alone. His helper saw Lenz a bit farther on, in Khoi, and postmen had reportedly seen the wheelman across the border. Alexander MacDonald, the minister in Teheran, affirmed: "We have certainly traced Mr. Lenz out of Persia into Turkey. Now it would be best to contact our minister in Constantinople."

Of course, the fact that Lenz had made it to Turkey was not necessarily welcome news, given the troubled state of that country. As the *Press* observed, "It almost gives a death blow to the last spark of hope." Graves, for one, gave a most somber assessment. "Your relative must have been robbed and made away with somewhere in the dangerous districts of Bayazid or Alashgerd," adding: "It will be difficult now to clear up the mystery of his disappearance."

The mere mention of Dyaden brought back bad memories to Sachtleben and Allen, who had stopped there four years earlier on their own tour. "Our little room was filled to suffocation," recalled Allen, "and the curious crowd was not disposed to heed our requests to be left alone. We threw them out bodily. Thirsting for revenge, they mounted the roof, and until far into the night stomped down the mud and earth from the unplastered ceiling." Allen sincerely hoped that Lenz had not been compelled to make a deferred payment "for our indiscretion."

Vanneman, whose cable arrived a few days after the letters from Graves and Chambers, offered an equally stark conjecture: he imagined that Lenz had gotten safely across the Alashgerd Plain, then "probably disappeared in Deli Baba Pass 80 Miles from Erzurum." Sachtleben submitted an eerily similar theory:

> In all probability Lenz disappeared about half way between Bayazid and Erzeroum. About midway between these two towns is the wild mountain gorge of Deli Baba. Mr. Allen and I were warned not to take this route when we were over there, but we had no choice. I remember well our feelings as we entered the pass. We traveled up the narrow defile and had to stop at a Kurdish village about half way up on account of a terrific hail storm. At this village we had several things stolen from us. Usually when this occurred we acted in a high manner and asserted our rights boldly. But on this occasion we swallowed our pill with the best possible grace. Discretion was decidedly the better part of valor. And Lenz's position would be more dangerous than ours. There were two of us and he was alone. We could watch all sides, while he could face only one way. But once our backs were turned the natives took courage and were equal to any murderous deed.

Worman, meanwhile, continued to hold out hope that Lenz was still alive, though he admitted to the State Department that his own inquiries "have as yet brought forth no satisfactory results." In fact, Cook & Son had yet to get anyone near the area of interest, given the heavy snow and the resistance of Turkish officials to foreign investigators. The London office warned Worman that even if it should manage to get investigators to the site, he should expect to pay a premium for their services: "The cost of traveling in Armenia is considerable, especially in the face of the existing troubles between the Turkish troops and the Armenians."

As 1894 came to a close, Worman faced mounting pressure to send an investigator to Turkey, as well as scathing criticism for his clumsy handling of the affair. "As far as we know," fumed one of Lenz's friends, "*Outing* has not taken the trouble to do more than write letters. They could offer no consolation to his mother worthy of the name." Nor did he care for the callous way in which Worman had discouraged Lenz's friends from making inquiries abroad, only to withhold the results of his own correspondence. The *American Wheelman* of New York City accused *Outing* of having recklessly risked Lenz's life, only to "pass around the hat" as soon as he vanished.

A defensive Worman sent out a circular vigorously defending his actions and denying that he was soliciting contributions. He insisted that Cook & Son was doing everything possible to get to the troubled region and appealed for the public's patience and understanding. He also tried to defuse his critics with a show of goodwill. He wrote Purinton offering to cover any expenses he had incurred in his correspondence abroad. When Lenz's old friend Ned Friesell dropped by Worman's office, he received a warm reception. "Our talk lasted over two hours and covered every phase of the Lenz case," Ned wrote his brother Charles. "The doctor went over with me a pile of correspondence a foot high. There were letters from British and other consuls, excepting American, bearing dates considerably earlier than the feeling of uneasiness in Pittsburg."

Still, Worman realized that he had to do more if he hoped to salvage his good name. He had no alternative left but to preempt the Pittsburgh committee and send an investigator of his own to Turkey as soon as possible, to prove his sincerity if nothing else. He had a practical incentive as well: the Mutual Life Insurance Company of New York would not pay the $3,000 coverage to Mrs. Lenz without indisputable evidence of her son's death.

But whom should he send? One obvious choice for a lead investigator was the British cyclist Robert Louis Jefferson, who had just published the book *To Constantinople on a Bicycle: The Story of My Ride*. *Cycling Life* of Chicago, which had been highly critical of Worman's inertia, claimed that Jefferson was eager to swing into action: "A cablegram would start him in two days. In a week he would be in Erzurum. In three weeks more he could ascertain all that it were well we should know."

Worman turned instead to a man he knew and trusted: Robert Bruce, the editorial assistant he had hired in 1890 fresh out of Oswego High School, and Lenz's former travel mate. For four years Bruce had performed his duties admirably, until he moved to Boston that past summer to write for rival *Bicycling World*. Though only twenty-one years old, he exuded remarkable poise and maturity. A Boston reporter described him as "cautious and cool, with plenty of reserve force, perseverance and patience; a man who maps out a definite purpose and strives to accomplish that end."

Worman figured that Bruce's intimate knowledge of Lenz might prove helpful, giving him special motivation to investigate if nothing else. Indeed, Bruce freely admitted that he would not even have considered the dangerous assignment had it not been for his devotion to the lost cyclist, whom he described as the bravest man he ever met. "I actually doubt if he knew the meaning of fear," Bruce reflected. "There was nothing in his mental or physical makeup corresponding to the timidity most men feel in the presence of danger." Still, Bruce conceded, that very daredevil propensity "to show fight regardless of consequences" might well have been Lenz's undoing.

Bruce's friends worried, however, that the young man was about to embark on a futile and possibly fatal mission of his own. His fellow students at Boston University, where he had just completed his first term, feared for his safety. Dean W. E. Huntington strongly advised his pupil to reject Worman's offer, insisting that "the people who send you would get the advertising and benefits while you would be running a great risk for a nominal sum."

Bruce nonetheless felt that he owed it to Lenz's mother and friends, not to mention his beleaguered former boss, to make the heroic effort. Even if he failed to find the man alive, he would at least give solace to Lenz's family and friends by uncovering the cyclist's fate and bringing back his remains for proper burial. And of course, if he should discover evidence of foul play, he would seek justice. Moreover, Bruce would have the high honor of completing the tragic but noble ride whose first several thousand miles he had covered with Lenz.

On January 7, 1895, the Boston papers announced Bruce's mission. The investigator discussed his itinerary with a local reporter. "I shall leave for New York in a few weeks as soon as my wheel is made for me. I shall then sail for Havre, then train to Constantinople. My wheel I shall leave there, to be taken up only after I have finished my search for Lenz." In the capital city, Bruce would meet up with escorts versed in the local languages, either native guides furnished by Cook & Son or volunteer missionaries. After crossing the Black Sea by steamer to Bantoun (Batumi), the party would head south to Erzurum, "the place where Lenz never reached," to begin its search.

"I shall work along to Bayazid," Bruce elaborated, "where Lenz is reported to have been seen. I shall carry with me a wallet with papers having his signature and photographs, to show to the natives while I inquire: 'Have you seen or heard of him?' I shall follow each road until I am satisfied that none of the natives have seen him." Added Bruce: "In case I don't find him in three months, I shall give up the search and have my wheel shipped from Constantinople to Teheran, where Lenz's narrative left off. There, I will take up the thread of the story and continue the journey to its completion."

As Bruce hastily began his preparations, he enjoyed an outpouring of goodwill. At the clubhouse of the Massachusetts Bicycle Club, he received a rousing round of cheers and a signed copy of Stevens's book *Around the World on a Bicycle*. He also had a long conversation with the Reverend James L. Barton, the foreign secretary of the American Board of Commissioners for Foreign Missions (ABCFM). Barton gave Bruce a letter of introduction to present to the agency's missionaries in the region. He also authorized two of his men to leave their posts, if necessary, to assist the cause: George C. Raynolds in Van and Chambers in Erzurum.

The public had barely received the welcome news of the Bruce mission when the Pittsburgh committee announced that it was about to dispatch an investigator of its own: none other than William Sachtleben, the famous globe girdler who already knew the territory of Turks. The sudden prospect of two distinct missions rushing off to Turkey after so much delay befuddled the public. Marveled *Cycling Life:* "How to reconcile the original state of masterly inactivity with the present fever to find Lenz is the subject of nightly discussions wherever wheelmen congregate."

For Worman, the Pittsburgh project spelled nothing but trouble. He had no desire to see a second search party in Turkey over which he would have no control, much less one that threatened to overshadow and outshine his own. Worman decided there was but one thing to do: meet with Sachtleben and, if possible, hire him away from the Pittsburghers, even if that meant reneging on the Bruce deal. And he knew just where to find his man: at the National Cycle Show, which had just opened in Chicago.

The massive show had given the strongest evidence yet that the country had truly gone bicycle-mad. Despite the bitter cold and abundant snow, tens of thousands of men and women had flocked to the "twin armories" on the lakefront to see the latest cycle designs and accessories. Hundreds of firms nationwide were now catering to the seemingly insatiable demand, and all the big brands were present. The typical machine cost under $100 and featured tubular tires glued to lightweight, American-made wooden rims. In all, it weighed about twenty-five pounds, or about half the weight of Lenz's antiquated mount. Among the novelties was a folding model and a strange self-moving contraption with a petrol-powered engine called the "motor cycle."

In the wee hours of January 11, Worman boarded a train to Chicago. The next morning, he rushed over to the armories to catch the last day of the show. The crowd was especially large thanks to the presence of Arthur A. Zimmerman, the great professional racer who had made an astronomical $40,000 the past season in Europe. Fighting his way to the stand of the Overman Wheel Company, Worman cornered Charlie Overman, Albert's brother. Hollering over the din of the brass band, the editor asked Char-

lie if he had seen Sachtleben. Told that the agent was expected to
pass by the booth sometime that morning, Worman asked Overman to detain Sachtleben for an urgent conference.

Later that morning, on cue, Sachtleben strolled over to the Overman stand. Charlie had barely delivered Worman's message when
he suddenly pointed into the crowd and gushed: "Here comes Mr.
Worman now!" Sachtleben spun around and spotted "an important
looking man" making a beeline toward him.

> "Mr. Sachtleben I presume?" the little doctor uttered with a
> perfect German accent.
> "It is a pleasure to meet you, Dr. Worman," replied the cyclist
> with a knowing smile as the two shook hands.
> "I'd like to talk to you about our lost correspondent, Mr. Lenz.
> Would you care to join me for lunch?"
> "With pleasure," Sachtleben replied.

During their meal, Sachtleben could readily see that Worman
was "full of anxiety" over the Lenz affair. Recalled the wheelman
many years later: "He was leaning toward the belief that Lenz had
been captured, and was being held a prisoner by the barbarous
Kurdish tribes." Sachtleben, however, would have none of that. "My
previous experience with these lawless Kurds led me to think that
they had secretly made away with Lenz." As the two argued back
and forth on the subject, Worman suddenly blurted out: "How'd
you like to go out in search of him?" Replied the cyclist without
flinching: "I would be glad of the opportunity."

Worman then outlined his offer. Although the payment exceeded that of the Pittsburgh committee, it fell significantly short
of Sachtleben's expectations. He politely pointed out that he would
require a larger sum to justify putting his life at risk, noble though
the cause was. The two amicably agreed to resume their discussion in a few days, once Worman was ready to present a new offer.
Sachtleben, meanwhile, returned to Alton to mull things over.

Certainly a major concern for the wheelman was the stark realization that Lenz "was past being found." It was fun to fantasize,

of course, about creeping into a Kurdish camp in the dead of night to slice the cords that had kept Lenz in bondage all this time. But Sachtleben knew well that there would be no joyous encounter in the wilds à la Henry Morton Stanley and David Livingstone. He had lost his opportunity to meet Lenz.

Still, the proposed mission to turbulent Turkey was not without possible benefits, especially if he could find Lenz's remains, unravel his fate, and bring about a measure of justice in the event of foul play. He would earn the eternal gratitude of Mrs. Lenz, the wheel world, and the American public. And if his work compelled the Turkish government to pay Mrs. Lenz an indemnity, he knew he could expect a liberal reward.

Even if he did not fully succeed in that mission, he reasoned, it would certainly satisfy his pent-up cravings for more adventure. It would also thrust him back into the international limelight and renew his reputation as a world wanderer and roving reporter par excellence. While in Turkey, he might even delve into the Armenian massacres and make himself an even more valuable commodity on the lecture circuit.

Besides, as he confided to a local reporter, he had long contemplated a "future career devoted to visits to foreign lands and the writing of travel books." While abroad, he could prepare a work illuminating "Armenia and its recent troubles," one that would cover "every phase of life." Yes, he told the journalist, he would almost certainly go to Turkey "if *Outing* will somewhat increase their offer of remuneration."

A few days later, Worman did just that, and a deal was struck. The editor agreed to advance his correspondent $1,300 and underwrite his expenses "to the farthest point east." After concluding his investigation, Sachtleben, rather than Bruce, would complete Lenz's trip all the way to Pittsburgh. Although he would be responsible for his own expenses during the cycling portion of the journey, he would share in all magazine and book-related profits. Satisfied with his terms, Sachtleben immediately began to plan for his long journey.

The revelation that Sachtleben would be taking Bruce's place caused a flap in the press. The Boston papers disputed Worman's claim that Bruce had voluntarily withdrawn in deference to his "widowed mother," charging that it was Worman himself who had withdrawn the promised financial support. *Bicycling World* affirmed that its writer "stood ready to proceed at once on his mission," adding that it was aborted "through no fault of his own." The *Wheelman's Gazette* surmised that Lenz's old friend had been "thrown overboard . . . simply because Sachtleben could command more advertising."

As Worman had anticipated, however, the general reaction was largely favorable given Sachtleben's seemingly stronger qualifications. Not only was he six years older than Bruce, but he was familiar with Turkey and its customs. The Pittsburgh committee threw its full support behind him. Declared Langhans: "If anyone in the world is able to find Lenz, Sachtleben will do it. If Lenz is alive he will find him. If not, he will discover what has become of him."

In early February, while Sachtleben was still at home waiting for Worman to give the go-ahead, grim news broke. *Le Vélo*, a Parisian cycling daily, published a dispatch from a "reliable source" in Armenia affirming that Kurds had shot and killed Lenz in the Deli Baba Pass between the towns of Kourdali and Dahar. "The news has long been expected," lamented the *American Athlete*, "and there is but small doubt of its authenticity."

Undaunted, Sachtleben vowed to find the murderers by tracking down telltale clues such as Lenz's "clothing or wheel." He was growing increasingly frustrated, however, with Worman, who had yet to give a green light. Moreover, the "five men on horseback" the editor had originally promised as an escort quickly dwindled to a single companion, an unidentified "young man from Chicago." Now it appeared that he would have to go it alone.

When Langhans called on Sachtleben in mid-February, the Pittsburgher felt compelled to reassure the folks back home that the mission was still on. "He has been so long getting started,"

Langhans conceded, "that most people have come to look upon his
trip as another bluff." Langhans insisted, however, that "there is
no bluff about it this time. I saw the contract signed by the *Outing*
people, and I know that he will leave for Turkey in a short time.
I saw his paraphernalia all packed and his route laid out. All he is
waiting for are marching orders."

Langhans took pains to exonerate Sachtleben and instead laid
the blame for the additional delay squarely at Worman's feet: "The
Outing people claim that it would be useless to start him out when
the country where Lenz disappeared is covered up in snow. But
Sachtleben himself says if he were there now he could be doing a
great deal of preliminary work that will have to be done anyway."

Meanwhile, as February slipped away, the news from abroad
became ever more discouraging. Cook & Son informed Worman
that it had made no headway whatsoever in the Lenz investigation. Moreover, it doubted that Sachtleben would make it as far as
Erzurum, even after the spring thaw, given the prevailing political
climate. "At present no one is allowed in the country," explained
a representative, "and although some newspaper correspondents
have ventured there, our agent feels sure they will be turned back."
Minister Alexander Watkins Terrell concurred, affirming to the
secretary of state: "I can see no prospect of such a mission being
successful."

Worman, however, was determined to stick to his plan. "I trust
our government is sufficiently strong," he wrote Secretary of State
Walter Q. Gresham, "to force a way into the country for our envoy,
where an American boy known and admired by thousands of his
fellow citizens, lies either in bondage, or is slowly wasting away by
disease, or worse yet, murdered."

Finally, on February 27, Worman instructed Sachtleben to head
immediately to New York, where his steamer was to leave in three
days for France. The wheelman bid hasty goodbyes to his family and friends. The *Telegraph* described his dramatic departure:
"A large crowd gathered at Union Depot and gave him an ovation
as the train moved out. Will's popularity in his native town was

at its height last night. His display of nerve at undertaking such a perilous trip and his undaunted determination were admired by all present. He expressed himself as having nothing to fear and started out on his journey with a cheery 'good-bye.'"

That same day, the Pittsburgh papers fanned yet another sensational rumor to the effect that Frank's mother had at last heard from her son, who was allegedly safe and sound in Russia! The shocking news drew more than one hundred anxious wheelmen to the Lenz residence that day. Alas, the papers soon clarified, Mrs. Lenz had simply received another letter from *Outing* reiterating its theory that Lenz might have sought refuge in Russia.

Sachtleben himself paid a quick visit to the Lenz home, where he met Mrs. Lenz, Langhans, Purinton, and a host of Frank's friends. Though he knew better, he promised them he would do everything in his power to bring Frank home alive. That failing, he vowed to bring back the wheelman's remains for a Christian burial and, in the event of foul play, to identify and prosecute his killers. He told them all how much he regretted that he had not lingered a while longer in Shanghai, so that he could have had the privilege to meet such a brave and noble man.

For Mrs. Lenz, the emotion was almost too much to bear. The day before, she had received a letter from Tabriz with a photograph of Frank seated on his bicycle in the royal gardens, taken by the crown prince himself. Waldo Wagner, the resident Austrian military adviser, conveyed His Excellency's deepest sympathies and his willingness to assist in the search. Though it was now apparent that Lenz had vanished in Turkey, not Persia, Mrs. Lenz was deeply touched by the prince's show of concern. And even though Frank appeared haggard in the photograph, she cherished it as the last image she would ever have of her beloved son.

A jubilant Worman announced Sachtleben's departure in the March issue of *Outing* and "the abandonment on the part of Lenz's personal friends of a direct search." Even Purinton, Worman noted, "has withdrawn from the search, satisfied that *Outing* is covering the field as thoroughly as it can be done under existing circumstances." Most satisfying of all, Worman affirmed, were the many letters he had received from Mrs. Lenz, expressing her gratitude for his "untiring efforts" to find her missing son.

Finally, in the wee hours of March 2—exactly ten months after Lenz's last communication from Tabriz—Sachtleben marched aboard the steamship *La Champagne*. All hopes for a satisfactory resolution to the Lenz saga now rested squarely on his broad shoulders. As the *Telegraph* put it, "The entire success of the trip rests with Will." He planned to return to New York that fall bearing conclusive, if unhappy, findings. Should he succeed in his onerous task, vouched the *New York Times*, he will "cover himself in glory."

❧ 11

CONSTANTINOPLE, TURKEY

March 23, 1895

Y OUNG MAN, YOUR FAME has preceded you," declared Alexander Watkins Terrell in a thick southern drawl from behind piles of papers stacked on his desk. Cracking a soft smile, the sixty-eight-year-old minister, who bore a strong resemblance to Samuel Clemens, waved a copy of the *New York World* as his long-overdue visitor made his approach. The opened page revealed Sachtleben's likeness, accompanied by a long article on his mission in Turkey.

After an exchange of handshakes, Sachtleben settled into a plush chair facing Terrell's desk. The portly minister politely inquired how the trip had gone so far. The correspondent replied that he had enjoyed a smooth transatlantic sailing, followed by a short but gratifying sojourn in bicycle-mad Paris. He relished his three days on the luxurious *Orient Express*, though he neglected to mention his brief stop in Vienna, where he met with a famous Arctic explorer to discuss his possible participation in an upcoming expedition. He was about to say how impressed he was by the crowded city's new train station when the minister suddenly broke off the conversation.

"Bigelow, come in here, please," bellowed the minister after spotting his assistant in the doorway. "I want you to meet Mr. Sachtleben. He's just come from America to look for Lenz's bones." The startled investigator dutifully rose to shake hands yet again, trying hard not to appear ruffled by Terrell's "plain style of introduction imported from Texas."

Once the awkward distraction was concluded, Sachtleben got straight to his objective: a passport from the Turkish government granting permission to travel to Turkish Armenia. At the very least, he hoped to reach Erzurum, the largest city near the presumed location of Lenz's grave.

"I'll do the best I can for you," Terrell intoned, his demeanor suddenly turning serious. "But I hardly think it is possible for you to get your permission—if you succeed in getting one at all—for several weeks." The minister stressed the severity of the ongoing unrest in Turkish Armenia and the sultan's resolve to bar all foreigners from that troubled region. He pointed out that several prominent foreign newspapers had been trying for months to send correspondents, to no avail.

In fact, the sultan had effectively sealed off Armenia since late August, when his soldiers and allied Kurds suppressed the Sassun revolt. The rampage quickly spread to neighboring towns before engulfing the entire province of Bitlis, a mountainous region in eastern Turkey. The situation remained extremely tense. The Europeans were already clamoring for an international investigation. It would eventually conclude that some ten thousand Armenian civilians had been massacred and scores of villages razed.

Terrell warned Sachtleben that even if he managed to get to the remote region awash in blood, he would probably learn nothing new about Lenz's fate. "The Turkish government has made two separate inquiries," the minister revealed, "without any result. They gave up the mystery as unfathomable." The minister observed that the porte was even suggesting that Lenz might never have entered Turkey in the first place, or that he exited it at some point. Terrell paused for effect, then shook his head vigorously. "No, young man, let me advise you to return the same way you came. Take my advice; use your wheel on the other side of the water in God's country."

Sachtleben could barely conceal his seething contempt for Terrell, whom he had already sized up as lazy and inefficient, if not downright corrupt. Before they parted, however, the investigator managed to extract a solemn promise from the busy minister: he would appeal directly to the grand vizier to get Sachtleben his travel papers, stressing the special circumstances of the mission. As the two rose, the wheelman started to thank Terrell, but the blunt minister snapped: "Don't thank me until you have something to thank me for."

In fact, Terrell had little desire to plunge into this hopelessly muddled affair. He had no pity whatsoever for a young man foolish enough to have tried to cycle through such hostile territory unescorted. Nor did he sympathize with an equally rash young adventurer who was itching to head off to that same wretched region to search for his hero's bones. Months earlier, when the first letters reached his desk inquiring about Lenz, he had blithely ignored them. The pile soon rose to about forty sheets, all begging for news about the missing wheelman. He would gladly have continued to steer clear of the affair altogether had he not received explicit instructions from Washington to investigate Lenz's "whereabouts and condition."

Terrell was already swamped with work. On his desk were some three hundred outstanding grievances from American citizens, mostly missionaries seeking compensation from the Ottoman government for alleged losses of property and life. And that pile, too, was bound to rise with the latest outbreak of violence. Pressing these claims was a time-consuming and thankless chore that had earned him nothing but scorn from the missionary community, which charged that he was soft on the vile sultan and remiss in his duties.

He had only just been through the headache of the celebrated case of Anna Melton. In June 1893, shortly after Terrell's arrival in Constantinople, this young American missionary had left the oppressive heat of Mosul (now in Iraq) for a peaceful mountain village, only to find herself assaulted one night by a bedside intruder. Bleeding profusely, she somehow managed to wrest away his club, whereupon he scampered out the window onto the rooftop. In the shadows she spotted an accomplice. A year after the ordeal, Melton complained to the American press: "It took long enough to make any arrests, although the guilty persons were well known." Finally, largely through the efforts of another American missionary, the Reverend E. W. McDowell, eleven Kurds were arrested. Eight were eventually convicted, but an appeals court in Baghdad had just released them all, citing insufficient evidence. The missionaries were now berating Terrell for his appalling "laxity" in the matter.

When he had embarked on his diplomatic career nearly two years earlier following a failed senatorial bid, Terrell had had far greater things in mind than the monitoring of American grievances or the rubberstamping of forms. Cashing in his political chips with the Cleveland administration, the loyal Democrat had sought the most influential position he could land. A prestigious post in western Europe being beyond his reach, he welcomed the opportunity to cultivate a rapport with the sultan. Although the Ottoman Empire had been in steady decline for decades, having recently lost its European foothold in the Balkans, it still ruled over large swathes of land in the Middle East and North Africa. And its future—known as the "Eastern question"—was of great strategic importance to other world powers.

Indeed, Terrell fancied himself a visionary elder statesman who was ready to leave his mark on the world. In truth, he was not without talent or credentials. An impressive orator, he had been for many years an effective power broker in Austin, crafting key legislation such as the charter establishing the University of Texas. Though largely self-taught, he was well-read and held surprisingly progressive views on some topical issues, such as favoring higher education for women. He was also an amateur archaeologist who planned, in his free time, to scour the region in search of ancient artifacts to send back to his beloved university.

From day one, however, the job had fallen far short of his expectations. For starters, he found himself assigned to a modest hotel room rather than the stately residence he had envisioned. Not only did he have no personal attendants, but his office staff was skeletal. He had to do much of the grunt work himself—including filing those interminable petitions from the miserable missionaries. Even more humiliating, he often found himself stewing in the palace parlor while the sultan gave priority to weightier European ambassadors.

Despite these aggravations, Terrell refused to keep a low profile. On the contrary, he vigorously curried favor with the sultan. He insisted that his controversial policy had already yielded important concessions, such as an unprecedented imperial decree allowing a woman, the missionary Mary P. Eddy, to practice medicine in the Ottoman Empire.

To his detractors, however, the former Confederate colonel was little more than a washed-up southern politician clumsily masquerading as a distinguished diplomat. To their minds, this would-be statesman was in fact a boorish, self-serving sycophant and a disgrace to his countrymen. Even his supposed admirer—the widely reviled sultan—reportedly deplored Terrell's raw demeanor and disgusting habits, especially his incessant tobacco chewing and spewing.

A story circulating among the missionaries epitomized Terrell's laughable limitations. Once, at a lavish state dinner held in the American's honor, His Excellency reportedly watched in horror as one of Terrell's wads landed on his precious carpet. The sultan wryly suggested to the minister that he take better aim the next time. The dense diplomat, however, failed to take the hint and continued his indiscriminate onslaught all evening long, mortifying the honored guests.

Terrell's dubious devotion to Christianity was another sore point with the missionaries. One American reverend went so far as to charge that "Minister Terrell has embraced the Mohammedan faith." Groused another: "We might as well have a Mohammedan as American minister, for all that Terrell does for us." Even fellow diplomats were often critical of their colleague. One consul recounted a disturbing display of irreverence: "At a gathering of Turkish officials Terrell said that he was not a Christian, but believed in God as the Turks do. The sentiment was loudly applauded by the Sultan's officers."

An American minister, upon hearing of that incident, fulminated:

> Terrell showed himself to be a cad by making such a remark. Christianity is the religion of this country, as far as it can be said to have a national religion. And in thus discrediting Christianity Mr. Terrell cast a reflection on his country. Even if Mr. Terrell himself is an infidel, and I don't know whether he is or not, it was not the act of a gentleman to say so under such circumstances. He did incalculable harm to the American missionaries in Turkey, and they constitute nine-tenths of the American residents.

That critic further alleged that the Turks were richly rewarding Terrell for his appalling acquiescence: "I hear that the Sultan has decorated Terrell's wife and daughter with jewelry, and that the minister himself cuts a brilliant figure in the court society of Constantinople to the neglect of American interests." As an example of a case crying out for Terrell's attention, the critic cited that of a missionary who had been waiting for two years for permission from the porte to add a chimney to his house. Summarizing the consensus among the local missionaries, the critic declared: "Mr. Terrell has allowed himself to be soft-soaped into forgetting what he is here for."

No, Terrell had no desire to add to his already oppressive workload. The last thing he needed was another high-profile trial involving an American citizen. To be sure, Lenz was no missionary. But Terrell was certain that the resident Christian community would rally to the wheelman's cause, making even more demands on his precious time and distracting him from weightier matters, such as the plight of Armenian refugees and the future of the Ottoman Empire.

On his second full day in Constantinople, Sachtleben visited the offices of Cook & Son. There he met the manager, Thomas Mill, the man who had alerted Mrs. Lenz about her son's unclaimed baggage. Mill led his visitor to Lenz's abandoned trunk. The wheelman was surprised by its ample contents, which included "clothes, correspondence and notebooks, and all manner of curios." Nearby was a large box Lenz had shipped amounting to "a small bicycle shop." It contained "worn-out parts of his bicycle and a full supply of new tires, pedals, inner tubes, etc."

Their conversation quickly turned to the stalled search for Lenz's remains. Mill affirmed that the porte had repeatedly spurned his petitions to send his dragoman (a native interpreter) to the area where Lenz was last seen, citing the need for the European commission to complete its investigation without hindrance. That highly charged and involved process had not even begun yet, on account of the fierce winter still prevailing in Armenia. And once it did, the investigation was likely to drag on for months.

Undeterred, Sachtleben vowed to hound Terrell until he had extracted the papers from the porte. In their follow-up meeting a few days later, the minister confirmed that he had made a personal appeal to the grand vizier. Although the authorities would not grant a passport that would permit direct transit to Armenia, they would allow Sachtleben to exit the country and reenter it at the Persian border, at which point he could retrace Lenz's route westward toward Erzurum.

To Terrell's great surprise, Sachtleben rejected the offer. The investigator feared a ruse. He reasoned that if he were to leave Turkey, the wily officials at the Persian border would in all probability either delay or bar his readmittance, prior assurances notwithstanding. No, thank you, he preferred to stay put in Constantinople. He asked Terrell to renew his efforts to secure a visa to the interior. The minister grudgingly consented.

In the meantime, Sachtleben vowed to make the most of his time in Constantinople, an ancient crossroad of civilizations where the

East perpetually tussled with the West. He was thoroughly familiar with the cramped quarters of the old city, a peninsula defined by the Sea of Marmara to the south, the Bosporus Strait to the east, and the Golden Horn to the north.

High on his agenda was a visit to the stately American Bible House in the heart of the old city. Its busy staff managed a network of missions stretching across Turkey and a bustling press dedicated to distributing religious matter to the masses. Despite a contentious rapport with the local officials—who had originally insisted that the agency's Bibles be marked "For Protestants Only" —the operation was thriving. There Sachtleben called on his old friend, the treasurer William W. Peet, who promptly introduced the wheelman to the missionary Henry Otis Dwight.

To Sachtleben's astonishment, Dwight revealed that he had perhaps unraveled Lenz's fate. In hushed tones, the reverend described a recent exchange with an Armenian lad of fifteen. The boy recounted that he had been out riding his bicycle the previous fall when a shower forced him to seek shelter in a guardhouse. One of the soldiers there examined the wheel and revealed that he had seen his first bicycle some months earlier while visiting his hometown. The soldier stated that he was conversing with several friends when an eerie figure atop spinning wheels suddenly appeared on the horizon. The frightened men debated whether the rider was a fellow human being or a devil. One of them spouted: "Let's shoot it. If it is a man it will fall and if it is a devil we cannot hurt it." One of the bystanders complied, and the figure collapsed to the ground. The men rushed over to it and discovered that the rider was a man—fatally wounded.

Sachtleben trembled with excitement. If this was indeed a true account, and the event had taken place near the Deli Baba Pass, the victim was almost certainly Lenz, for cyclists were virtually nonexistent in that remote territory. The wheelman pressed Dwight for more details, but the missionary said that the boy had refused to reveal anything more about the incident.

Determined to follow up on this clue, Sachtleben again called on
Terrell. The minister patiently listened to the tale and agreed that
it might represent a true breakthrough. He suggested that Sachtleben "put the clue in the hands of Constantinople's chief of detec-
tives." If necessary, the minister suggested, Sachtleben could hire a
Christian investigator to pursue the matter with authorities.

The wheelman promptly called on the chief of police to explain
the matter and enlist his help. "Although he treated me with pol-
ished politeness," Sachtleben lamented, "I could get no aid from
him. 'If there is a soldier in the case,' he told me, 'we can do nothing.' I was forced, reluctantly, to relinquish this clue. I began to
learn how impregnably the Turkish soldier was guarded from the
clutches of the law."

A frustrated Sachtleben concluded that he would get nowhere
with the Lenz case until he managed to get to the interior, where
the wheelman was presumably buried in a shallow grave. He resumed his campaign to secure travel papers, visiting Terrell on a
daily basis. But the minister offered only bland assurances that the
porte was still reviewing his petition.

Finally, after having languished in the capital city for nearly a
month, Sachtleben decided to take matters in hand. He knew the
authorities would gladly issue him a *teskere*, or visa, to visit the ancient capital of Broussa (now Bursa), just south of Constantinople,
across the Sea of Marmara. Although he would still be far from
his destination, he reckoned that he would be better off having at
least one official paper in hand rather than nothing at all. Perhaps,
upon his return to Constantinople, he could slyly have his passport extended so that it authorized transit deeper into the Turkish
interior.

In mid-April, Sachtleben toured Broussa and found it one of the
most captivating places he had ever seen. One evening he returned
to his cozy hotel to find a letter from Terrell awaiting him. "In a
few days I will procure a teskere for you," the minister wrote, "allowing travel to Erzeroum and Bayazid via Trebizond [Trabzon]."

Sachtleben was ecstatic. The next morning he boarded a boat back to Constantinople to claim his prize.

"Good morning, Mr. Terrell," chirped the investigator as he strolled into the minister's office. "What's the good word?" The minister sat up, but did not return the cheer. On the contrary, he frowned, before muttering: "I'm afraid the good word's not very good, after all." He then confessed that the promised papers had not materialized after all. In a somber voice, he declared: "I think I can do nothing for you."

Sachtleben was crestfallen. After a moment of silence, the wheelman began to protest. Terrell cut him off. "I do not demand a pass," he explained. "I merely request it, if the Turkish government has no objections. I have no war ships at my command to sway their decision." His temper at the boiling point, Sachtleben fumed: "I must go. I will not have anyone say that I am neglecting my duty." As he stormed out of the office, Luther Short, the consul general who had been silently witnessing the exchange, blurted out: "You'd better take care, young man, or your bones, too, will find a resting place in some Armenian grave."

The next day, to calm his nerves, Sachtleben took a contemplative stroll up one of the highest cliffs overlooking the Bosporus. "I have seen many beautiful things," he wrote a friend afterward, "but the panorama before me was the most exquisite view I ever saw. What an enchanting picture; the large city with its thousands of houses rising from the water's edge, the huge mosques with their dazzling white minarets, the blue waters of the Bosporus, the distant sea of Marmara, and the snow clad mountains of Asia Minor lost in the clouds."

Sachtleben had timed his visit to coincide with the sultan's prayer ceremony (*selamlik*) held every Friday, his only regular public appearance. The wheelman described the distant spectacle:

Six thousand Turkish soldiers, infantry, cavalry, artillery, and marines marched into position for the ceremony. Countless musical

bands played sweetly. Promptly at noon the salute of cannons began, and the Sultan appeared in a carriage attended by several
hundred officers. He disappeared into the mosque for half an hour
of prayer. When he came out the army passed in columns of four.
After the revue, an hour later, the Sultan returned to his palace.

Returning to sea level, Sachtleben plotted his next move. Meanwhile, he vented his frustration in a letter home, denouncing Terrell in no uncertain terms. "He is thoroughly incapacitated to discharge the duties of the office. It is a mystery to me why the U.S.
ever appointed such an ignorant fellow." The cyclist also hinted
darkly that he had the goods on Terrell and was prepared to use
them. Reported the *Telegraph:* "Sachtleben says he is in possession
of facts that would lead to the minister's recall."

Vengeance aside, Sachtleben was in a terrible fix. Owing to
Terrell's ineptitude and the sultan's intransigence, the wheelman
found himself stranded in Constantinople, hundreds of miles from
Lenz's grave. "Had I possessed no other resources my difficult mission would have ended right there," he would later confess, "and I
would have been forced to return to America entirely discomfited,
the laughing stock of my friends."

Fortunately, the resourceful investigator had a trump card up
his sleeve. He discreetly cornered Mr. Dernetriades, a Greek employee of the American consulate, whom the wheelman had met
four years earlier during his first visit to Constantinople. Slipping
him $50 in cash, Sachtleben implored the clerk to procure the elu-
sive papers through his private channels at the porte. The next day
the Greek greeted the cyclist with a "knowing grin" and handed
over a passport permitting travel as far as Trebizond on the Black
Sea.

Although he would still be a good two hundred miles north of
Erzurum, Sachtleben reasoned that, once in Trebizond, he could
seek permission to travel along the caravan road to Erzurum.
Once he had reached that destination, he planned to meet up with

Chambers and Graves, the missionary and the diplomat who had been investigating the Lenz case for some time. They could brief him on their latest findings and help him travel the remaining one hundred miles to the approximate location where Lenz had disappeared.

Sachtleben decided, however, that he would not leave Constantinople until he had engaged the services of an able interpreter — someone who was prepared to accompany him throughout the dangerous journey ahead. At the recommendation of his friends at the Bible House, he interviewed an elderly Christian Arab from Mosul named Khadouri. "His visage was a study in wrinkles," Sachtleben related. "He sported a fierce looking pure white mustache, and his snow-white locks were covered by a bright red fez, decorated with an Arab turban. His costume was exceedingly picturesque. Bright red shoes were followed by gray checked cloth leggings which he had inherited from some English pastor who had long since joined his forefathers in some quiet churchyard."

Despite his age, Khadouri seemed remarkably vigorous. And being a citizen, he was relatively free to travel in Turkey even without special papers. Most importantly, he spoke "every language and dialect of Turkey," with one glaring exception: Armenian. Still, Sachtleben reasoned that it would be some time before he would have to face that language. In the meantime, Khadouri's lack of Armenian might actually help persuade Turkish authorities that the two of them had no intention of traveling to that troubled region.

During his long career, Khadouri had worked for numerous diplomats, missionaries, writers, and travelers of all stripes. Recalled Sachtleben: "He came with a valise full of letters and recommendations in many languages. He treasured them greatly and was fond of looking them over. He was very happy when I added mine to the list, saying I was the youngest master he had ever had. He took it upon himself to write letters to my sisters in beautiful but unintelligible Arabic, telling them how much he loved me. That was before I settled with him."

Anticipating that Turkish officials might balk at his debarking in Trebizond, despite his papers, Sachtleben sent his flamboyant dragoman ahead to alert Mr. Longworth, the local British consul, of his imminent arrival. That way, should he encounter any trouble at the port, the consul could come at once to the American's aid. At last, on April 27, the day after the Arab's departure, Sachtleben boarded the *Tebe*, an Austrian steamer bound for the same destination. "My friends who saw me off wished me all sorts of good luck," Sachtleben recalled, "but they prophesized lots of trouble."

As the ship pulled out on the Bosporus, Sachtleben was in a pensive mood. From the deck he watched as "the domes and minarets of Constantinople gradually faded from view." He took one last look at Dolmabatchi, the sultan's magnificent palace along the waterfront. Some distance beyond, he detected the sultan's favorite hideout, Yildiz (meaning "star"). Farther on, perched on a hill, was Robert College, a prestigious institute of higher learning founded a generation earlier by American Unitarians. After a brief stop on the Asian side to collect Turkish officials, the ship "ploughed her way into the dark night and the darker waters of the Black Sea, bearing me to an unknown fate."

Over the next two days, Sachtleben was a fixture on deck, gazing at the picturesque and heavily forested Turkish coastline. "The farther eastward the vessel proceeds," Sachtleben noted, "the loftier the mountains become, until their summits are so high as to be covered with perpetual snow." On occasion, the *Tebe* would stop in the open sea to allow the approach of fleets of small rowboats manned by "wild looking natives representing various stages of the nude, jabbering in their barbarous tongue."

Finally, the ship reached the harbor of Trebizond. Since the port lacked wharves, the captain had to drop anchor two miles from the shore. Once again, the vessel was instantly surrounded by rowboats. Sachtleben engaged a boatman to take him and his baggage ashore. Meanwhile, he braced himself for a rude reception.

"Being very doubtful of the Turkish officials' willingness to let me land from the rowboat, I stationed myself at its prow as it slowly approached the customs house," Sachtleben recalled.

This landing spot consisted of a flight of stone steps, the lowest one being in the water. Right there stood a Turkish official in a great blue coat armed with the traditional long sword and revolver. He raised his hand and shouted "yassok," which means "forbidden." I jumped right into his arms and held on. He was taken totally unaware and nearly fell over with my weight. But I was safe on Turkish soil.

After recovering from the shock, the humiliated officer marched Sachtleben into the customhouse, where he was "roughly" searched and questioned. All his belongings were confiscated, including his gun and cartridge belt. Khadouri, who had witnessed the entire scene, raced up the hill to enlist Longworth. The British consul immediately dispatched two guards on black horses, who managed to free the American, albeit sans baggage. Sachtleben was relieved nonetheless as he chatted with the minister over a hearty meal.

The next day, thanks to Longworth's timely intervention, Sachtleben recovered all his belongings—with the exception of his pocket book of Byron's poetry, which the local authorities had deemed seditious literature. On Sachtleben's behalf, Longworth also asked the local vali for permission to proceed to Erzurum. To the American's astonishment, the vali furnished the papers and even bade his guest a safe and successful transit.

Before embarking on the weeklong journey, Sachtleben retired to his hotel room to dash off a round of letters. At the same time, he sent Khadouri out to buy supplies. The Arab returned with a plethora of provisions, ranging from dried fruit to canned salmon, as well as a wealth of accessories, including "a little charcoal stove, an alcohol lamp, and a patent cork mattress." Groused Sachtleben: "Khadouri thought I was made of money, and I thought he would bankrupt me. So I had to call a halt to his extravagance."

For transportation, Sachtleben engaged two Armenians with three horses. The heavily loaded party left Trebizond on May 6, in gorgeous spring weather. As they headed into the pristine countryside, Sachtleben took in the "beautiful trees and foliage, full of birds twittering in the branches." He admired the large flocks of sheep as they peacefully grazed by the lush mountainsides and riverbeds. He watched with detached amusement as a host of industrious men and women tilled the fields with crude implements.

Suddenly, Sachtleben envisioned poor Frank Lenz, who had entered this beautiful but tragic country exactly a year earlier. He thought of its oppressed citizens who suffered so under the sultan's cruel tyranny. "I wondered how these poor people could respect an authority that ruled them with a rod of iron and left them with nothing," Sachtleben recalled. "They had little to eat, no beds, and scarcely any clothes."

At one village, where the party had stopped for lunch, Sachtleben met an innkeeper's son, "a very bright and obedient little fellow. . . . I asked the father what he would make of his son. The man replied, 'First, he'll learn to be a soldier. Then I don't know what.' I thought to myself that if the little fellow remains in that village he must of necessity become an innkeeper, a farmer, or a loafer."

A few days later, halfway through their journey, the party reached Bayburt, a city of about eight thousand residents. "I never saw a city of such size look so poor," Sachtleben lamented. "The place was full of beggars, and the houses were wretched shanties of squalor and destitution." Even the cattle "looked as if they were in the last stages of starvation." That night Sachtleben stayed at the same decrepit inn he and Allen had patronized four years earlier. He found everything "exactly the same," except for the "burning incense of myrrh," introduced to "neutralize the dreadful odor."

For the next several days, the party trudged over snow-capped mountains. Occasionally they encountered large caravans of camels passing between Trebizond and Tabriz. A few of the creatures

were so cold and exhausted that they simply drifted away from
the pack and curled up to die on a bed of snow. Mercifully, the
men soon emerged in a lush valley alongside a stream. From time
to time, they paused to enjoy a hot sulfur bath. Finally, the party
entered Erzurum. At long last, Sachtleben's search for Lenz was
about to begin in earnest.

~ 12

ERZURUM, TURKEY

May 13, 1895

SACHTLEBEN WASTED NO TIME calling on the missionary William Nesbitt Chambers. When the good reverend kindly offered a "light and airy room" in the mission house, Sachtleben accepted without hesitation. He knew well that the next-best alternative, Erzurum's premier hotel, was nothing more than "a ramshackle three story structure, the first story of which was devoted to beasts and filth, and the upper ones to men and filth."

The investigator could hardly have asked for a better host or ally than the forty-two-year-old Canadian national. Chambers was thoroughly versed in the local languages and culture, having already served sixteen years at his post. A graduate of Princeton Theological School, he had come to Erzurum in the aftermath of the Russo-Turkish War. He promptly founded a Protestant church and school for girls, catering primarily to Armenian Christians. A widower at the time, having lost his first wife and child in childbirth, he soon met and married Cornelia Williams, the daughter of American missionaries. The couple had two children, Kate and Talcott.

The handsome reverend cast an imposing figure. Tall and fit, with bright blue eyes and a full graying beard, he looked every bit the stern pastor. Sachtleben nonetheless readily detected his host's gentle and humorous side, and soon became quite comfortable in his presence. The missionary, in turn, relished Sachtleben's bright and energetic company. Writing Barton to announce the young man's long arrival, Chambers pronounced his houseguest a "nice fellow."

Neelie, a petite but strong figure in her own right, likewise took an instant liking to her houseguest. In a letter to her brother, the journalist Talcott Williams of Philadelphia, she remarked: "He falls into our ways and makes no extra trouble." His escort was no less striking. "And who do you think is his interpreter and servant?" she queried her brother. "Why, none other than father's old servant Khadouri! He is white haired now, says he is 75 but he is still hale and strong. He inquired after you and sends special salaams. He takes great interest in the children and takes them on walks. They are both fond of him. How sweet to have one's own childhood linked with that of one's children."

As much as the reverend admired Sachtleben, he had comparatively little affection for his boss. "If Mr. Worman had only shown the energy he ought to have shown," Chambers lamented to Barton, "this case could have been settled long ago." The reverend had been downright incensed when he received a request from Worman, relayed through Barton, asking that he cease his correspondence with Mrs. Lenz and that he write to him, Worman, instead. Chambers was not about to break his promise to the grieving mother to keep her informed of developments, and he had a message of his own for the controlling editor: "Please let Mr. Worman know that I will communicate to whomever I please what I please."

Nor did Chambers have any desire to correspond with the *Outing* man. "As Mr. S. is here and in communication with Mr. Worman," the reverend wrote back tartly to Barton, "no further correspondence need fall to me." He did, however, suggest how Worman might show his appreciation for the hospitality he was extending to the *Outing* correspondent: "If Mr. Worman wants to recognize services, he might make it possible for me to buy a good bicycle. I have long wished for one. It would be very handy here."

As soon as Sachtleben was comfortably settled, Chambers took his guest to meet Robert W. Graves. The local British consul had likewise lodged with the Chambers family when he settled in Erzurum two years earlier. Since then, the two British subjects had become great friends and collaborators. At present, they were coordinating relief efforts on behalf of young Armenians in the region orphaned by the latest wave of violence. And of course, the two were in close consultation regarding the Lenz matter.

For the time being, until the opening of an American consulate, already approved by Congress, Graves was the closest thing to an American official in the vicinity, and he regularly represented American interests. He even told Sachtleben that if he had an urgent message for Terrell, he could cable Sir Phillip Currie from the consulate, and the British ambassador would relay the message to his American counterpart, saving considerable trouble and expense. Sachtleben was impressed by Graves's evident willingness to help, in sharp contrast to Terrell. The official, in turn, judged the young investigator "very capable and enterprising."

Graves had a shocking piece of news for Sachtleben. Two weeks earlier, just as the American left Constantinople, the British consul had sent Currie the names of Lenz's alleged murderers, to pass on to the American legation. Graves charged that six Kurds, three sets of brothers from the village of Dahar, in the middle of the Deli Baba Pass, shot Lenz dead in the same pass on or about May 10, 1894. As the consul explained to his boss, the names came from a Kurdish informant who was "usually reliable." Moreover, Graves asserted, the Kurd was not an enemy of the men he accused, nor were their respective tribes at odds with each other.

According to the informant, Lenz had stopped for the night in the village of Kourdali, about a quarter of the way, as one headed west, into the twenty-four-mile-long pass. The next morning the six Kurds allegedly helped Lenz cross a raging river, only to shoot him as soon as they reached the other side. They took his belongings and left him for dead by the roadside. Several villagers from Dyaden purportedly passed by the body shortly thereafter and recognized it as that of the man who had cycled through their village some days earlier.

Sachtleben sat in stunned silence before an overwhelming feeling of relief kicked in. The informant's account confirmed exactly what he had suspected all along, namely, that Kurds had killed Lenz in the treacherous Deli Baba Pass. But he had hardly expected such a gratifying breakthrough so soon after his arrival in Erzurum. Chambers summarized the encouraging situation in a letter to Barton: "We have furnished Mr. Sachtleben with all information important to the prosecution of the case: the place, time, and almost the circumstances of the murder."

This astounding revelation culminated a rigorous six-month investigation conducted jointly by Chambers and Graves. Initially, both men had been reluctant to get involved, so appalled were they by Lenz's recklessness. "It is most unfortunate," lamented Graves in his first letter to Purinton, "that I was not warned in time of Mr. Lenz's rash intention, or I should have protested against his uselessly risking his life by traversing alone a region which was comparatively safe at the time of Messrs. Allen and Sachtleben's journey, but is now swarming with heavily armed and ferocious brigands." Echoed Chambers in a letter to a colleague, "If young men will take such risks they ought to at least inform those residing on the route—either consuls or missionaries—so that such a mishap as this could be known in time."

Determined nevertheless to unravel Lenz's fate, the pair worked their special channels to track his progress through Turkey. Chambers in particular tapped his many Armenian friends residing along the Silk Road. One vouched that friendly Turkish officials at the Persian border had waived Lenz's passport fee and had even served him a cup of coffee. A Turk who saw Lenz the next day in Dyaden reported that the American had spent a tranquil night there in a government building before resuming his ride the next morning across the Alashgerd Plain.

Since Sachtleben had left the United States, the men had communicated additional details to Pittsburgh. They confirmed that

Lenz had reached Karakalissa, the third town west of Dyaden, on the afternoon of May 9, 1894. Fifteen miles farther on, just before sunset, according to Chambers's Armenian witness, Lenz stopped in the village of Chilkani. There he found refuge in the home of an Armenian farmer named Avak Parsegh. "Lenz was in good health and spirits," Chambers relayed. "A number of villagers called to see him and his wonderful machine that evening. He spoke two or three words of Turkish and made them understand that he came from Persia and was going to Erzurum. He left early the next morning. About a month later the villagers heard that he had been killed in the vicinity of Koord Ali."

The pair had collected other testimony affirming Lenz's demise. Parts of his bicycle had reportedly been sold as silver at local bazaars. A rumor in Erzurum held that sometime after the murder a Kurd had discreetly approached a merchant in the Alashgerd, telling him he had something very valuable to show him. The merchant followed the Kurd to a village and was shown a bicycle. Asked what he would pay for it, the merchant replied that it was worthless metal. The dejected Kurd warned the merchant not to breathe a word about what he had seen. Even more chilling, several residents of Zedikan, the last village on the plain, claimed to have seen Lenz's naked body the previous spring, after it had washed up from the Sherian River.

To be sure, the Kurdish informant's account differed slightly from Chambers's previous findings on one point. It asserted that Lenz had spent the night of May 9 in Kourdali, in the pass, rather than in Chilkani, on the plain. Still, the distance between the two towns was only about thirty-five miles. Conceivably, Lenz had slept in both towns, and the given dates were simply off by a day or two.

Most persuasively, the Kurd's account was eerily consistent with the dispatch published some months earlier in *Le Vélo*. It also agreed with a report from the Armenian correspondent of the *Daily News*, a London paper. Dated March 30, 1895, it read: "I am now informed by a merchant of Karakalissa that he knows three inhabitants of the village of Zedikan who saw the body of Mr.

Lenz in China, wearing traditional Mandarin dress.

OCCIDENTAL & ORIENTAL
STEAMSHIP CO.

S.S. Oceanic — Nov 5th 1892.

Mr. Fred Lenz,

Dear Sir; — Your letter to San Francisco was duly received, but with 30 other letters put off answering until on board the steamer.

I will reach Japan the 15th and go through China in Dec. & Jan.

If you see my mother always try to drive the fear from her as I will no doubt get through everywhere without trouble.

Regards to all,

Yours truly
Frank

℅ Oriental Hotel
Calcutta
India

Above: A letter from Lenz to his step-uncle Fred, written aboard the *Oceanic* en route to Japan. He expected to be out of China by February 1893, but he was still there in late June. *Right:* Lenz's calling card.

FRANK G. LENZ,

OUTING World Tour

SPECIAL REPRESENTATIVE,
OUTING,
AMERICAN AMATEUR PHOTOGRAPHER,
239-241 FIFTH AVENUE, NEW YORK.
170 STRAND, W.C., LONDON.

With Wheel & Camera.

Scenes from the Great West, summer 1892. *Above:* Lenz reflects in the woods. *Left:* Lenz watches a train go by after another close call. *Below:* Lenz marches his wheel along the tracks during a sandstorm, probably in Oregon.

Above: Lenz fixes one of the four flats he suffered in the United States. *Left:* Lenz poses for a local photographer in Missoula, Montana, August 1892.

Lenz heads up a mountain road as he nears the Pacific coast in California.

Lenz in front of the royal palace in Honolulu, shortly before the overthrow of the monarchy.

Lenz in a contemplative mood aboard the *Oceanic*, en route to Japan.

Considering that this casting was done six hundred and forty-two years ago, it is a wonderfully perfect piece of work. The casting is smooth and fifty feet high. The waist measures ninety-eight feet in circumference. The face is eight feet six inches long; eye, four feet; ear, six feet six inches ; nose, three feet eight and a half inches ; mouth, three feet two and a half inches. Other curiosities of this section of Japan are a lacquered gold idol in one of the many temples, and the tomb of the once-famous Prince Yoritomo. About 737 A. D. the Emperor of Japan, Shomu, had monasteries built all over the country ; Kamakura was one of them. One Goroyemon was the famous bronze caster of the Kamakura Daibutsu. No matter if any foreigners a r e at the i d o l, the natives go to it at all hours of the day and offer u p prayers. T h e reader will doubtless smile

when I say that an effort was actually made to procure this idol for the World's Fair—of course, without avail.

The hotel at Kamakura is run on the American plan by a Japanese, and I certainly had no reason to complain of my accommodations.

After I had cleaned the mud off the wheel next morning, my friends started in jinrickishas while I led the way. From Kamakura the road winds up over a short hill, then down to the beach, continuing near the water for a considerable distance.

I passed many Japanese, old and young, bearing huge burdens on poles. Ever polite and smiling, they would say "*Ohayo*" (good-morning) or "*Sayonaro*" (good-bye) as I w h e e l e d along. Again I passed thro' H a s e, and turning to the right followed the Enoshima road to the beach. Here the sand was very deep, so leaving t h e w h e e l at a small tea and

WITH BUDDHA, BUT NOT OF BUDDHA.

A page from *Outing* showing Lenz and friends by a giant Buddha.

Japan, November 1892. Lenz hired coolies to help him cross a mountain.

A crowd observes him as he stops on the national highway.

Lenz crosses the famous Five Arch Bridge in southern Japan.

Lenz crosses a much
narrower bridge in China.

Chinese villagers strain for
a view of the foreigner
adept at using chopsticks.

Top: Lenz cycles past a group of onlookers in China. *Bottom:* Lenz crosses a stone bridge, probably in western China.

Lenz's route around the world (east to west), ending prematurely in Turkey.

Middle: Lenz in a city of temples, possibly in Burma. *Bottom:* Lenz admires the fortress in Agra, India.

Lenz unpacks his new bicycle frame and parts in Calcutta, September 1893.

Lenz's abandoned trunk, marked "Hold Until Arrival."

Middle: Lenz chats with a local. The Taj Mahal looms in the background.
Bottom: Lenz rests at a milestone on the way to Allahabad.

Above: Lenz with camels, probably in Beluchistan or Persia. He relied on them to cross the desert between India and Persia. *Below:* Lenz photographed himself at rest. He was probably at a government bungalow in India.

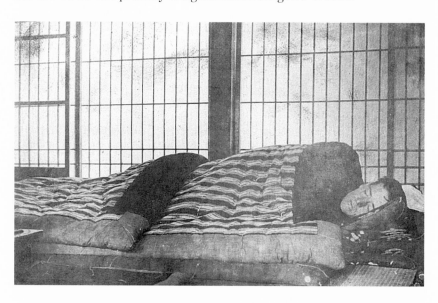

The Selamlik ceremony at the sultan's mosque near Yildiz Palace in Constantinople.

Left: The Reverend William Chambers interviews locals in Erzurum about the Lenz affair while Sachtleben takes notes. *Middle:* Shakir Pasha, Sachtleben's escort to Alashgerd. *Right:* The future sultan Abdul Hamid II, on a visit to London in 1867. In July 1895 he would discuss the Lenz case with the American minister Alexander Watkins Terrell.

The prison at Erzurum where five Armenians implicated in the Lenz murder were held. Two of them died in captivity.

The Armenians of Erzurum bury their dead, October 31, 1895, a day after the massacre. Photo by Sachtleben.

The contents of Lenz's trunk. Sachtleben recovered it in Constantinople
and brought it to Lenz's mother in Pittsburgh.

The last known photo of Frank Lenz, taken by the crown prince of Persia in Tabriz in late April 1894, about two weeks before Lenz's death.

AROVND THE WORLD
WITH WHEEL AND CAMERA

BY FRANK G. LENZ.

The envelope that contained Lenz's last letter to Petticord, sent from Tabriz.

The graphic published in *Outing* in the fall of 1892 announcing Lenz's series.

Lenz after he was killed. The unfortunate gentleman was shot on the road between Kourtali and Dahar, but nearer to Kourtali."

Sachtleben was determined to get to the Deli Baba Pass as soon as possible. But as he explained in a letter to Langhans, "I do not merely want to find Lenz's grave, I want to see these murderers punished and an indemnity paid." Of course, he knew well that he would need to secure at least a measure of Turkish cooperation to accomplish any of these objectives—and that would be hard to come by. The authorities would be unlikely to grant him a passport, much less permission to search homes and make arrests.

Indeed, Sachtleben anticipated that the Turks would go to great lengths to protect the Kurds, their allies in the Armenian repression. Graves had even withheld the names of the accused men from the local vali for fear that the official, who had yet to assist the investigation, might try to tip off the culprits that the foreigners were closing in on them. At least two of the accused had close ties with the Hamidieh regiment, an irregular mounted force named after the present sultan. Formed four years earlier at the suggestion of the field marshal Ahmed Shakir Pasha, the regiment was fashioned after the Russian Cossacks. The hope was that it would give the government not only a fit and flexible fighting force, but also a means to gain some control over the Kurds, a notoriously independent lot.

Sachtleben promptly called on the vali of Erzurum to determine just how helpful he was prepared to be. Alas, the official, Hakki Pasha, was not the congenial man the American had met four years earlier, the one who had commanded the cycling demonstration. The present ruler, in the wheelman's estimation, was instead "an infamous scoundrel—who cared nothing about one Christian more or less."

Predictably, their meeting was tense. The governor questioned whether the cyclist had even entered Turkey, and "he had the impudence to suggest that Lenz might have been a drinking man who simply got drunk and fell off a cliff." The vali nevertheless offered a surprising concession: two zaptiehs to escort Sachtleben to the Deli Baba Pass. As it turned out, the vali was motivated more by duty than goodwill. Shortly after Sachtleben's departure from Constantinople, the porte had acceded to Terrell's prodding and cabled the vali with instructions to provide Sachtleben with an escort, provided he agree to stay within the district of Bayazid, which included the Deli Baba Pass.

The investigator turned down the offer, however, asserting that he needed at least a dozen zaptiehs. He knew well that his was a tall order. Had the suspects been Armenian Christians, he reasoned, the vali would have been only too happy to meet his demands. But since they were Kurds, the government would do all it could to shield them from justice. Sachtleben was hardly surprised when the vali refused to up the force, claiming that he could not do so without the porte's explicit permission.

Sachtleben was nonetheless confident that if the American legation in Constantinople leaned heavily on the porte, the vali would be forced to furnish a larger force. It remained to be seen, however, whether Terrell would be willing to push the demand. Chambers, for one, was skeptical. Confided the missionary to Barton: "I fear Sachtleben's efforts will be greatly hampered for want of backing by Mr. Terrell. We laugh at the Moslem cholera doctor who examines the patient through a spyglass. But when that same absurd incompetence appears in one of our own people what can we do?"

Sachtleben, in fact, fully expected Terrell to balk at his demand. The minister had insisted all along that the wheelman should focus on finding Lenz's grave, in which case two zaptiehs could conceivably suffice. The Texan argued that if Lenz's bones were recovered and identified, the American government would have proof that he had been murdered in Turkey and could therefore insist on the arrest of the murderers, their trial, and the payment of an indemnity. Sachtleben countered that if he were to go to the region simply to search for the body, the suspects would learn of his investigation and destroy any remaining evidence of their crime. They would thus elude justice, and without a conviction, the Turks would have a pretext to refuse payment of an indemnity.

The solution, Sachtleben concluded, was to whip up enough popular support back home for his demands so as to compel the State Department to force Terrell's hand. It was therefore imperative to inform the public at once that the killers had been identified and that he, Sachtleben, was within striking distance of their homes. Americans would naturally expect their representatives in Turkey to ensure that he was properly equipped for this mission of mercy on behalf of Mrs. Lenz.

The wheelman took several initial steps to implement his plan. Mrs. Chambers described the first: "After consultation between [William] Nesbitt, Mr. Graves, and Sachtleben, we sent a cable to Constantinople to go from there to London and from there to New York. If properly taken up by the press, it ought to work up something." The bulletin read:

> Constantinople May 21, 1895. Advices received here from Armenia say that the names of five Kurds, who are said to be the murderers of Lenz killed while attempting to ride around the world on a bicycle, are known. It is announced that William L. Sachtleben, who has gone in search of the missing bicyclist, in hopes of recovering his body, or obtaining definite information as to the cause of his disappearance has arrived at Erzurum.

To put even more pressure on Washington, Sachtleben wired Worman asking him to induce Mrs. Lenz to make, as publicly as possible, three demands of the Turks: first, the immediate arrest of the accused Kurds; second, the dismissal of the local authorities who had stymied the Lenz investigation; and third, the payment of an indemnity totaling $50,000.

While he waited for these initiatives to bear fruit, and for his men to materialize, Sachtleben acquainted himself with his environs. Chambers gave his guest a whirlwind tour of the fortress city where the investigator was likely to be entrenched for some time. Nearly a third of its forty thousand residents were Armenians, and other large percentages were of either Persian or Russian extraction. The American noticed the frequent passing of camel caravans plying wares between Persia and the Black Sea, as well as scores of soldiers patrolling the streets. Ostensibly they were guarding against the Russians, who had already invaded the city twice within living memory.

As it turned out, Chambers had little affection for this remote outpost, despite its picturesque setting at the foot of a lofty mountain chain. Graves was equally down on his adoptive city, branding it "somber and unattractive." He would lament in his autobiography that Erzurum offered

> no fine buildings, broad streets or smiling gardens. The narrow, ill-kept streets are a huddle of crowded mean-looking dwellings with dull grey stone walls and flat mud roofs. The ancient walls, of which some vestiges remain, were replaced after the Crimean war by a rampart and ditch with four principal gates, enclosing an area of three square miles. The town only occupies about one square mile, the rest being mainly deserted graveyards, waste land, and a few meager vegetable gardens. Shops are virtually nonexistent, the retail trade being confined to the narrow alleys of the bazaars.

Until his men appeared, Sachtleben resolved to gather whatever evidence he could find in Erzurum. The dragoman of the Russian consulate introduced him to an Armenian named Hagob Effendi, who attributed Lenz's murder to the same Kurds Graves's informant had accused. Effendi, however, offered a new detail that he had gleaned from an Armenian friend of his from Chilkani, a certain Garabed Hovagemian. This man claimed to have seen Lenz when he passed through Karakalissa, and he stated that Lenz had made an indiscreet show of money, catching the attention of a Kurdish chief named Moostoe Niseh, also from Chilkani. Hovagemian claimed that Moostoe, who subsequently tried to sell parts of Lenz's bicycle, was the one who had ordered those Kurds to kill Lenz the next day.

Sachtleben was intrigued. Certainly, Moostoe should be checked out as well, even if he was not among the names given to Graves.

Sensing that he might be closing in on the "arch-murderer," Sachtleben hatched a plan to speed up the investigation. In advance of his own visit to the Deli Baba Pass and the Alashgerd Plain, he would send a spy to those places to interview the locals and, if possible, to locate the culprits. His agent would also be instructed to purchase, as evidence, any items he could find that might have belonged to Lenz. That way, Sachtleben would be better prepared once he got to those places himself with his armed force.

On May 20, with Chambers's assistance, Sachtleben interviewed a Protestant Armenian named Khazar Semonian whom Chambers had recommended for the mission. "He wore blue jeans, loose trousers, variegated stockings and approached us in stocking feet," Sachtleben recalled.

> But he had not been long in our presence before we wished that he had left on his shoes and instead had taken off his red fez and dark turban so we could see his face. He sat bolt upright with his hands tightly clasped in his lap. The first question that Mr. Chambers put to him in Armenian was "Have you common sense?" Khazar laughed dryly and vouchsafed a long explanation proving that common sense was his most precious possession.

Khazar, who made his living as a guide to visiting Kurds around the bazaars of Erzurum, assured the two that he knew Moostoe personally. The candidate was hired on the spot. "We judged him to be an excellent person to ingratiate himself into the good graces of Kurdish women," Sachtleben related, "by making small gifts of mirrors, needles, yashmaks, etc. And from the Kurdish women one can learn a great deal, as they are very independent. They are good gossips."

The next day Khazar, disguised as a vendor and with a companion, left Erzurum on a donkey "loaded with all sorts of knick-knacks." Sachtleben described their plan: "The companion was to do most of the selling, while Khazar was to take his time and inquire about Lenz. We gave him all the information we already had. He was to go as far as Chilkani, about 100 miles, and search about that neighborhood, following Lenz up from the time of his leaving the house of Avak Parsegh."

Meanwhile, Sachtleben tried to dig up some dirt on Moostoe. "I looked up this man's history as far as I could," the investigator wrote Langhans. "He is a villain of the deepest dye. A description of all the murders of this Kurd would fill a volume. He is the terror of all the Armenians of Chilkani, whom he robs and kills as he pleases. The government takes no notice of his misdeeds, they practically share in the booty." Indeed, Moostoe was "an inferior officer in the Turkish army, that wretched Hamidish Corps of irregular cavalry who are practicing all kinds of oppression upon the Christian inhabitants."

The more Sachtleben found out about the Kurd, the more evil he appeared. "Four years ago there was not a Kurd in the village of Chilkani when this bloody rascal came and settled there by force," Sachtleben wrote home. "He treated the helpless Armenians with great cruelty and oppression. They were all afraid for their lives and had to obey his slightest wish." Shortly after his arrival, the Kurd had allegedly slit the throat of a resident Armenian. Afterward, he was said to have dismembered the body and left the parts by the roadside, as a show of force.

On June 8, Sachtleben dashed off his first letter to Terrell from Erzurum, just in time for the weekly mail pickup. The wheelman inquired if the minister had received Graves's dispatch naming the six Kurds, sent to the British embassy a month earlier, and if so, what he intended to do with the information. Sachtleben added that he had since discovered the name of their ringleader, an officer in the Turkish army, though he did not mention Moostoe by name.

Sachtleben also reported that the vali had offered him a paltry force consisting of two zaptiehs. "A weak prosecution of this case is worse than none," he warned Terrell, "and will only embolden the Koords to kill the next American that comes this way. That will be me, because I am preparing to go over the road in a few days." He closed with a veiled threat: "If you won't help me I will go to head-quarters in America when I return."

Later that same day, Khazar returned from his three-week road trip with stunning results. He confirmed that Lenz had spent the night of May 9, 1894, in Chilkani at Parsegh's home and that Moostoe and his men had killed Lenz the following day. He even claimed to have found physical evidence of the crime and to have discovered the whereabouts of Lenz's grave. Sachtleben, naturally, was overjoyed.

Khazar concluded that Lenz had not gotten as far as the Deli Baba Pass after all, but was slain only a few miles out of Chilkani, at the crossing of a stream between the villages of Musertee and Shamian. At that spot, the locals had recovered a number of small items they suspected were part of Lenz's camera. Although Khazar was unable to view the hardware, he surmised that Lenz's assail-ants had smashed the camera to see if it contained valuable parts, before doing away with Lenz himself. Moroever, the spy discov-ered, Moostoe's accomplices were not the men Graves had named, but rather a sordid band of associates living in and around Chilkani. One, a certain Alayee Chavdar, reportedly had articles of Lenz's in his home.

In fact, in retrospect, it seemed unlikely that Lenz would have made it as far as the Deli Baba Pass after leaving Chilkani on the morning of May 10. It was a rainy day, and the muddy terrain would have forced him to walk much of the way. Moreover, accord-ing to Der Arsen, the Armenian priest of Chilkani who claimed to have been with Lenz that morning, the cyclist was not feeling well, contrary to the testimony of Chambers's Armenian witness.

More tellingly, Khazar could find no witnesses in Zedikan who recalled seeing a wheelman pass through, as Lenz would have needed to do to reach the pass. In fact, the villagers of Chilkani, who had heard about Lenz's killing within days, not weeks, were under the distinct impression that Lenz had been killed just out-side their village near the Hopuz River.

Further evidence pointing to an ambush just outside Chilkani
came from an Armenian resident named Varshabed Ohannes. He
confided that in May 1894 a naked corpse was found in the river
Sherian, about a mile west of town. The locals promptly notified
the *kaimacam* of Toprakaleh, who had jurisdiction over the territory. The *medjelis* (a council of mullahs) went to see the body and
determined that it was that of a young man of medium height,
sandy complexion, and strong build. They could find no signs of
a wound. The body was secretly spirited to the Kurdish village of
Kolah and buried under cover of darkness.

Khazar was convinced that the body in question was that of
Lenz. Although the evidence strongly suggested that the cyclist
had been killed near a different branch of the Sherian, Khazar theorized that the wily Kurds had taken Lenz, dead or alive, across
the fields before throwing him into the larger river. In so doing,
they hoped to cover their villainous tracks.

As if all this were not stunning enough, Khazar had one more
revelation: several informants in Chilkani had told him that the
Kurdish chief was using Lenz's inner tubes as saddle girths. Reported the spy: "I managed to get on friendly terms with Moostoe's family, giving them presents of looking glasses and other
things. They invited me to meals several times." Sure enough, the
spy spotted the incriminating articles dangling from Moostoe's
horse. Khazar settled in the village and awaited his opportunity.

Finally, Khazar found a ripe moment. "I approached Moostoe
and, putting my hands on his shoulders and looking him lovingly
in the eyes, said, 'Moostoe, promise not to refuse me.' He appeared
quite overcome by this burst of affection and said: 'Speak. I will do
anything for you that is in my power.' 'I want to buy that saddle
of yours, put it on my horse, and ride it back to Erzurum.'" After
some haggling, the two came to terms. But just then an Armenian
friend stopped by to see Moostoe, distracting the Kurd. By the
time he refocused on Khazar, the Kurd had changed his mind. The
spy, not wishing to raise suspicions, reluctantly abandoned his bid
to buy the saddle.

For the next few days, Khazar continued to hunt for other elements of Lenz's gear. While peddling his own knickknacks, he sent out word that he was looking to buy small metal articles. Unfortunately, no one came forward with anything of interest save a Kurd in the village of Tchurmouk. He produced half a bicycle bell, which Khazar promptly purchased on the assumption that it had belonged to Lenz.

Sachtleben was now utterly convinced that Moostoe was the arch-murderer. After all, the tubes in his possession were brown, a color distinct to the Overman products Lenz employed. The investigator immediately cabled a summary of Khazar's findings to Mrs. Lenz to serve as proof of her son's death. At the same time, he sent another letter to Terrell, asserting: "It will be a very easy matter to discover the real culprits as soon as a strong order is sent from Constantinople to the Vali here authorizing him to give me the power and sufficient force to arrest these men, search their houses, and bring them to trial in Erzeroum." Sachtleben added a stern warning:

> Do not divulge any names I have given you. This would be very
> foolish. If you do, you will destroy in a moment the results of all
> my work. For as soon as the authorities at Constantinople have
> the names they will secretly telegraph them to the Governor here,
> who will give the murderers warning and they will not be able to
> be found when wanted, and they will destroy every trace. If you
> disclose the names of the Armenians they will either lose their
> lives by the hands of the Koords or be robbed of all they possess.
> Do not disclose the names of the towns, but secure an order from
> the government to order the Vali here to give me immediately the
> power and permission to do what I wish in this case.

A few days later, Sachtleben finally received a terse cable from Constantinople in response to his earlier letter: "Your letter of 8th June received. The facts we reported to our Government. I await its instructions. *Haste cannot restore the dead.* Therefore, get all the facts you possibly can before I move here. It would be better not to start at all than to fail. *I would write more fully but in the condition of the mails, prefer not to.*"

Terrell's patronizing plea for patience irked the investigator, who felt that he had been waiting long enough for action. A few days later, Terrell cabled again, this time in response to the second letter: "Remain if you can. British Consul will assist. Measures are afoot to secure justice." Eager to learn just what those measures were, Sachtleben dashed over to see Graves. The consul revealed that he had agreed to represent the American government in case of a trial, but he knew of no other developments.

Sachtleben reluctantly concluded that he had made little headway with the lethargic minister after all. In fact, Terrell had sat on Graves's report for a good month. Finally, on June 20, the minister wrote Currie to apologize for "the failure of this Legation to promptly acknowledge its appreciation," citing his "absence in the Mediterranean." He then cabled Washington to announce that Lenz's killers had been identified. He also declared that he would demand that the porte act on this new information.

The substance of Terrell's cable was published in numerous American newspapers, sending shock waves across the country. For despite all the previous reports affirming Lenz's demise, including Sachtleben's recent cable, nothing had seemed quite so definitive as this telegram from the American minister in Turkey asserting that Lenz was dead. Now it was official, though it would be another few months before Mrs. Lenz actually filed his will. A reporter with the *Dispatch* rushed to the Lenz residence to get Mrs. Lenz's reaction, and his report appeared in the paper the next day:

> Mrs. Lenz is a comely German woman. She lives comfortably with her husband at 4701 Liberty Avenue. "Frank was always wild to go off on this trip and talked of it all the time," she said in broken English. "He wrote to *Scribner's* and they said their force was made up for the year and they could not take up the scheme. Then he tried *Outing* and they agreed to send him. I told him how danger-

ous it would be and he would never come back alive. But he said he would be all right. After he went away he wrote every week till he got to China, when it took six weeks to get a letter home. A friend of his who had been in Little Asia told me the people were very treacherous. I wrote and warned Frank and told him not to go there. He wrote back that he was all right, that there was no danger. That's the last I heard."

Mrs. Lenz declared with tears in her eyes that she would still hope. Frank was her only child, and she had tried every endeavor as had his employer, Mr. Cadman, to induce him not to make the trip. Her last letter from him was dated April 28. She received it May 27. About a week later began the rumors of his murder. Since then she has laid awake nights weeping, but will not give up hope.

A few days later, she faced yet another grim task. Worman had written her to request a description of Lenz's dental structure so that Sachtleben could confirm her son's remains. She dutifully composed a letter in German, which Worman translated and forwarded to his correspondent in Turkey. It read:

Filled teeth Frank never had before his departure from home. That I know definitely, but it is barely possible that while he was traveling he had some filled for he had suffered often from toothache. But it seems to me he would have written me for he was always accustomed to tell me such things.

Frank's teeth were very uneven. On the upper row he had on each side a crooked crown tooth somewhat protruding and beside that, one too large outside of the tooth row. I often talked with Frank about it, whether we should have it removed because it pushed forward the upper lip a little in consequence. But I begged him not to have it done as I feared it would do him harm, because it was a very strong tooth. Two eye teeth Frank had drawn before he left home.

I write all this that it may possibly help to find my son. I had continued to hope that we might find him alive. Oh! How hard it is to be so near your goal; to have suffered so much and then to lose one's life. My poor Frank.

I thank you many times for all the pains you are taking to find my poor son.

Respectfully,

Signed, Mrs. Anna Lenz

A few weeks later, Langhans received a direct request from Sachtleben, asking for a photograph of Lenz revealing his teeth. A Pittsburgh paper described the successful search: "Mr. Langhans went out to the home of the mother of Lenz yesterday and the matter was canvassed. She happily recalled the fact that she had a picture of her son taken by himself in comical attitude. The portrait shows his teeth, which is a first-class means of identifying the remains."

Just after cabling Washington with the news that Lenz's killers had been identified, Terrell made good on his promise to demand action from the porte, addressing a note to the Turkish foreign minister. Rather than request more firepower for Sachtleben, however, the minister divulged the names of the six Kurds listed in Graves's report and asked the porte to "arrest the parties named." He made no mention of the newly accused Moostoe or his alleged accomplice per Khazar, Alayee Chavdar.

The Reverend Dwight got wind of Chambers's note and wrote Chambers to inform him of Terrell's action. He added that he had recently run into the minister, who told him in no uncertain terms that it would be "impossible" to demand ten zaptiehs for Sachtleben. Chambers promptly related the information to Sachtleben. Of course, the wheelman went into a rage. Not only had Terrell revealed the names of the Kurdish suspects, contrary to Sachtleben's explicit instructions, but he was also evidently maneuvering to delegate the responsibility of conducting house searches and making arrests to the Turks themselves.

Evidently, Sachtleben was not having his way with the authorities. Despite his frequent and impassioned appeals to public opinion, he had yet to gain any visible sway over the State Department or Terrell, let alone the Turks. Moreover, his relationship with Worman was rapidly deteriorating. The editor was taking great pains to disassociate himself from his outspoken investigator, who rarely wasted an opportunity to blast Terrell in his letters home, much to the dismay of Washington. "We wish in no wise to be responsible for anything Mr. Sachtleben has chosen to say," the editor assured the State Department. "We are not willing to share in the insinuations made against Mr. Terrell or other employees of the Government."

Worman also practically apologized to the State Department for Sachtleben's vociferous grumblings to the effect that the American government was not doing enough to secure him a larger protective force. "We had hoped that Mr. Sachtleben, who knows that country, would go into it quietly," Worman wrote to Acting Secretary Alvey A. Adee, "and obtain proofs of the death and identify the body. We were disappointed to learn that he could not go without an escort."

Worman emphatically refused to ask Mrs. Lenz to make public demands of the Turkish government, as Sachtleben had stipulated. Read Worman's telegram in reply: "Cable worthless. Convincing data of death and body wanted from you." Instead, the editor all but commanded his correspondent to abandon his efforts to make house searches and arrests and to focus instead on finding Lenz's remains or other irrefutable proof of his death.

Some even doubted the significance of Khazar's findings. "Charlie Petticord smiles grimly when talking about the report that Sachtleben has found Lenz's bell," a Pittsburgh paper reported. "Said he yesterday: Lenz never carried a bell on his wheel. He wouldn't do it here and he never took any away with him either. I am certain that he did not get a bell while en route else he would have told me in his letters for he knew that I knew his antipathy for bells. I think this is another fairy tale and I will not yet believe the boy is dead."

Feeling increasingly embattled, Sachtleben went on the offensive again. He fired off a barrage of letters back home to Lenz's family and friends urging them to contact the State Department to voice their support for his demands. "I know where Lenz's grave and possessions in part are," Sachtleben wrote to Langhans, "but I have no power to get them. I have done all that can be done without official support." If he did not receive the necessary escort, he threatened, he would be forced to return to the United States empty-handed.

Lenz's loved ones responded quickly and forcefully. Wrote Langhans to the secretary of state:

> Mr. Sachtleben knows all but cannot move from Erzurum. The governor of the province only offers him two Turkish soldiers. To undertake such a dangerous mission he must have at least ten well armed body guards. He informs us that if sufficient support is not granted him soon he must return. You no doubt understand what a blow it will be to the begrieved mother if he should return without bringing the remains with him.

Echoed Purinton: "Cannot your Department direct Terrell to demand that the vali provide Sachtleben with sufficient support and protection? Terrell seems to fail to realize that he is dealing with as treacherous a nation as exists on the face of the globe. Their promises are as plentiful as water and not half as reliable." Wrote Mrs. Lenz herself: "I pray that your Department makes an immediate demand on the Turkish government to furnish Mr. Sachtleben with sufficient protection so that he can proceed to Chilkani, to examine and secure the remains of my only child."

At the same time, Sachtleben continued to send long letters to Terrell demanding not only the armed squadron but also immediate action on the indemnity front. Sachtleben maintained that he had already submitted sufficient evidence to prove Lenz's death and the failure of the Turkish government to provide him with adequate protection. The investigator argued that Terrell had no need to defer this action pending the discovery of the body or ex-

plicit instructions from Washington. Indeed, Sachtleben feared
that if he left Turkey before such a demand had been lodged, Terrell might never get around to it.

Anticipating another lull, Sachtleben tried to make the most of
his time in Erzurum. Mrs. Chambers described his doings to her
brother in a letter dated July 9: "Mr. Sachtleben is still with us. He
is a pleasant guest and making the best of his time reading up on
the country and laying by a good store of information. The police
have been watching him lately, as they did not at first. We wonder
if his letters have been opened. It began one day when we went on
a ride and he took a camera with him for the sake of photographing
us. But they pretend to think he tried to photo the fortifications!"

Sachtleben made several follow-up visits to the vali, but the results were invariably disappointing. The governor revealed that
he had sent gendarmes to Chilkani, Karakalissa, Zedikan, and Dahar to interview the locals, but all denied seeing a wheelman pass
through. At one point, Sachtleben divulged the names of the suspects, already known to the porte. The vali was furious to discover
that Sachtleben had been withholding that information. "Why
did you not give these names to me?" he stammered. He then demanded to know Sachtleben's source, but the investigator coyly
refused to reveal the names of his Armenian informants.

The vali then launched into a tirade, cursing Lenz's stupidity.
"Why did he go traveling among the Kurds without a zaptieh on
a jansizat [soul-less horse]?" he shouted. "Of course he would be
killed!" In the midst of his rant, Khadouri handed the vali a photo
of Lenz. The official suddenly fell silent as he examined the image.
"Oh, he was quite young!" the governor remarked at last in a much
softer tone. Replied the interpreter: "Young, yes, but very strong."

On July 12, unbeknownst to Sachtleben, Terrell visited Yildiz,
the sultan's fortified palace, to discuss the Lenz case with the supreme ruler himself. Terrell described his host, Abdul Hamid II:
"The sultan is over fifty years old, of medium height, with clear
olive complexion, dark hair, high forehead, and large dark brown

eyes. His habitual expression is one of extreme sadness. Though his pashas are decorated with regal splendor, he always appears in plain garb, wearing a red fez, a frock coat, dark blue trousers and leather shoes. A broad sword which he holds sheathed in his hands completes the costume."

The American minister found the sultan "agreeable in conversation" and, unlike most European sovereigns, "free from that stilted dignity that repels confidence." The despot was indeed a man of many eclectic interests, ranging from opera to wrestling. And he loved nothing more than a good mystery, being a voracious reader of the Sherlock Holmes novels. Indeed, the sultan took great pride in his vast spy network, and he was reportedly obsessed by the fear that would-be assassins were forever lurking in the shadows. He listened intently as Terrell's dragoman recounted the Lenz case.

When Terrell concluded, the sultan inquired about Lenz's gear. Indeed, that past fall, he had asked Terrell to procure from America "two bicycles of the best sort." The minister relayed the request to Uhl, stressing that the wheels were not to exceed $150 each. Abdul Hamid was also a photography buff, having commissioned thousands of photographs throughout his empire. He had only recently presented the British Museum and the Library of Congress with a collection of fifty albums chock-full of images depicting the progress of the Ottoman Empire.

Terrell finally steered the conversation to Lenz's assailants. This time, however, the minister referred to Khazar's report, telling the sultan that Lenz's bicycle tubes had been found in the hands of the Kurdish chief Moostoe Niseh, a resident of Chilkani and an officer in the Hamidieh regiments. Terrell demanded that the porte instruct the vali of Erzurum to arrest at once the Kurd and his accomplices.

Visibly shaken, the sultan replied that anyone could have purchased those articles. He declared that it was his duty to provide justice under his reign, and he insisted that nothing would be done contrary to justice. Therefore, nobody would be arrested without reasonable and definite grounds. Terrell countered that if the suspects were arrested and interrogated, the elusive truth could be established.

Unmoved, Abdul Hamid reiterated that the mere possession of those articles was insufficient grounds to arrest the Kurd. He maintained that before anyone could be arrested the authorities had to determine if, and where, Lenz had entered Ottoman territory. Terrell replied that Lenz had come from Tabriz, Persia, and had even sent him a postcard from that place. Upon reaching the border at Kizil Dizeh, Lenz had sent him a letter stating that he had been well treated by Turkish authorities.

Abdul Hamid expressed incredulity that Lenz would have come that way, insisting that he must have debarked at a port such as Batum on the Black Sea (now Batumi, Georgia). Told that Lenz had come all the way from China almost entirely overland, the sultan stared incredulously. "How could he possibly have cycled across the vast deserts of central Asia?" he gasped.

In any case, the sultan asserted, even if Lenz had crossed the Persian border into Turkey, he could easily have gone back to Persia or headed into Russia. His officials would therefore need to consult with their Russian and Persian counterparts to make sure that Lenz had not wound up in either of those countries.

As their animated meeting came to a close, Abdul Hamid expressed his deep regret that this "small affair" had become such a sore point between the two countries. He expressed his concern, judging from the ambassador's insistent demands, that the American government was simply using the Lenz affair as a pretext to compel the porte to arrest and perhaps execute a few token Kurds from the Hamidieh regiments—a reprisal of sorts for their alleged abuse of the Armenians. For his part, he insisted that his government would not be cowed and would adhere to proper legal procedures.

Terrell's initiative seems to have spurred the porte into action, at least temporarily. The day after his visit, the grand vizier cabled the governor of Erzurum to remind him that the Lenz case was not an ordinary one and that the suspects should be arrested immediately. The day after that, however, the sultan's chief official cabled the vali again and ordered him to suspend all action in the case until further notice.

Sachtleben, meanwhile, continued to press for his men. On July 23, he returned to the vali and was astonished when the official indicated that he was now prepared to supply a dozen zaptiehs. An elated Sachtleben wrote Langhans: "At last, at last, I am triumphant over the Vali! I hope to leave shortly for Alashgerd to search for Mr. Lenz's remains personally." Alas, a few days later, the vali reneged, maintaining that he was still awaiting permission from the porte. Per the vali's suggestion, the investigator again cabled Terrell asking him to press the porte on the matter.

On August 1, Terrell wired back: "I will answer your cable in three days." Not until August 6, however, did he send a second cable reading: "Unless the Vali is taking effective steps to arrest and punish the guilty, your stay there is useless. In returning to the Wheelmen of America come by this city." Sachtleben was stunned. He could not fathom turning back now, not after all this time and tribulation. He cabled back: "I do not propose to abandon search until you inform me that you cannot obtain such instructions without which nothing will be done here."

The investigator was hardly cheered, a few days later, when he received a rare letter from the minister written several days before his latest cable. "You must be aware that no American Minister has the authority to demand indemnity, or, as you term it, 'blood money,' until his Government instructs him," Terrell admonished. Nor would he demand the ten zaptiehs: "To give you a force to search suspected parties and houses is not to be thought of. No government can be expected to authorize a foreigner to go to the houses of its people and search them. Their government can find the murderers *if it will*. To demand that it *shall* do this is all that I can until I hear from Washington."

Terrell, however, suggested that Sachtleben might yet receive a force sufficient to retrieve the body, if only he exercised patience: "The business methods of the Turkish officials at the Porte are always slow, and I cannot wonder that you are impatient," the minister consoled. "But you must have realized this before you agreed to undertake the present work." The minister pointed out that the recent Armenian troubles were now absorbing the porte, making their response time to minor issues even slower than usual. On a more positive note, the minister added: "As soon as you hear from America and have the means of identifying the skeleton of Mr. Lenz, I will see that you are authorized to exhume it."

Up to this point, the State Department had been largely supportive of Terrell's handling of the Lenz case, virtually apologizing to the minister for Sachtleben's "impetuosity and ill-temper." By mid-August, however, Sachtleben's overtures to the American public were beginning to pay off. The new secretary of state, Richard Olney, successor to the late Walter Q. Gresham, felt increasing pressure to demonstrate that the department was doing everything possible to resolve the case.

On August 13, Acting Secretary Adee instructed Terrell to demand a larger force for Sachtleben, although he stopped short of specifying the number of guards. Read the cable: "Governor of Erzerum offers Sachtleben inadequate guard of two soldiers. Ask escort to insure and permit practical investigation of Lenz murder."

Terrell cabled back: "I have renewed demand for a guard to protect Sachtleben in identifying Lenz's skeleton." He stressed, however, that even with a larger force, Sachtleben's plan to search the homes of the Kurdish chiefs for evidence was pure "folly." Huffed the minister: "It would require an army to protect Sachtleben in his scheme. Though Turkey has armed that race she has never been able to control it." He also expressed doubts that Turkish soldiers would respect Sachtleben's authority, pointing out that "German officers of the highest rank employed in the Turkish service are never allowed to utter a word of command to their soldiers, it being degrading for even a private to move at the command of a Christian officer."

Terrell was nonetheless determined to placate the State Department. A few days later, he paid a visit to the foreign minister to make a personal appeal for a larger force. The minister pointed out that the United States had vouched for Turkey's sovereignty, having thus far refused to back European demands to intervene in Turkish affairs on the Armenian question. Naturally, he expected Turkey to show its appreciation by facilitating the arrest and conviction of Lenz's murderers. Warned the minister: "Sixty million Americans are carefully following this affair, and any further delays will certainly have harmful effects on public opinion."

Terrell then cabled Sachtleben promising to send another cable shortly detailing "final action." Though unclear on what exactly that phrase meant, Sachtleben hoped it signaled that he was about to get his men at long last. He was more eager than ever to conduct the house searches, even if they were unlikely to turn up evidence. In any case, a large force would come in handy in the search for Lenz's grave. He had just received the revealing photo of Lenz's teeth along with his mother's graphic description and was now confident that he could identify the bones once recovered.

As August closed, however, no further word came from Terrell. Writing a friend in St. Louis, Sachtleben expressed his exasperation.

> I am sorry that governmental affairs move so slowly. I had hoped to return to the United States by September at the latest and enjoy in company with the boys a few trips out of town on the bicycle. But fate has decided otherwise. I am still here trying to induce the stubborn Turkish officials to travel in the ways of justice. I am eating to keep up my energy for so difficult and hopeless a task, and silently praying for a speedy release from so trying a position.

Meanwhile, Sachtleben continued to search locally for more evidence. On August 20, he received word from two Armenian informants that one of Moostoe's gang was in town, a certain Achmet of Chilkani. He was in fact visiting with the Armenians, unaware that they were discreetly assisting Sachtleben. Per the investigator's request, the Armenians had themselves photographed with their visitor. Achmet had allegedly told other friends that he personally killed Lenz, and one witness even claimed to have seen Lenz's silver revolver in Achmet's possession. Sachtleben was pleased to obtain an image of the murderer. A short while later, another person of interest, Moostoe's servant Garabed Hovagemian, also came to town. Sachtleben instructed his informants to induce the man to talk about the Lenz affair, but they failed to extract any testimony.

Finally, in late August, Terrell cabled: "Sufficient guard has been ordered for you. See governor." Sachtleben rushed over to the official residence. The vali, in fact, promised to give him as many zaptiehs as he wished. Elated, Sachtleben began to make preparations for his trip to Alashgerd. Once again, however, the vacillating official reneged at the last moment, saying he still needed the porte's approval. Sachtleben was "dumbfounded." He immediately cabled Terrell: "Vali declares he has received no orders and still refuses me escort. How much more delay must there be?"

Sachtleben dashed off another irate letter to Terrell. "I do not see why there should be any more delay in this Lenz case. Even if there were a dozen mighty questions, like the settlement of Armenian affairs, before the Porte, any able government should have the necessary force of officials to carry out minor affairs, as you term this Lenz case. It seems to me that the murder of an American citizen is about as important a case as can arise in international relations."

The wheelman proposed that the minister stage a show of force to budge the Turks, such as sending a warship into the harbor of Constantinople. He again explained at length why Terrell should immediately demand an indemnity. Although Terrell did not respond to Sachtleben right away, he forwarded a copy of the letter to the State Department, remarking dryly: "Its disquisition on International Law will give you a faint idea of the embarrassments I have to face." Added the minister: "The bold effrontery shows that it is intended for publication."

As tensions between Sachtleben and Terrell mounted, even Lenz's friends back home began to worry that the outspoken cyclist might be pushing the State Department a bit too far. Wrote Purinton to Adee: "I know that Sachtleben has chaffed under delay and has been pretty blunt in some of his remarks. But I am sure that his position at Erzurum is calculated to make one crabbed. You will no doubt take this into consideration before passing judgment upon him."

When September opened, Sachtleben appeared destined to stew indefinitely in Erzurum, while the hopes for any consolation in the Lenz affair continued to fade. On the sixth of that month, however, Sachtleben at last received some encouraging news. Graves delivered a terse telegram from Terrell reading: "Postpone your departure until the arrival of Shakir Pasha, who will furnish suitable escort."

13

ERZURUM

September 9, 1895

S HAKIR PASHA ARRIVED in Erzurum "amid a great deal of trumpet blowing and firing of cannon." This distinguished soldier and diplomat was about to embark on a tour of troubled Armenia to implement reforms mandated by the three overseeing powers—France, Russia, and Great Britain—designed to improve the condition of Armenians and to stem the rising tide of regional violence.

By all accounts, he was the best man for an impossible job. A contemporary review described him as "about fifty, modest and plain in his appearance," adding that "one could hardly realize that this man had been one of the great captains of the Turkish army." During the Russian-Turkish War of 1877–78, in fact, he "had taken part in all the great battles, inflicting terrible losses upon the Russian troops." Ironically, after the conflict, he was sent to St. Petersburg to serve as the Turkish ambassador. Far from being an unpopular figure there, he became, according to the review, "a great favorite at court and in society" thanks to his "urbanity, amiability, imperturbable humor, and ready wit."

Before leaving Constantinople, Shakir had informed Terrell that, as part of his tour, he would be willing to escort Sachtleben to the suspected site of Lenz's grave and provide him with all the protection and authority he required. Sachtleben was elated to

learn that his prospective escort was a man of such power and influence, affirming: "To arrest a few Kurds whom every one knew
to be criminals or to discharge a *kaimacam* or two was not more to
him than snapping his fingers."

True, the wheelman did not fully trust the Turk, despite his dis-
arming charm. "I did not relish the idea of his accompanying me,"
the investigator would later reveal, "because I knew if he were inclined to shield the culprits he could most effectively do so if he
were on the spot himself. I thought if I were allowed to go to Chilkani alone with a guard, I should be able to fasten Lenz's murder
on the true culprits."

Still, Sachtleben had little choice but to accept Shakir's proposition, in the hope that the Turk would see a resolution of the Lenz
case as a timely means to improve relations with the United States.
The American was tired of playing the waiting game, and he knew
well that this was probably his best—perhaps only—opportunity
to arrest the suspects and search their homes—even if his chances
of finding anything incriminating at this point were slim. Indeed,
Khazar had heard rumors that Turkish officials had already visited
the region to tip off the suspects and intimidate potential Armenian witnesses.

On September 9, Sachtleben called on Shakir, who had taken
over a room in the vali's residence. He was a big, bearded man who
could not mount his horse without the help of three assistants.
The numerous medals pinned on his chest added to his aura of importance. "He rose from his chair, shook hands, and saluted me in
French," Sachtleben recorded. "He opened his cigarette case saying
'je vous donne un cigarette d'abord' ('First I give you a cigarette.')"
He then inquired in a most pleasant manner whether Sachtleben
had ever been to these parts before. The investigator briefly described his round-the-world bicycle tour. "Indeed," gasped Shakir,
glancing at his assistant. "Now there's a journey for you!"

The investigator, however, was anxious to get down to business. He asked Shakir if the vali had briefed him about the Lenz

case. The diplomat shook his head and then listened intently as Khadouri launched into a long description of the Lenz affair in Turkish. Afterward, Sachtleben handed the diplomat a photo of Lenz. He studied it for a few seconds, before bursting into tears. He said that he wished he had never seen that picture. "The idea that this young man had journeyed through nearly all the uncivilized countries in the world only to meet his death on Turkish soil," Shakir lamented, "is a thought too terrible to bear."

Sachtleben, however, was unmoved by what he dismissed as crocodile tears. He would later affirm: "I was not deceived; I knew Shakir did not care a rap about Lenz." Still, Sachtleben reasoned, he did not need Shakir's compassion, just his cooperation. Promising to contact Sachtleben in the next few days, the cordial diplomat escorted his guest to the door.

Three more days went by with no word from Shakir. Sachtleben was beginning to fear that this proposition was just another ruse. He sent Khadouri to the governor's palace to inquire about developments. The dragoman came back with an answer that "fell like a knell on my ear. It was the same old story. Shakir said that he had telegraphed the minister of foreign affairs and would let me know the answer as soon as it came."

On the evening of September 15, Shakir was still lingering in Erzurum, attending a dinner in his honor at the Russian consulate. Graves took the opportunity to corner the Turkish diplomat and impress upon him the urgency of Sachtleben's mission. Graves mentioned that he would be heading to Constantinople in a fortnight and that "it would be a good thing if I can report to the American minister that this case is at last being settled."

Graves's plea was apparently heard. "At last, it seems as if something will be done," Sachtleben wrote home a week later.

Shakir Pasha is a very high official and a special favorite of the Sultan. I called on him in great style, with my own interpreter and interpreter of the English Consul. Twice I've seen him now.

He is extremely polite, affable, and all that. The Turks know so
well how to put on when they wish to do so. For some time it
looked as if he would put me off also, but today I have just received the joyful news that he is going in person to Alashgerd,
and will take me with him.

Sachtleben hastily assembled a team to accompany him, consisting of Chambers, who had volunteered his services as an Armenian interpreter; Khadouri; an Armenian driver named Misag;
and Aram, a young Armenian who was tapped to perform "any
and all kinds of spywork." The American braced himself for an adventure. "Being a high Turkish pasha," Sachtleben explained to
friends back home, "he will travel very slowly, in the finest style,
with a small army of soldiers and servants. I expect to have an interesting journey out there now, but whether he will investigate
this case in earnest the event alone will prove."

Finally, on the morning of September 24, Sachtleben and Chambers left the mission house to embark on their climactic journey.
The pleasant Indian summer had come to an abrupt end the night
before as the temperature plummeted. As the pair made their
way down the snow-covered path toward an awaiting carriage,
Sachtleben suddenly felt the thumping of snowballs on his back.
He wheeled around and identified the mischievous hurler: Chambers's precocious daughter Kate.

Sachtleben's small group soon merged with Shakir's immense
entourage, led by eight soldiers on horseback and followed by a
like number. Another eighteen officers rode on horseback, while
Shakir and his secretary, Danish Bey, traveled in their private carriages. At the gate to the city, the procession stopped to receive
the parting salaams extended by the local officials. In unison, they
held their right hands low to the ground. Then they slowly lifted
them to their stomachs, their hearts, and finally their heads to in-
voke "a healthy stomach, a good heart, and a clear mind."

Once the small army struck the caravan road, it covered only
about twenty miles a day, even on the perfectly flat plain. On the

third day out, the procession approached the entrance to the infamous Deli Baba Pass, guarded by rocky walls abruptly rising 1,500
feet. The road soon led to a narrow valley, through which a stream
of clear water flowed. Along the way, the pilgrims passed through
a number of Kurdish villages filled with mud huts and dugouts.
From time to time, villagers joined the procession on foot, only to
drop out after a short distance. That night the group camped in
Dahar.

The next day, September 27, Sachtleben and company reached
Zedikan and the Alashgerd Plain. They stopped a short while later
at Hoshian, a village just west of Chilkani with both Armenian and
Kurdish residents. Failing to find an Armenian host, Sachtleben
and Chambers stayed with a Kurdish sheik named Abdul Kerim
Bey, whose name meant "the mighty servant of God." "If the last
word were changed to devil," Sachtleben mused, "the appellation
would be strictly true. He was sweet as sugar to our faces, but a sly
knave when out of sight."

Sachtleben and Chambers learned that a number of Armenians
had tried to call on them that evening at the Kurd's residence but
were turned back by the zaptieh posted at the door. The furious foreigners, determined to hear what the Armenians had to say, sent out
Misag to interview them. But the driver returned empty-handed,
having been thwarted by swarms of Turkish soldiers who impeded
any contact with the villagers. The investigator was thus deprived
of the Armenians' testimony, save for a few smuggled notes.

Sachtleben and Chambers called on Shakir in his tent to protest
the injustice. The affable diplomat promised to review the matter
with the local *kaimacan*. He then cheerfully proclaimed: "Demain
est votre affaire" (Tomorrow it's your business). He explained
that he had formed a commission, consisting of themselves, three
Turks, a Kurd, and an Armenian. One of the Turks, Tewfik Bey,
the procureur-general of Erzurum, was to preside over the proceedings.

Although the commission's findings would be reviewed during
a trial in Erzurum, it had the authority to gather evidence and

recommend arrests, subject to Shakir's approval. The pasha added that he would stay in the area a few days to give the commission time to conduct its business. Should it require more time, he would arrange to stop by this place again on his return from Bayazid in about a fortnight, at which point the commission could reconvene.

Arising early the next morning, Sachtleben gazed out his bedroom window and took in an expansive view of the fertile plain where Lenz had lost his life. "The day was perfect," he would recall. "A deluge of sunshine filled the half garnered plain with a flood of gold. The gloomy distant mountains and Ararat's silver tip stood silent witness over it all." Suddenly his five fellow commissioners appeared at the door. The men marched in and sat down on two parallel carpets, directly across from one another, to begin deliberations.

Tewfik Bey pulled out a large packet of papers and began to read them in silence. After a long lull, he suddenly asked Sachtleben: "The man's name was Lenz, Frank Lenz?" The Turk repeated the name multiple times until at last he got the pronunciation right. He then asked a myriad of questions about Lenz's background: How old was he? How old was his mother? Did he have children? Then the questioning turned to the trip itself: When did Lenz leave the United States? Through what cities did he pass? Sachtleben tried to truncate the meandering interrogation, skipping over entire segments of the trip. Tewfik persisted, asking about remote cities in China. Finally, Sachtleben began to answer every question with a terse "I don't know."

Only when Tewfik had at last traced Lenz as far as Tabriz did Sachtleben start to give more detailed answers in order to dispel the absurd notion that Lenz had never entered Turkey. Then Tewfik pressed Sachtleben about Lenz's friends and family, before posing a host of personal questions about Sachtleben himself. The American refused to divulge the names of his Armenian informants, citing only those of the accused Kurds. He produced the bell that Khazar had purchased as evidence of the Kurds' culpability.

By the time the opening session concluded, Sachtleben could

barely stand the sight of Tewfik, whom he characterized as "an insolent, lazy scoundrel who was everlastingly at prayer." Confessed the investigator: "several times I came within a breadth's of striking him." He would summarize his initial ordeal: "They spent eight hours trying to pump me dry on the plea that I should let them know all, so that they could effectively prosecute the case. Their plan was to learn all I knew, and then by secret means to destroy its value when we appeared on the spot."

After a break for lunch, the proceedings resumed. Tewfik called five villagers from Hoshian and two from Zedikan. All swore that they had not seen or heard anything about a man riding a bicycle through their villages. Sachtleben concluded that it would not be easy to induce the terrified Armenians to talk. He wanted to ask them directly if they had been warned by the police to keep their silence, but Tewfik insisted that the question could be asked later. "These men are telling what they saw," the prosecutor explained, "not what they heard."

At about four o'clock, the commission suspended its proceedings to call on Shakir, who dutifully looked over the papers. Despite the lack of testimony supporting Sachtleben's accusations, the pasha suddenly pushed the papers aside and announced: "Well, it is the proper thing to go at once and arrest these men." He then detailed a squad of ten soldiers to accompany the commissioners to nearby Chilkani. Sachtleben could hardly contain his joy: at last, he was about to come face to face with the arch-murderer himself, Moostoe.

An hour later, arriving in the village of Chilkani, the group sought out the *mukhatar* (village head), who pointed out Moostoe's house. "We went there at once and found him at his door," Sachtleben related, "washing his feet in preparation for evening prayers. He was a devilish looking Kurd, and his son was just as bad. Moostoe was a dark complexioned man of 38 years, with dark coarse hair and piercing, evil-looking black eyes with a decided squint. He was athletic and sinewy built. He and his imp of a son, like all Kurds, wore their daggers in their belts."

Moostoe did not appear entirely surprised by the invasion; indeed, Sachtleben was certain that the Kurd had been expecting them. The two men exchanged cold glares. Sachtleben wished he could throttle the murderer on the spot. The Kurd began to mutter a few menacing words to his pals at his side. "Do you know what he is saying?" an anxious Khadouri whispered to Sachtleben, knowing full well that he did not. "He says he would like to run his sharp knife across your throat. And if it wasn't for the big Shakir Pasha that's exactly what he would do."

Undaunted, Sachtleben led the house search while the soldiers stood guard.

> We all entered the house and searched every nook and cranny for an hour or more. Moostoe, meanwhile, pretended to be sick, though he was not too sick to express his anger at my man Khadouri, who turned up everything. Moostoe groaned as we turned his saddle bags inside out, looking for the smallest trace of Lenz's baggage. We saw the saddle, of course, but as I suspected the rubber tires had been taken off.

The search, alas, turned up nothing. Sachtleben was keenly disappointed, but not surprised. He knew well that the "ripe time" for a house search had long passed. "Neither Mr. Chambers nor I had expected, after four months of delay, to find any better result," he admitted. The American remained determined nonetheless to have the last laugh, as he cast one last hateful glance at Moostoe. The party proceeded to the home of Mehmet, one of Moostoe's suspected accomplices. Once again, they found nothing.

The commission then broke for supper. Sachtleben and Chambers headed to the home of the priest Der Arsen, who had invited the pair to dine with him. "We were sitting on the floor talking," Sachtleben recalled, "when a local church member knocked on the door and requested to talk to Mr. Chambers. They both left and about twenty minutes later Chambers returned alone. He said to me, 'I bet you can't guess what I've got in my pocket?' I told him

I couldn't and he pulled out the brass clockwork machinery from Lenz's camera by which he could take his own pictures."

The hardware, which had been hidden for months in the altar of the Armenian church, consisted of two brass screws and a six-inch rod. The Armenian had explained that a twelve-year-old shepherd boy named Bido found the articles, along with fragments of film, near the Hopuz River sometime after Lenz's disappearance. Der Arsen had saved them to present as evidence of foul play, even though the terrified villagers would initially deny that they had seen a cyclist pass through town.

Sachtleben was thrilled to have these items, which all but confirmed that Lenz had been attacked just outside Chilkani. The Armenians, however, were extremely reluctant to acknowledge possession of the articles, fearing that the Turks would immediately charge them with the murder. Sachtleben took the objects and promised to keep the matter secret for the time being. He added that when the time came for the Armenians to testify and reveal this evidence, he would see to it that they received adequate protection.

Of course, Sachtleben never seriously entertained the idea that the Armenians themselves were the murderers. As he would later explain: "While the machinery was found on the altar of the church, this did not in any way prove that the Armenian Christians had killed Lenz. On the contrary, they knew who had killed him and in their simple minds they wanted to keep this bit of evidence where it would not be lost."

As night fell, the commission continued its marathon proceedings. It examined Avak Parsegh, whom Sachtleben described as a "common peasant about thirty-five years of age." Although he was evidently confused and frightened, he acknowledged that he had hosted a foreigner matching Lenz's description something like a year and a half earlier. Tewfik asked the witness to describe Lenz's appearance and "the kind of man he was." Parsegh became flustered, saying that he had only met the man briefly and could not recall much about him. Under pressure, he also admitted that he did not know for certain in what direction Lenz headed the morning of his departure.

Sachtleben observed that the farmer's testimony "fell like a thunderbolt on Tewfik, who had expected him to lie as the rest had done. I felt like slapping Parsegh on the shoulder and saying 'Bravo!'" Although he had offered few details, the farmer had at least confirmed Lenz's presence, putting an end to the Turks' absurd claim that Lenz had not even entered their country.

The following morning, five more witnesses were called, all from Chilkani, including the *mukhtar* and Der Arsen, the priest. Lenz's visit to the town having finally been established, they all acknowledged that they had seen the stranger arrive on his bicycle. One by one, however, they insisted that they knew nothing more about him or his fate. Lamented Sachtleben: "They had not heard anything since what had become of him; they had not seen any of his things since." Nor would they implicate Moostoe in the American's disappearance, for they professed not to know if the Kurd had been in the village the day Lenz arrived. Convinced that the witnesses had been intimidated, Sachtleben refused to sign the official papers at the conclusion of the proceedings.

"I was greatly disappointed at the result of our efforts in Chilkani," Sachtleben wrote. "Every one of the witnesses had perjured themselves. The Christians [Armenians] lied for self-preservation as they feared for their property and their lives, and they had no assurance that they would be protected. The Moslems [Kurds] had perjured themselves for the sake of saving their fellow countrymen, the guilty Kurds."

The next day, Sachtleben took Der Arsen aside and expressed his keen disappointment with the priest's guarded testimony. Retorted the Armenian: "Oh, you Europeans—you don't know what fear is." The American warned Der Arsen that he would call him back as a witness upon his return to Chilkani, and he implored him to implicate Moostoe the next time, promising that he would do everything in his power to ensure the priest's safety.

After a few more fruitless house searches, the commission headed to Mollah Osman, a small village six miles east of Chilkani. Along the way, Tewfik, who was chafing from Sachtleben's refusal to sign papers, took Chambers aside and complained: "Mr. Sachtleben is young and hot-headed, and has not much experience with Turkish law." Reaching the home of Alayee Chavdar, the other Kurd whom Khazar had implicated, they could find no trace of its owner. They proceeded to search the premises and again found nothing.

Over the next few days, the commission conducted several more house searches in the area, all without success. Nor could they find any more witnesses willing to attest that they had seen the "soulless horse." The party even traveled to Kolah, in search of Lenz's grave. But the Muslim residents all testified that the only corpse they had seen at that time was that of an old man without teeth. No suspicious grave was found.

One evening, by candlelight, the commissioners searched the home of the Kurd in Tchurmouk who had sold the bell to Khazar. Again they found nothing. While in that village, however, Sachtleben met another Kurd, Kassim Agha, who confided to the American that he knew all about Lenz's disappearance. He promised to tell all in return for a decoration from Shakir. The two agreed to meet again when Sachtleben returned from Bayazid.

Heading back to Chilkani, the commissioners reunited with Shakir and his entourage. Sachtleben told the diplomat he was not satisfied with the results of the proceedings. Shakir replied that he, too, was troubled by the failure to unravel Lenz's disappearance. Though they would have to continue on to Bayazid, the Turk promised to leave some of his men in Chilkani to conduct further interviews and also to send secret agents to search for Lenz's grave. When the commission returned to Chilkani, it could act on any new intelligence. Sachtleben accepted the proposal.

As Shakir's entourage resumed its march eastward toward Bayazid, Sachtleben and his men once again tagged along—with the exception of Aram, who remained in Chilkani to conduct discreet inquiries of his own. The American had concluded that he could do nothing more to advance the Lenz case until the commission reconvened in Chilkani. In the meantime, he took in Shakir's curious spectacle, watching with detached amusement as "the natives streamed to the wayside to make low salaams to the pasha." Soon, the procession swelled into a gigantic parade that included more than one thousand men on horseback and "all the brigands of the Alashgerd Plain." Many of the participants were members of the Hamidieh regiment, who were only too pleased to show off their horsemanship to their founding patron.

Reaching Karakalissa, Sachtleben and Chambers quickly discovered that the Lenz case had become a cause célèbre in that city. "In every coffee house and all over the bazaars," Sachtleben recounted, "it was the topic of conversation that two pashas, one Turkish and one American, had come to look for a man who was lost in Alashgerd. Everyone knew and talked about it."

They had barely settled in the home of their host, an Armenian priest named Der Garabed, when a messenger came looking for them. He informed the foreigners that Shakir wanted them to report immediately to the local government building. The men dutifully abandoned their dinners and dashed off to find the pasha. When they arrived at their destination, they found Tewfik preparing to grill a witness. They soon learned that the subject was a Greek doctor of the Hamidieh regiment who claimed to have examined, on May 16, 1894, the corpse of a man who had drowned in the vicinity. They immediately deduced the Turk's objective: to prove that the victim was Lenz, and that he had died of natural causes.

Sachtleben related the doctor's full testimony:

The body had been found in the river Achmet Bey, near Toprakaleh. One foot and one hand were in the water and the head was partly submerged. It was taken out and washed free from sand; no marks of violence were found on it. The hair was cut in military style, and it and the mustache were of a sandy color. The body was about medium height and perfectly white, and the age appeared to be about twenty-two years. On the upper back part of the head was a ridge as if made by a heavy cap. He judged that the body had been dead for four days. He further testified that the river was high and the current strong at that time, and this stream had destroyed many people.

After the doctor had completed his account, Tewfik handed him a photograph of Lenz and asked if the man in the photograph could have been the victim in question. Sachtleben took a deep breath, fearing that the doctor would answer in the affirmative. The witness studied the image "long and earnestly," as a heavy silence prevailed. At last, he answered firmly: "No, sir, not at all. No resemblance whatever." Tewfik winced while Sachtleben heaved a sigh of relief.

Moments later, the beaming American approached the doctor and greeted him in his native tongue, a gesture that "went right to his heart." Sachtleben, in fact, recalled meeting the doctor four years earlier. The investigator coyly asked the man if he had ever seen any bicyclists pass through this city. The doctor's face lit up, once the recognition was mutual. "He described the visit Allen and I had made in '91," Sachtleben would record with satisfaction, "how we had asked in French for various things to eat; how he brought us some honey."

Shakir suddenly emerged, and he asked Chambers and Sachtleben to come straight away to his private quarters. Once the party had settled there, the pasha asked his guests if Der Arsen had given them screws to Lenz's camera. The two men looked at each other in utter shock. How did Shakir know about this? They had sworn to the Armenians that they would tell no one about these compromising possessions until the trial was under way. As it was, they had no choice but to admit to Shakir that they did indeed have those parts.

"I learned afterward that the Kurdish bey of Toprakaleh, Ali Pasha, had played a trick on the Armenians," Sachtleben explained. "He went to Chilkani pretending that the priest Der Arsen had sent him to get all the things that belonged to Lenz. In one Armenian house he found an inner tube belonging to Lenz's bicycle, and in another the ground glass from his camera. He was told that the priest had already given us the screws."

Sachtleben reluctantly turned the hardware over to Shakir, who promised to return the items following the trial. He knew the Turks would now do their utmost to implicate the Armenians. "The Turks naturally tried to make much of the fact that these items were found in Armenian hands," Sachtleben reported to Langhans, "whereas nothing was found in the Kurdish houses. But to me it was a point in the Armenians' favor that they kept these articles which they knew belonged to the murdered man, whereas Moostoe had carefully destroyed the two pieces of the outer rubber casings, and Lenz's revolver was not to be found anywhere."

Shakir also told Sachtleben that the men he had left in Chilkani had learned nothing more about Lenz. "The witnesses strangely told the same story," the pasha lamented. In particular, "the Armenians continued to deny any knowledge of Lenz's fate." For his part, Moostoe had admitted that he had used bicycle tubes as saddle girths, but he vigorously denied that he had had any contact with Lenz. Indeed, he asserted that he had been bedridden the day the cyclist came to town. He maintained that his son Abdal had purchased the tubes from an Armenian, who had found them by the Hopuz River. He asserted that they had worn out about a year earlier, at which point he threw them away.

Shakir was unswayed by the suspects' professions of innocence. "They will not tell the truth until they have seen the inside of a prison," he asserted to Sachtleben. Accordingly, he had ordered the arrests of Moostoe and the five Armenians who had been found with bits of Lenz's gear. The men would be transported at once to a jail in Toprakaleh, and eventually to Erzurum to stand trial.

For Sachtleben, the news of the arrests was bittersweet. He was elated that Moostoe would soon be in custody, but deeply concerned about the plight of the Armenians, whom he judged completely innocent of any wrongdoing. To his mind, the importance of the rendezvous in Chilkani loomed even larger. It was now imperative to gather all available evidence exonerating the Armenians and implicating Moostoe and his men.

The next day, an utterly distraught Der Arsen appeared at Der Garabed's home in Karakalissa to speak with the foreigners. The Chilkani resident recounted that Shakir's men had accosted him the day before and had tried to make him confess to Lenz's murder, or at least place the blame on the arrested Armenians. Sachtleben revealed that the Turks had discovered the camera parts in his possession and were evidently redoubling their efforts to pin Lenz's murder on the Armenians. But the American insisted that they would all be exonerated—and Moostoe convicted—during the upcoming trial.

Once again, however, Sachtleben stressed that he needed Der Arsen to testify against Moostoe once the commission returned to Chilkani. The priest replied that he and his family would suffer severely if he dared breathe a word against Moostoe or his men. Sachtleben again assured Der Arsen that the American government would see to it that all Armenian witnesses received adequate protection.

The priest appeared little relieved by Sachtleben's promise. "He asked me what I was going to do with him," the American would later recall. "I told him that his presence was needed as a witness in Erzurum, after which I hoped that the reforms would have been instituted so that he could be reasonably safe when he returned to his home."

Recognizing that he had little alternative but to cooperate with the American, Der Arsen agreed to testify against Moostoe at the next opportunity. In the meantime, the priest promised to assist Aram in a search for more evidence against Moostoe and the Kurds. The two men would meet up with Sachtleben when he returned to Karakalissa and brief him on their findings, just before the commission reconvened.

Over the next few days, Sachtleben and Chambers continued to travel with Shakir's entourage. Upon reaching Bayazid, they de-

cided to take a relaxing hike up Mount Ararat. Mrs. Chambers
was glad to learn of the expedition. "Mr. Sachtleben has been urging Nesbitt all summer to climb Ararat," she wrote her brother,
"and it is a thing Nesbitt has so much desired to do. I am very glad
he should have the trial." In her next letter to Talcott, she would
reveal the somewhat disappointing outcome: "The ascent of the
mountain was enjoyable, but they did not have good weather and a
snow storm prevented their reaching quite to the summit."

On October 9, the pair rejoined Shakir's entourage and followed
it back to Karakalissa. There, as planned, Aram and Der Arsen
met up with Sachtleben. Alas, the investigators had found no more
traces of Lenz's bicycle, baggage, or body. The local Armenians
had no idea where his remains were buried, or even if they were indeed buried. The Kurds, in contrast, knew all—or so the men believed—but they refused to divulge the dark secret.

Their inquiry, however, had not been entirely fruitless. On the
contrary, they had gathered testimony against Moostoe. Parsegh's
wife confided that about a month after Lenz's visit, she saw Moostoe's son wearing a coat strikingly similar to the one the cyclist
had worn. Other villagers affirmed that they had seen, at about the
same time, foreign clothes on Moostoe himself. Still others claimed
to have overheard Moostoe quarreling with his men about how to
split the money found on Lenz's person. The wives of Moostoe
and his servant had allegedly alluded to Lenz's murder during a
fight. "Your husband murdered an American," snapped the former,
to which the latter supposedly retorted: "Well, if he did, your husband gave the order."

Aram had even visited the prison where Moostoe was being
held, to interview the Kurd himself. The suspect had said that he
would tell all, including the location of Lenz's grave, for $500.
Sachtleben was certain that the miserable Kurd would sing for half
that sum, but he was loath to offer the murderer any reward at all.
After some reflection, he decided to pass on the offer.

For his part, Der Arsen had procured a testimonial signed by
himself and twenty-two fellow Armenian residents of Chilkani. It

not only implicated Moostoe but also identified his alleged accomplices and even offered a motive for the murder. It read:

> The American cycler, the day he halted in our village, passed the night in the house of Parsegh Avakian. In the evening, Moostoe and his men visited him. These were Dahar, the son of Gallo, Simbelzor Mamoud, the [two] sons of Avdele Niseh, the brother of Moostoe, whose names are Nabone and Hodo. These criminals examined one by one the revolver, the watch, and all Lenz's other possessions, and with rude oaths returned them to their possessor, saying "These things suit us and not you." Although at this moment they made movements to strike the American, because of the beseeching of us, the villagers, they did not accomplish their design. That same night the criminals mentioned met the sons of Alayee Chavdar of Mollah Osman, who had followed the American to Chilkani, evidently with the purpose of harming him and robbing him if a favorable opportunity presented itself. On the morrow, before the American started, all the mentioned criminals had already disappeared from the village. Some time after this event, we saw several times the revolver and watch, which we had seen and recognized in the hands of the American, in the possession of Moostoe, who had not yet found out how to open the revolver. The shepherds of our village found the worthless goods of the murdered American, since found in Armenian houses, by the abundant waters of the spring, in the sands of the river Hopuz.
>
> We have carefully kept concealed these things in order to produce them when necessary with the idea that innocent blood should not go unavenged.

Sachtleben was elated to have all this new evidence against Moostoe and his men. With the Kurd already in custody, however, the American deemed it best to keep these findings under wraps for the time being. He did not want to tip his hand to Turkish authorities in advance of the upcoming trial, so as not to give them an opportunity to tarnish his evidence in the interim. In particular, he did not want Der Arsen to say much after all. "I directed the priest to keep his mouth shut until the trial in Erzurum," Sachtleben would later reveal. "Shakir was given only the names of the culprits, and I demanded their arrest."

Before leaving Karakalissa, Sachtleben revisited Kassim Agha, the Kurd who had claimed to know all. Although the American could not as yet produce the promised decoration, he extended a fistful of coins to get the Kurd to talk. Kassim proceeded to name the same Kurds the Armenians had cited in their testimonial, with the exception of his relative Dahar, whom he insisted had played no part in the ambush. The Kurd also revealed that Lenz was not buried in Kolah after all, but by the Hopuz River, near the spot where he was killed. He could not, however, give an exact location.

Sachtleben was now satisfied that he had unlocked the secret of Lenz's death, even if the grave had yet to be identified. He was eager to arrest any of Moostoe's alleged accomplices that he could lay his hands on. Shakir obligingly furnished the American with a party of twenty-five guards, assuring the American that they "will do anything you order and arrest any man you may point out."

Stopping in Mollah Osman, on the way to Chilkani, Sachtleben sought out two residents said to be Moostoe's accomplices: the sons of Alayee Chavdar. Alas, both men had already bolted. The investigator took the opportunity to recall the local witnesses who had been mum the first time around. "This time they told the truth," Sachtleben related, "saying that Lenz had passed, did not stop, and that every man, woman, and child had come out to see him from their house-tops." Chambers would later comment in his autobiography: "The village notables did not seem to think there was any inconsistency—not to say moral obliquity—between the villagers' solemn oath that they knew absolutely nothing about the matter and ten days later their declaration under oath that they knew all about it."

"On reaching Chilkani," Sachtleben reported, "we found that the other Kurdish suspects had also bolted. It was evident that the murderers had made themselves scarce." His soldiers did manage, however, to nab one of the suspects in the nearby village of Tchurmouk: Dahar. "He was a young Kurd between twenty-six and thirty years of age," Sachtleben recounted. "He swore that he had not seen or heard anything about Lenz, and that he did not know where the grave was." Sachtleben decided to arrest him anyway, despite his previous assurances to Kassim that his relative would be spared. If nothing else, he might prove a valuable bargaining chip.

As planned, Sachtleben reexamined the Armenian witnesses of Chilkani. This time, their testimony reflected the account given in the Armenian testimonial. Yes, they had seen Lenz and his bicycle, and they had reason to believe that Moostoe and his men did away with the wheelman shortly thereafter. Evidently, concern for their co-villagers in captivity, if not Sachtleben's promises of protection, had loosened their lips.

Although Sachtleben continued to offer the Armenians assurances of protection, he privately doubted that he could deliver on his promises once he had left their presence. "The homes of Armenians in Chilkani are in danger of being wiped out of existence," he appealed to Terrell,

> and it is the prayer of all these poor people that you protect them from the accursed Kurds. The Armenians besought me on their knees with tears in their eyes. The honour of the American name is at stake and something must be done and lively threats made if a single Armenian of that village is harmed. I am keeping close watch on what occurs and will report right away. If something is not done in such a case, I'll appeal to the English power whose influence I know I can rely on.

Sachtleben, who was growing increasingly homesick, was not even sure that he would stick around Turkey long enough to participate in the trial. He nonetheless prepared a final account of Lenz's murder, incorporating all the information he had gathered during his tour of Alashgerd, to serve in the eventual trial, even if he would not be there himself. It read:

> The 9th of May, 1894 was a rainy day. Lenz had passed Mollah Osman late in the afternoon, probably an hour before he arrived

in Chilkani where he went to a house on the main road and sat down to make a few notes in his journal. Moostoe came along and said "Get up and leave that place." So Lenz arose, asked for a lodging, and was led to Avak Parsegh's house. He was not well. He asked for a chicken and gave the priest Der Arsen some money to buy it for him and have it prepared with a little butter. Lenz also wrote down the priest's name and promised to send him a photo. He divided with the priest some raisins he had in his pocket.

While his chicken was being prepared Lenz fell asleep, but he was rudely awakened by the two sons of Alayee Chavdar, who were among the crowd of visitors with Moostoe. Lenz's revolver was lying by his side on the floor. Moostoe tried to pick it up, and Lenz wished to stop him; but Moostoe already had it in his hand. He asked Lenz to open it, which Lenz refused to do. Moostoe became angry, cursed Lenz in Kurdish, and threatened to kill him; which of course Lenz didn't understand, and the Armenians could not explain it to him. Lenz ordered the Kurds out of the room, but they wouldn't go so he curled himself up and slept.

The priest, as well as other Armenians said to Moostoe "Why do you treat a stranger like this—a Christian gentleman who is traveling in our country[?]" "Is he a king," said Moostoe, "that he cannot sit up and talk with us?" Lenz was probably irritable for the priest had tried to find out where he had come from on that day, and Lenz tried to explain but couldn't and became out of humour.

While Lenz was quietly sleeping through that fatal night, Moostoe had a gathering of his minions at his own house. Besides himself there were two sons of Alayee Chavdar, Nabone and Hamid, the two sons of Moostoe's brother, Nabone and Hodo, the servant of Moostoe, Simbelzor Mamoud, and Dahar, the son of Gallo Tehroukh. Under the guidance of Moostoe this gang plotted the foul murder. Their plan was simple enough. They left the village before daybreak to wait for Lenz on the road. Their object was plunder as they had seen Lenz's money, revolver, watch, etc. They imagined his camera contained money and that the nickel plate on his bicycle was silver.

The following morning, May 10th, 1894, Lenz asked for another chicken. When it was ready he drank the broth, then pulling some rice out of his pocket, he asked for some. They had none, so he rolled the chicken up in a bundle and made ready to depart. It was also a rainy disagreeable day. The crowd pressed around him to see him ride, but it was probably too muddy for he even threw stones at them to get them away. And he also put water on his tires to keep the mud from sticking in the crotches. The soil here is dark and loamy, very sticky in muddy weather.

The natives saw him pushing his bicycle a long way off across the plain.

About five miles from Chilkani is a place called Topik, which means a knoll. This was on the highway and marked the division between the towns of Chilkani and Mussuri. Beside this mound ran a small rivulet. In the spring of 1894 all the streams of Alashgerd were unusually high and the rivulet was swollen to quite a stream several feet deep. Lenz could not ride his wheel in the deep mud. After this knoll the seven murderers awaited their victim. Lenz arrived at Topik and was preparing to cross when the Kurds attacked him. One of them drew his sword and severely cut Lenz in the right hand, breaking his arm, so that he could not draw his revolver.

Lenz begged them not to kill him, saying "ben mussulman — I'll be a muslim. Take all I've got but spare me." Moostoe said: "Don't kill him, I told you to rob him!" Thereupon the Kurds seized him and his baggage and took him, wounded as he was, across the fields about twenty minutes walk to the right bank of the Hopuz river about halfway between Chilkani and Shamian. Here they robbed him of everything, and at Moostoe's order put him to death with their knives, so that he would not reveal their names. They buried him and his bicycle on the bank.

Sachtleben had, by this point, done everything in his power to ensure a conviction in the upcoming murder trial in Erzurum, even if a favorable outcome was still in considerable doubt. He had also done his level best to advance Mrs. Lenz's case for an indemnity from the Turkish government, though that, too, loomed as a large question mark. Sachtleben was confident that he had, if nothing else, assembled sufficient evidence of Lenz's death to enable Mrs. Lenz to collect on her son's life insurance policy. Still, he knew that there was only one—albeit faint—hope left to crown his mission with at least a resemblance of success: the recovery of Lenz's remains.

The investigator was now convinced that Lenz had been buried, in all probability, near the spot where he had been slain, and he was determined to make one last heroic effort to recover the remains. "Before leaving Chilkani for the last time," Sachtleben related, "I had it announced throughout the village that I would give $50 to any man who would show me where Lenz's grave was, but it was of no use."

Finally, on the evening of October 11, Sachtleben made one last desperate bid, with the help of Aram. "We stopped at a place on the Hopuz river where the articles had been found," Sachtleben recounted, "and near which it was almost certain that the body had been buried." The American began to case the barren field, looking for any hint of a grave. He would later assert that he had probably walked over Lenz's bones "many times"—but, alas, "there was nothing to mark the spot." Aram, meanwhile, showed his unwavering devotion, "digging in any place where a grave might be." As the sun began to set, the sullen investigator reluctantly gave up his quest.

Sachtleben paused to take a photograph of the eerie setting. "It was at the close of a beautiful Indian Summer's day," he would later reflect. "A brilliant sunset left a thousand varied tints on plain and mountain alike. A beautiful panorama met my eyes. As I stood at that lonely bend in the river looking at the sparkling stream wending its silent way eastward, a most somber sadness affected me. I pictured to myself that awful, cold-blooded scene that had probably been enacted there. Here my investigation came to a close."

14

ERZURUM

October 19, 1895

S ACHTLEBEN WAS GLAD to return to his little room in the mission house after a three-week absence. Although he was deeply disappointed by his failure to find Lenz's remains and worried about the fate of his Armenian witnesses and their peers accused of the murder, he nonetheless informed Graves that the mission had been "partially successful." The arch-murder Moostoe was, after all, in captivity and awaiting trial, even if his accomplices were still at large, with the possible exception of Dahar.

The American was still hopeful that he could secure a conviction against Moostoe and return home with his head high. At the same time, of course, he also hoped to protect and exonerate the Armenians. He was equally determined to secure an indemnity for Mrs. Lenz. Perhaps he could even find Lenz's grave after all, if Moostoe or his fellow Kurds were eventually forced to reveal its location.

Sachtleben recognized, nonetheless, that his situation was precarious. He had little faith in Turkish justice and was certain that the Turks would do everything possible to pin the crime on the innocent Armenians rather than Moostoe. Moreover, there was no telling when the trial would actually start. Worman had already withdrawn his financial support, and Sachtleben himself was increasingly eager to head home. He resolved to do the best he could to help the American legation prepare for the trial for as long as he remained in Erzurum, even if he did not stick around for it.

A week after his return to Erzurum, Sachtleben sent Terrell a long report detailing his trip to Alashgerd. He gently reminded Terrell: "I rely on your zeal to push American interests, which are at the same time Mrs. Lenz's interests." He included a copy of his final account of Lenz's murder, marked "Confidential," and defended its reliability. "I have not assumed any one point without a witness," he insisted, adding: "For me it is a matter of indifference whether Armenians or Kurds murdered Lenz. I am after the murderers, and I don't care who they are."

To clear the way for his return to America, Sachtleben asked Terrell to send an official representative to Erzurum as soon as possible—someone who could ably manage the upcoming trial. Affirmed the investigator: "This man ought to be a lawyer, well versed in the practice of Turkish law." Still, the investigator insisted he was not about to run away from the matter: "I am perfectly willing to remain here and help such a man in his difficult task. I shall watch the case very closely as long as I am here."

Chambers, meanwhile, was also readjusting to life back in the mission house. Upon his return, he had happily discovered that he was not the only one in the household defying his age. Neelie, his forty-four-year-old wife, revealed that she was expecting their third child. "You cannot be more surprised than I," she wrote her brother Talcott. "I had given up all thought of welcoming another little stranger to our house. Who would ever imagine such a thing at my age! Two or three years ago I'd have been very glad at the prospect, but at this late date, it has been hard to make myself accustomed to the thought. To be sure, I feel as young as ever. But I know I am not. I try to be glad for the sake of the little one and I am taking every care."

The personal anxieties pervading the Chambers household were soon superseded by the terrible events of October 30. That morning a horrific massacre, similar to those that had visited other Turkish cities, came right to their doorstep. "Reports that the Kurds were coming flitted through the city like lightning," Sachtleben recounted, "and the greatest excitement prevailed. The Armenians knew well the awful intentions of the invaders, and they fled for their lives in desperation. They barricaded doors and windows and hid with their families. But the Turks and Kurds fell upon them before they had taken any steps for defense."

Hearing the clamor, Sachtleben, Chambers, and Graves rushed to the rooftop of the mission house, where they became "eye witnesses to the fearful massacres." Sachtleben watched below in horror as the attackers "burst through doors and windows and threw the inmates of the houses into the streets, where they were shot to death and brutally mutilated. The murderers were everywhere. The riflemen and swordsmen went in first to conduct their festival of murder and pillages, then the thieves followed closely behind, stripping the dead of valuables and robbing stores and homes."

The trio soon realized that they, too, were targets, as bullets began to whiz by their heads. They scurried into the building, but even there they came under fire. "I saw soldiers suddenly turn and discharge their guns directly at the window at which I was standing," Sachtleben recounted. "Before I had time to dodge, one of the bullets struck the casement, about an inch and a half from my head." The murderous rampage raged for two hours and claimed nearly a thousand lives, "leaving the dead where they had been killed."

The next day, Sachtleben visited the Armenian cemetery, where many of the victims' bodies were stacked in preparation for a mass burial. "He counted three hundred and fourteen bodies," Mrs. Chambers wrote her brother, adding, "The scene is too horrible to describe, so many marks of hellish cruelty." With the help of an Armenian photographer, Sachtleben photographed many of the mutilated bodies belonging to men, women, and children. "A crowd of a thousand people, mostly Armenians, watched me take the photographs," Sachtleben recounted. "Many were weeping beside their dead fathers or husbands. The Armenian photographer recognized one of his own relatives among the dead children."

The Graphic, a London weekly, would soon publish a selection of Sachtleben's grisly images.

Suddenly, Sachtleben had ample material for a lecture on Armenian massacres, which he hoped would underscore the diabolical complicity of the Turkish government. "If he succeeds in escaping with his plates," the *Telegraph* reported, "he will have several hundred splendid pictures of the murderers and the unfortunate people murdered. He will hasten home with his materials just as rapidly as possible, and the people of Alton will be the first in America to see pictures of the terrible doings in Armenia, and hear them described by an eye witness."

A few days later, Sachtleben ventured out into the streets with a foreign friend when shots suddenly rang out again. The terrified pair ran for cover. "Had we been caught out a little later when the fire became general and the fanaticism fully aroused," Sachtleben wrote home, "we would have fared badly." For some weeks after that, he dared not leave the mission house without an armed escort. "The city is ruined," Sachtleben wrote to his father. "Nearly every store has been robbed or burned and trade has almost ceased." Added the investigator: "The horrible scenes which I have beheld will haunt me through life."

The week following the massacre, Sachtleben tried valiantly to refocus on the Lenz case. His hopes for a successful conclusion, however, were rapidly fading. In his weekly report to Langhans, Sachtleben wrote: "The only hope of seeing Moostoe condemned is to bring the proper pressure on the Porte and the Sultan. But it would seem, from the lack of aid from Mr. Terrell, that I am destined to see this trial slip through my hands and the blame fastened on innocent Armenians. My witnesses are in the terror of their lives all the time."

On November 8, Sachtleben appeared before the examining judge to accuse Moostoe and his men of the murder of Frank G. Lenz. The judge agreed to indict Moostoe but dismissed charges against the other Kurds, citing lack of evidence. Against Sachtleben's vehement protests, the judge also indicted the five Armenians in custody. The general prosecutor accepted the judge's findings and scheduled a trial to be heard in Erzurum by the Criminal Court of the First Instance.

Before long, Sachtleben suffered another jolting setback: the awful news that Moostoe had somehow broken out of his cell in Toprakaleh and was nowhere to be found. The Armenian suspects, meanwhile, had been marched to Erzurum and were now languishing in the local jail. As he explained to Langhans: "Prisoners in a Turkish jail are not fed by the government. Their friends are supposed to feed them. I must send them some bread and cheese occasionally so that they may live." Sachtleben's star witness, Der Arsen, was likewise in a terrible bind, though Sachtleben had managed to keep him out of prison. The priest's family, fearing the revenge of the Kurds, had been forced to flee Chilkani to start life in a new village.

Sachtleben made a spirited effort to recapture Moostoe and find his accomplices. "After things had quieted down somewhat," the *Telegraph* reported, "Mr. Sachtleben attempted to recapture the Kurds. But Mr. Terrell shows no disposition to help him. Will is well-nigh discouraged, being powerless to work alone. The guilty men have friends everywhere who would willingly kill him should he become too aggressive in his eagerness to imprison the Kurds again."

Meanwhile, Shakir sent his report to the grand vizier upon his return to Erzurum:

> Four Armenians and two Muslims have been arrested as suspects. The interrogations were made in the presence of Mr. Sachtleben and his interpreters and he signed the documents. Up til then, he had claimed that Kurds had murdered Lenz, but he now admits that some Armenians were also involved. Nevertheless, the evidence against the murderers is not decisive on legal grounds. There are signs that the Armenians may have commited this murder for political fodder to be used against Muslims. Obviously, this is a grave matter, and it will be necessary to expand investigations to reveal the truth so that no one can object to the outcome.

Clearly, Shakir and the Turks were determined to pin the murder on the Armenians at all costs. Admitted Sachtleben to Langhans: "Conviction of the Kurds depends on the finding of the exact spot of Lenz's grave." And although the investigator claimed to have "located it within a radius of several hundred square feet," he conceded that the recent massacres would make it "impossible for some weeks to hold any secret conversation with Kurds and Turks who are the only people who know definitely about Lenz's murder."

On December 7, Sachtleben sent the Pittsburgher more troubling news. Graves's replacement, Henry A. Cumberbatch, was threatening to skip the upcoming trial unless he received explicit instructions from Terrell asking for his presence. The American minister, however, was still holding his silence. Meanwhile, the Armenian prisoners were growing weaker by the day. Even Dahar, the only Kurd still in captivity, was ailing. His father and uncle had come to Erzurum, demanding his release, but Sachtleben refused to comply. He nonetheless admitted to Langhans: "Dahar is not the main agent in the murder, so far as I know."

Sachtleben wrote yet another lengthy letter to Terrell imploring him to take an active role in the Lenz case. "I cannot understand why you have not answered my letters," the investigator complained. "You have asked me to inform you of my progress, and I have done so. But I have no answers from you. What is worse, I see no evidence out here that you are using your influence to assist me."

Writing to Langhans on December 14, Sachtleben expressed his growing frustration with the ever-silent minister. "He tried to call me back three months before I got permission to go to Alashgerd," Sachtleben recalled. "If I had followed his advice, I would have been in the United States long ago, completely outwitted and suckered out of everything by the insolent and corrupt Turkish officials." A week later, Sachtleben vented to Langhans: "It is a great pity that after all the labor which has been devoted to this case, and all the time and money spent on it, that it should be allowed to drift along in such a disgraceful fashion by our Minister at Constantinople. His conduct to me I consider little short of insulting."

In fact, Terrell wanted nothing more to do with the Lenz case. Following a fresh wave of violence in Constantinople, he affirmed to the State Department: "Every moment of my time is employed in safeguarding the lives of our countrymen." Added Terrell: "I deeply sympathize with the feeling that prompted Americans to send Sachtleben on his mission. But they surely cannot understand his situation. Out there, he is surrounded by lawless Kurds, the Apaches of Asia. Neither the Turkish Government nor our own has any ability to protect either him or the four Armenian witnesses he has discovered in his zeal. His persistence can do no good." On the contrary, the minister predicted, Sachtleben's blind perseverance "will end in his own destruction." Terrell saw no prospect for a legal victory in the Lenz case until "the dawn of a new peaceful era."

Terrell at last wrote Sachtleben, bluntly explaining why it had taken him so long to reply: "The events which led to a massacre of many thousands in Asiatic Turkey, the pressure on my time during the last sixty days to provide for the safety of our people while a Christian race is being butchered and missionaries are in danger, and other pressing duties have left me with no time to correspond with you." Far from offering support, Terrell suggested that he had already done all he could for the beleaguered investigator: "I obtained every necessary order to facilitate your inquiry into the question of who killed Mr. Lenz. If you have not been able to find his bones or secure punishment for his murderers, I do not perceive how this Legation can further assist you."

The minister also bitterly alluded to Sachtleben's relentless and highly public criticism. "All your letters have been forwarded to the State Department as received, with your frequent references to the disgraceful conduct of your Government, your interesting advice to me regarding my duty, and your lengthy arguments on international law and the proper policy of the United States abroad." Terrell also lambasted Sachtleben for his appalling ingratitude. "While hunting for murderers among wild Kurds where even Turks exercise small control, you should remember that your own bones would now be in an unknown grave, were it not for the forethought of the Government, which you have more than once maligned. Frankly, it doesn't become you, sir, to criticize your government for inaction, when you had the assistance of Shakir Pasha, the chief officer in the six provinces. But no doubt you will satisfy yourself that your personal influence secured his services."

The minister also asserted that he could do little to assist the incarcerated Armenians, placing the blame for their predicament squarely on Sachtleben himself. "Before producing Armenian priests and witnesses in the country of the Kurds to prove that Kurds were murderers," he admonished the investigator, "you should have weighed the consequences to those witnesses." He closed with a blunt piece of advice: "If you can get safely out of Turkey and return home, it would be well for you to do so."

Sachtleben conceded to Langhans that the situation in Erzurum had become intolerable. "One of the Armenians has succumbed to the horrors and torment of the Turkish prison, and is now dead and buried beside the 600 odd victims who were massacred in this city not long ago. Another prisoner, I understand, is almost dead and the other three are quite sick. Even Dahar, the Kurd, is sick." Meanwhile, the villagers of Alashgerd "are threatened with destruction unless the one Kurd here is released." Confessed Sachtleben: "I cannot keep this up many days more. I'm sick of the entire business and have lost all hope. I am seriously thinking of letting the Kurd and the Armenians go until all the Kurds can be captured. It is useless keeping them here unless the true murderers of Lenz are brought in."

The plight of the Armenian prisoners was indeed lamentable. Wrote Chambers to Barton at the close of the year:

I am sorry to say that two of the Armenians arrested in the Lenz case have died in prison and the remaining three are in serious danger. These men are absolutely innocent, I am convinced. It was sad that Lenz was murdered, but it increases the sadness greatly to think that these innocent men are sacrificed for the sake of a murdered American. Their families have been robbed and left in most destitute circumstances, and now this sorrow is added. Oh, what infinite sadness hangs like a pall over this land.

In early 1896, the Criminal Court of the First Instance formally accused Moostoe and the surviving Armenians of Lenz's murder. It recommended sentences of fifteen years in prison and ordered them to stand trial in Erzurum for the final verdict. For Sachtleben, the preliminary decision offered little satisfaction. With Moostoe on the lam, his conviction would mean little. Meanwhile, the three incarcerated Armenians, barely clinging to their lives, faced more torment.

Sachtleben determined that the best he could do for the surviving Armenians was to prevail upon Shakir to release them on bail pending the advent of the trial. Meanwhile, he would leave the task of exonerating them to Leo Bergholz, the newly appointed American consul in Erzurum, who had agreed to take up the case. Sachtleben also hoped that Bergholz would eventually force Moostoe's recapture and conviction.

On January 4, 1896, Sachtleben confirmed to Langhans that he had secured the release of the Armenians. "After the death of the two Armenians, we renewed our solicitations to Shakir Pasha to have the others, who were all sick and likely to die, released. At length he consented, but on the peculiar grounds that he thought the two who had died in prison were the men who had murdered Lenz."

In mid-January, Cumberbatch, who was monitoring the case until Bergholz could take over, wrote the British minister Currie to explain the status of Sachtleben's preparations. "When things are in a more satisfactory state, I would suggest that the United States Legation should insist on the arrest and trial of Moostoe. A certain Kiazim Agha and another Kurd named Tahar [Dahar] as well as a priest called Der Arsen, are, I believe, in a position to

throw considerable light on the proceedings regarding Moostoe,
but they have, so far, preserved a stubborn silence owing to fear of
that individual."

Confident that he had done all he could to advance the Lenz
case, Sachtleben began to plan his return to the United States. Of
course, given the prevailing chaos, he had long ago abandoned the
idea of completing Lenz's journey by bicycle. He would be lucky
simply to get out of the country alive, especially since he would be
smuggling incriminating photos. He wrote his father to explain
that he would leave as soon as he could, but that he might have to
wait many weeks before conditions improved. Noted Sachtleben:
"Brigands and road agents infest the highways. Every step taken
by the innocent traveler is full of peril and very liable to end in
death."

Even if conditions had permitted a bicycle ride, Sachtleben was
through working for Worman. Some months earlier, the editor
had written Sachtleben with instructions to return home, but the
correspondent had chosen to ignore them. He was determined to
wrap up the Lenz matter as best he could, while pursuing his new
duties as a correspondent with the *Times* of London. He was also
intent on gathering materials for his upcoming lectures on Armenian massacres. Indeed, his agent, Will Sauvage of Alton, was already in New York booking engagements for the spring.

Finally, on the morning of February 24, Sachtleben judged conditions safe enough to leave Erzurum. He bid a fond farewell to his
hosts and began to retrace his way back to Trebizond. Joining him
on the journey was a twenty-two-year-old Armenian cigarette
maker named Mihran Sieaganiam. The young man had begged
Sachtleben to take him to America, offering $30 to cover his travel
expenses. He longed to find work there so that he could relocate
his relatives, who had barely survived the recent massacres. Despite the heavy snow, the travelers opted to go by horseback rather
than by sleigh.

The Alton papers announced that their hometown hero was at
last heading home. One reporter stressed the positive:

Mr. Sachtleben's mission, though not entirely successful, has been of such a dangerous and patriotic nature that America has watched every movement he has made. He went into a lawless country and he learned not only that the American had been murdered but also who his murderers were. With a daring and determination characteristic of blue blooded America, he did not pause until he had landed every one of them behind bars. But it was there that he faced insurmountable obstacles. The massacre of Armenians and the state of war into which the country was thrown gave the friends of the prisoners opportunity to liberate them.

Two months later, after brief stops in Vienna, Paris, and London, Sachtleben debarked in New York City. A correspondent with the *American Wheelman* was "surprised to see to what an extent Mr. Sachtleben had aged, several new wrinkles having made their appearance on his face." Conceded the wheelman: "This trip has added about ten years to my age. When I left New York I felt young. Now I feel like an old man; all my boyishness is gone."

Still, Sachtleben cheerfully asserted, "I am glad to get back here, where I can occasionally see a smile on the face of my fellow men." As for the Lenz matter, he affirmed: "The only thing to be done now is for the United States government to compel the Turkish government to pay an indemnity to Mrs. Lenz. I have done all that could possibly be done under the circumstances."

Sachtleben sent Mihran ahead to St. Louis to assist his partner Homer Canfield in the bicycle store. A local newspaper snidely remarked upon his arrival: "Sachtleben could not bring back Lenz, but he brought a substitute." The investigator, meanwhile, lingered in New York to tend to various business matters. At one point, he met with Worman and offered to write up his recent experiences for *Outing*, but this time the two failed to reach an accord.

In late April, Sachtleben finally headed west. He made a brief stop in Pittsburgh to meet once again with Mrs. Lenz and Frank's friends. No sooner had he stepped off the train than a swarm of reporters surrounded him. To the *Leader* man, he expressed his profound admiration for the lost cyclist:

In my opinion he was the bravest man that ever strode a bicycle. Had he survived another week, chances are he would have lived to tell exactly what it feels like to travel around the world alone on a wheel. His undertaking was an awful one, and it is really surprising that he could have gotten as far as he did. No one can realize the hardships of such a journey unless they try it. When more than one go at a time it is different, but when a man tries it all by his lonesome I tell you it is risky. Allen and I were not bothered much, but Frank had plenty of trouble coming through Asia, and was killed in the worst portion of the whole country.

Sachtleben delivered Frank's abandoned trunk to the grieving mother and told her all he knew about her son's fate. He was gratified to learn that the Mutual Life Insurance Company of New York had consigned a check for $3,000 to Mrs. Lenz's lawyer, Arnold Schneider, though the company insisted that it was not obligated to do so in view of the insufficient evidence of Lenz's death. Sachtleben predicted that the Turkish government would eventually be compelled to pay an indemnity, if the American government took the matter in hand. He spent the afternoon with Langhans, touring the Carnegie steel works in nearby Homestead, before resuming his journey.

When Sachtleben dismounted in St. Louis, he reunited with his younger sister Minnie. Once again, his aged appearance became a topic of general conversation. "He was hardly recognized here," affirmed a St. Louis paper, "such a change has been wrought in his countenance by the hardships and dangers he has gone through and the terrible outrages he has been compelled to witness." When he reached Alton later the same day, he strolled down the street toward his father's house, shaking hands with a sea of admirers. They, too, were startled by his haggard look.

Feeling the need for a prolonged rest, Sachtleben canceled his spring lectures and postponed his tour until the fall. The wheelman nonetheless agreed to keep two important impending engagements: one in Pittsburgh at the end of May to discuss the Lenz case, eagerly anticipated by Lenz's friends, and another in Alton a few weeks later to expose the Armenian massacres.

Once he regained his health and vigor, Sachtleben also planned to devote time to his bicycle store, where business was better than ever. Reported a St. Louis paper:

> The reputation of Canfield and Sachtleben extends further than any other local firm, thanks to the prominence of its junior member, whose fame is world wide. Its quarters at 421 Seventh Street are being fitted up in lavish style. On the first floor is the display room, on the second floor is the sales room for ladies' wheels, and on the third floor are the storeroom and repair shop. The basement is provided with lockers and baths for the use of wheelmen, quite an acceptable innovation.

Sachtleben had barely settled back in Alton when yet another attractive option came his way. The *Times* of London wrote to propose sending him to Cuba as a war correspondent. "The offer was entirely unexpected," a local paper reported. "Sachtleben corresponded regularly for the *Times* from Erzurum during the Armenian massacres, and visited their headquarters at London on his way home. But nothing was said to him at that time about going to Cuba." Affirmed Sachtleben: "The *Times* makes me a splendid offer and I am more than half tempted. I understand that their present representative in Cuba is not giving entire satisfaction. I presume they want someone who will face personal danger and get right out where the fighting is. But I hardly like to leave home so soon after getting back from Asia. If my departure can be delayed a bit I may accept."

On May 15, just as Pittsburghers were eagerly awaiting Sachtleben's return to their city, they were surprised to hear that the embattled American minister to Turkey himself, Alexander Watkins Terrell, had been spotted in town. "He was decidedly averse to talking or even of saying who he was at first," the *Dispatch* reported, "and would only indulge in some general observations when he did consent to speak." The diplomat spent most of the interview defending his controversial tenure in Turkey. Affirmed the reporter: "Mr. Terrell acknowledged he had tried to make himself *persona grata* with the Sultan, but he insisted that he always had the good of the country in mind. He appeared to think the judgment against him was of the snap-shot order."

Naturally, the reporter brought up the subject of Lenz.

> Mr. Terrell said the case had given him a great deal of trouble and he had worked hard and long to find the young man and something about his fate. Lenz, he thought, had really acted in a foolhardy manner in insisting upon entering that part of the country. Mr. Terrell was satisfied the young man had met his death for the money he had. Lenz had shown his money too freely, and the Kurds spotted him and made short work of him when he resisted them.

About a week later, Sachtleben arrived in Pittsburgh, where he stayed at Langhans's home. The old city hall, the *Press* reported, was lavishly decorated with flags and flowers in preparation for his lecture, billed as "The Search for the Missing Wheelman." When he took the stage, the overflowing crowd erupted in cheers. Langhans immediately stepped forward to offer the visibly moved lecturer an enormous bouquet of flowers.

The presentation would effectively mark the end of Sachtleben's mission of mercy. Like so many other aspects of the sad affair, however, the result was largely disappointing. Commented the *Press:*

> Several hundred riders, mostly old friends of the lost wheelman, turned out to hear Sachtleben. The *Press* had announced the lecture in good faith, believing that it would be an interesting account of his perilous journey to find the remains of the missing Pittsburger, with details of the murderers. But that was not what was given last night. The subject was simply the Armenian massacres. Sachtleben referred briefly to Lenz once or twice, and

showed one stereopticon view of Lenz in China. But there was no description of the search, of which Pittsburgers are so deeply interested. The crowd that left the hall about 10 o'clock was sadly disappointed.

In fact, Sachtleben was eager to put the Lenz case, as well as the stigma of failure, behind him. He passionately believed he had a new and vital mission to perform: to inform the American public about Turkish atrocities and the plight of the Armenians and to insist that the United States and the European powers force the sultan to enact at once far-reaching reforms. From that time forward, he intended to address the situation in Armenia, making only tangential references to the lost cyclist.

Sachtleben's lecture at Alton's Temple Theater a few weeks later drew another large and enthusiastic crowd. Projecting his photographs on a canvas, he described the region and its customs. He claimed that Armenian "thrift, abhorrence of bloodshed, and submissiveness" had left them vulnerable to Turkish wrath. The local newspapers gave the lecture rave reviews. Wrote one critic: "His vivid picturing of the recent atrocities almost transferred one to the scenes and the horrors." Echoed another: "Portions of the lecture were thrilling, especially the scenes thrown on the canvas of the dead and the dying." Mihran gave a stirring conclusion as he stood up in native garb and sang a soulful Armenian wail.

Once again, Sachtleben only briefly alluded to Lenz, showing a map of the route he had followed in Turkey in search of the missing wheelman. He projected the photograph he had taken of the barren spot near the Hopuz River where he believed Lenz had been killed. He noted that the body had not been found and suggested that it never would be. He speculated that Lenz's bones were resting at the bottom of the river into which his mutilated body had been thrown.

Though Sachtleben tried valiantly to distance himself from Lenz, the two were by now inextricably linked in the public con-

sciousness. Wherever he went, Sachtleben was pelted with questions about the missing Pittsburgher. In his own serialized
accounts of his adventures in Turkey, published in various newspapers, Sachtleben repeatedly eulogized the kindred spirit he had
never actually met:

> No one will ever realize his terrible sufferings, his narrow escapes,
> his sensations while he lay ill with fever in a strange land among
> barbarous and hostile people without medicines or doctor. The
> critical moment of danger, when intense excitement sometimes
> carries a man through an ordeal despite himself, are as nothing
> compared to the daily endurance of the menace in stealthy forms.
>
> I sympathized deeply with the mother in her bereavement of
> her only son, a young man full of promise, just entering upon a ca-
> reer that bade fair to be one of exceptional usefulness, called in the
> spring of life to his eternal rest. Friends he had many, who mourn
> with me the loss of a true comrade. It seems the very irony of fate
> to snatch away at an unexpected moment the fruits of a difficult
> undertaking, the accomplishment of which would have brought
> him much honor. Few voluntarily set before themselves so ardu-
> ous a task, especially when they have an easy pathway to wealth
> and influence at home. But that is the true American spirit, the
> spirit of the pioneers of our great republic, and its results have
> made our nation famous the world over.

Robert Bruce, the man Sachtleben replaced, likewise paid tribute to his erstwhile travel companion. In *Bicycling World*, he shared
a moving vision of Lenz approaching Constantinople, where the
two men were supposed to have reunited:

> For months now my "other self" has stood morning and evening
> upon the European shore of the Bosporus, commanding the best
> attainable view of the highlands of Asia Minor, with eyes ever
> strained to catch a glimpse of a ghostly rider, mounted upon a
> wheel of now antiquated pattern, loaded like a pack horse—a
> phantom cycler whose spirit is as yet unbroken, upon whose face

there is no trace of fear or hatred or revenge, but only a look of mingled kindness and determination. Illuminating the whole countenance is a cheerful half-smile, born of the consciousness that each revolution of the faithful old wheel brings him nearer to the misty ocean that alone lies between the old world and his home in the new.

III
Epilogue

15

REPERCUSSIONS

I N JULY 1896, some months after Sachtleben's return to the United States, Mrs. Lenz asked the State Department to demand $40,000 from the Turkish government in recompense for the loss of her son. She asserted that Lenz had asked Turkish officials for protection while en route from Tabriz to Chilkani but was denied, even after showing his passport. Noting that he had earned between $1,200 and $1,400 a year as a bookkeeper, she affirmed: "My son had always taken care of and provided for me and would have done so in the future, as he well knew that I entirely depended on him." As proof of the "future prosperity" now denied her, she cited his "high grade of intelligence, splendid education, good behavior, and perfect health."

A month later, the State Department informed Terrell: "You are instructed to bring this matter at once to the attention of the Turkish Government and to demand in the name of the United States a suitable indemnity to the mother of the murdered man." In September, Terrell wrote the Turkish foreign minister to repeat Mrs. Lenz's claim that Turkish officials had denied her son's request for protection. He further faulted the Ottoman government for its lax investigation and its failure to apprehend the murderers. Affirmed Terrell: "I shall, if necessary, at a proper time insist on the payment of an indemnity to Mrs. Maria Anna Lenz. At present I desire only to call the attention of Your Excellency to this unfortunate matter in hope that the Ottoman Government will voluntarily express its willingness to pay some indemnity, the amount of which may hereafter be agreed between Your Excellency and myself."

Several weeks later, having received no response from the Turkish government, Terrell made a formal demand for an indemnity totaling 200,000 francs. At the close of the year, the Turkish foreign minister signaled to Terrell that the porte had no intention of paying such a sum:

> Your Excellency cites the case of Lenz, who disappeared in a remote locality of the Empire. The Sublime Porte naturally decries any violation of law, and it desires to settle every incident in accordance with the precepts of justice. Facts of the kind in question, however, even those connected with the most horrible murders, are committed in every country in the world. Your Excellency is certainly not ignorant of the murder of Galeb Abdullah, an Ottoman subject, which was committed near Susanville, California. This murder was not committed recently but about the 15th of June, 1891, and notwithstanding the efforts of the American authorities, the murderer is still at large, and probably happy to have escaped with his life, unless he has since died a natural death.

Meanwhile, Bergholz pressed for a new trial to exonerate the convicted Armenians and preclude their return to captivity. At the same time, of course, he expected the court to find Moostoe and uphold his conviction.

Finally, that November, the consul informed Secretary of State William Woodville Rockhill that the appellate court had agreed to rehear the case, owing to various "irregularities." The five-man panel of judges consisted of the president of the court and four associate members, comprising two Christians and two Muslims. For a murder conviction, four votes would be required. In preparation for the trial, the authorities issued fresh warrants for the arrest of Moostoe and the three Armenian suspects known to have survived their captivity in Erzurum.

The trial finally opened in Constantinople, on March 17, 1897, though none of the accused men had been apprehended. In particular, Moostoe was rumored to have fled to Russia. Two days later, Bergholz sent Rockhill a report describing the trial and the verdict:

> The clerk read all the proceedings in the case, including those of the Criminal Court of the First Instance. Afterwards, the Public Prosecutor addressed the Court and stated that there was not sufficient evidence to convict and demanded that the court enter a verdict of acquittal. The President and one Christian and one Moslem found all the accused guilty of the charge of murder, but the other two members voted for acquittal. As it required four votes to convict on a murder charge, a verdict of not guilty was entered.

In essence, the court ruled that the suspects' possession of Lenz's belongings, found scattered about the banks of the Hopuz River, was insufficient proof of their complicity in his death. It considered Der Arsen's damning claim that he had seen Moostoe wearing the dead man's clothes, but it found the testimony unreliable.

Although the verdict cleared the Armenians, it was an obvious setback for the indemnity demand, given that no Turkish subject stood convicted of the crime. Moreover, the exoneration of Moostoe and his men left the American public deeply dissatisfied. "Turkish Justice a Farce," ran one headline in the *American Wheelman*. It pronounced the verdict "rather surprising," given that the evidence Sachtleben had spent months gathering implicating the Kurds was "almost conclusive of their guilt."

In April 1897, facing intense pressure from the American public, Terrell pressed for an appeal. Confirmed the State Department in a letter to the *American Wheelman:* "Our Minister to Turkey has taken steps to obtain a rehearing of the case at Constantinople." Terrell, however, would not see the process through. Earlier that year, he had indicated his intention to resign his post. On July 15, he left Constantinople for the last time, bound for Austin. The

matter of the appeal thus fell to his successor, James Burrill Angell, formerly a professor of languages at Brown University.

That September, Angell wrote to Secretary of State John Sherman to confirm that a new trial had been granted: "I take pleasure
in reporting to you that the judgment of acquittal in the criminal case against the supposed murderers of Mr. Lenz, which was
originally tried at Erzeroum, and appealed to the Court of Cassa-
tion at Constantinople on March 17, has been annulled, and that
instructions will be transmitted through the Public Prosecutor to
the proper Court at Erzeroum for a new trial." Once again, the Justice Department issued warrants for the arrest of Moostoe and
the Armenian suspects. It also summoned nine witnesses who had
previously testified in the case.

As the December trial date loomed, however, some began to
question the wisdom of pursuing an appeal. Bergholz was especially critical of Sachtleben and his handling of the accused Armenians. The consul feared that a new trial would only reopen old
wounds, as he explained to Angell:

> When examined privately by Mr. Chambers and Mr. Sachtleben,
> the Armenians frankly admitted having certain articles of Lenz
> in their possession and just as frankly explained how they had
> come into their hands. They felt, however, that if they should ad-
> mit to having these things to the Commission they would be ac-
> cused of the murder. Under the verbal promise of Mr. Sachtleben,
> I am told, that he would see to it that no harm should befall them,
> they were induced to give their testimony freely. I fear that Mr.
> Sachtleben gave these poor fellows the impression that he rep-
> resented the United States in the examination, and that when he
> promised them protection they firmly believed that he was speak-
> ing as an official of the government.

Chambers was equally convinced that a new trial would only
lead to more misery for the accused Armenians and their families. He wrote Angell requesting that the minister withdraw the
demand for an appeal. "I was much impressed by Mr. Chambers's

statements," Angell conceded in his reply to Bergholz. "Possibly if his views and the facts he presents had been known to the government at the close of the first trial, no steps would have been taken to secure a review. But as that review has been taken at our instance, we are unable to take any steps to prevent a new trial." Angell nonetheless expressed his hope that the local authorities, following the verdict, would "refrain from punishing the innocent."

The trial took place on December 27. The next day Bergholz summarized the proceedings to Sherman. The witnesses "gave practically the same testimony as they gave in Chilkani before the Commission of Shakir Pasha." This time four of the five judges ruled against the defendants. Consequently, "the men were found guilty, and a sentence of fifteen years imprisonment was imposed."

The verdict, coming nearly four years after Lenz's disappearance, gave little consolation to either Sachtleben or the Lenz family. Although it reaffirmed Moostoe's guilt, the Kurd was seemingly nowhere to be found; he was "probably hiding in the mountains," in Angell's estimation. Moreover, although the accused Armenians were likewise absent, having fled to Russia, they were once again fugitives in the eyes of the law.

Nor did the decision do much to enhance Mrs. Lenz's demands for an indemnity. True, the court affirmed that "the heirs of Lenz have the right to appeal to the Religious Court for blood money." Angell, however, dismissed this avenue: "Since the only persons from whom this 'blood money' could be obtained are the condemned criminals, all of whom are absent, and none of whom, it is safe to say, are possessed of property of much value, the privilege of applying to the Religious Court would be of little consequence." Edwin Pears, a prominent British barrister and Mrs. Lenz's representative in Constantinople, concurred. He noted that even if Mrs. Lenz managed to extract a reward from the culprits, it would not even cover her legal costs.

The only hope left for Mrs. Lenz was to collect an indemnity from the Turkish government through diplomatic channels, a painfully slow process that had yet to show any promise. Angell

believed that even that route was a long shot. As he explained to
Secretary John Hay in July 1898: "That there was culpable delay,
according to our ideas, in bringing the real criminals to trial, and
that there was great reluctance to deal rigorously with Musteniseh,
the Kurdish culprit, there can be no doubt. But a regular trial has
now been had, and the Ottoman government will undoubtedly
point to that as a sufficient reason to decline payment of damages."

In February 1899, Angell's successor, Oscar S. Strauss, reiterated to Hay that Mrs. Lenz stood little chance of collecting an indemnity from the Turks: "In view of his taking so hazardous a
journey, in such an exceptional manner, through provinces far distant from the central government, where disorders are chronic,
and where travelling even with the best of safeguards is surrounded with danger; and in view of the criminal procedure instituted by the authorities, I seriously doubt whether a good ground
for a claim for indemnity exists."

Strauss nevertheless hatched an elaborate plan that, if successful, would at least net some payment for Mrs. Lenz. Noting that
numerous American citizens had lodged similar claims against
the Ottoman government, he suggested that the State Department press the Turks for a lump settlement—"a round sum, say,
from twenty to twenty five thousand pounds Turkish." Upon re-
ceipt, the State Department could "apportion the amount among
the claimants as it may seem equitable and just." He stressed that
it would be "easier and more practical to come to an arrangement
on this basis than to press these individual claims."

Although Strauss would leave his post before his scheme could
be implemented, his successors saw it through successfully. In
mid-1901, after a personal appeal from President William McKin-
ley, the sultan finally agreed to pay a lump sum to settle all outstanding claims, without any formal admission of guilt. The monarch discreetly attached the sum to a scheduled payment on a
warship under construction in Philadelphia, and the settlement
money was then turned over to the State Department for distribution. Mrs. Lenz's share, paid early the next year, amounted to

$7,500. Though only a fraction of her original demand, it was a sizable sum nonetheless.

By all accounts, she desperately needed the money. For the past several years, following a work accident, her husband had been a virtual cripple, leaving the couple devoid of any income. Her own health had deteriorated markedly, not to mention her morale. Reportedly, though she knew better, she still expected her son to appear one day at her doorstep with his loaded bicycle.

Even after Mrs. Lenz received the payment, her husband's deteriorating health prevented her from acting on a long-cherished dream: to travel to Turkey herself to find her son's bones and return them for burial in Pittsburgh. On January 7, 1902, the *Dispatch* explained her sad predicament:

> Mrs. Lenz will not be able, as she had hoped, to use the $7,500 indemnity just received to go or send a representative to Turkey to find the body of her boy. Only a few days ago her husband was stricken with paralysis and physicians say there is little hope of his recovery, although he may be a hopeless invalid for years to come. Efforts yesterday to secure his admission to a hospital failed on account of the case being pronounced incurable. If Mrs. Lenz was not able to go to Turkey she expected to send Charles Petticord, a close friend of her dead son. But the increased expenses occasioned by her husband's illness will prevent that, and Frank Lenz will rest in his unmarked grave in the Orient until his body crumbles to dust.

Charlie, in fact, was not doing so well himself. After Lenz's departure, he had thoroughly immersed himself in cycling. He finished the 1892 season with a staggering 6,300 miles, the second-highest total among the Allegheny Cyclers. The following year, while Lenz made his way across Asia, Petticord registered an incredible 10,000 miles. Along the way, he smashed Lenz's twenty-four-hour regional record, logging 216 miles in one day. That fall he somehow found time to pedal to Chicago, with his sister Amelia, to take in the Columbian Exposition. His troubles began, however, the following spring. Announced the *Dispatch* in April 1894: "Petticord has been very ill for several days." In fact, cycling had become so painful that he was forced to desist.

Petticord tried gamely to shrug off his mysterious ailment. He diligently prepared for his rendezvous with Frank that fall, confident that by then he would be fully recovered. That June, *Bicycling World* affirmed his plans: "Sometime in October, Mr. Lenz expects to reach Germany. Petticord has conceived the idea of meeting Lenz on the German frontier and will accompany him home." Charlie had even gone so far as to order a gold-plated bicycle for the festive occasion.

Alas, Charlie was heading nowhere. By fall, when news of Lenz's disappearance broke, he was a virtual shut-in. Reported the *Washington Post:* "The lower end of Petticord's spine has become diseased from his incessant riding, and a sympathetic nerve in his left limb has been injured. As a result, the leg has been drawn up, and is much shorter than the other." Charlie even traveled by train to Chicago to consult mystified medical experts.

With millions actively riding, cycling's health risks and benefits had become a hot topic. Petticord quickly became something of a symbol of excess. Declared one paper: "The results of over exercise are no more clearly shown than in the case of Charles Petticord, champion long distance bicycle rider of Pennsylvania. The man has wasted away to a skeleton. Being a bicycle crack has its drawbacks, and the athlete is foolish who fails to take warning from such examples."

William Sachtleben, too, had slowed down considerably by the start of the new century. Following his return to Alton, he did not go to Cuba after all. After enjoying a few months of much-needed rest, he embarked on a lecture tour focusing on the Armenian massacres. But it failed to gain much traction. When 1897 opened, he resolved to settle down to his still-thriving bicycle business. He even assumed the editorship of a local cycle magazine called *The Pedal* and occasionally entered local bicycle races. But before long, he became restless once again.

In June 1897, Sachtleben's famous temper flared again. A local paper reported:

> Martie Duddy, aged 17, employed as a driver applied for a police summons yesterday against William L. Sachtleben, a bicycle dealer. Duddy alleged that he delivered goods to Sachtleben in the morning. There was a money transaction and Sachtleben accused the boy of giving him a counterfeit dollar. Martie denied the charge, and the bicycle man, it is alleged, then assaulted him. "He punched me in the face and kicked me out of the shop," said the boy. "I didn't pass any counterfeit money on him and he had no reason for beating me."

That fall, as business began to fade, Sachtleben exempted himself once again from his shop duties. He spent a relaxing four months touring Germany and England with a friend from Alton. By the time he returned, the boom had gone bust, and his chief supplier, the Overman Wheel Company, was bankrupt. Sachtleben briefly toyed with the idea of promoting professional cycle racing, but soon decided to bail out of the moribund business altogether.

After languishing for a year, Sachtleben decided to revive his lecture tour in 1899. Once again, however, he enjoyed only modest success. He himself was tiring of the topic. "He says he deserves a new subject," the *Telegraph* affirmed in the spring of 1900. It outlined his plans for a new adventure. He would travel to Cape Nome, Alaska, the site of the "richest finds" during the recent Klondike Gold Rush, which had attracted thousands of prospectors. Sachtleben explained that he would go in the interest of *Outing*, which was no longer in Worman's hands. In Alaska, he would "secure materials and a series of pictures for a new lecture."

In the spring of 1901, Sachtleben prepared for yet another journey, one worthy of his old self. Reported the *Telegraph:*

> Will Sachtleben is seriously considering a proposition to join the Baldwin-Ziegler expedition to the North Pole. Because of the valuable experience Will has gained in roughing it in his two trips to Asia, and on his last trip to the Cape Nome gold fields, he has

been sought by Mr. Baldwin to join the expedition. But so far the two have not been able to come to terms. Will is holding out for a good salary, as he would not be allowed to write or lecture on his trip on his return, all rights being reserved by Baldwin.

For Sachtleben, the idea of being among the first men to set foot on the North Pole was simply irresistible. He soon reached a verbal agreement with the leader, Evelyn B. Baldwin. A short while later, however, Sachtleben wrote Baldwin to convey a stunning reversal. "I presume that you will not entertain any hard feelings against me, if I tender my resignation. I do so with the deepest regret, because my mind was set on going. I must candidly tell you that the only reason is the determined opposition of a certain young lady whom I have known for several years. I cannot overcome this opposition without causing her great suffering."

Baldwin was incensed. "You have not treated me fairly," he wrote back testily. "I recall very distinctly our conversation in St. Louis relative to the very point in question which you give as an excuse for your withdrawal. At that time you promised, indeed you assured me, that a matter of this kind would positively make no difference with you. This was upon my statement to you that I would take no one who would not willingly part with his dearest friend on earth."

Two and a half years later, in December 1903, Sachtleben married that certain young lady, Mae Merriman, the daughter of a wealthy St. Louis merchant. The two promptly moved to New York City, where Sachtleben took a job with a publisher, before eventually settling in Houston to run the Majestic Theater. The wheelman's days as a world-famous adventurer and correspondent were well behind him.

And what about Frank Lenz? Where might he have been at the start of the new century had he completed his circuit? Certainly, the timing of his return would have been most fortuitous. Pittsburgh, like every other American city, had become bicycle-mad. Declared a downtown retailer in early 1895: "The increase in the sale of bicycle goods is wonderful. We have sold three times as much goods compared to the same period last year." That summer, the *Dispatch* mused: "The disease is absolutely incurable, and unless something remarkable happens soon the major part of the atmosphere promises to be pumped into pneumatic tires. The many growlers who have cried down the bicycle amusement since its inception will consequently have to utter their protests in indistinct gasps. It will make but little difference. The bicycle has come to stay."

Without a doubt, Lenz would have been welcomed home a hero and deservedly honored as an early proponent of the safety bicycle. Had he written a book, it would have enjoyed brisk sales. Had he embarked on a lecture tour, he would have been in high demand. It seems unlikely, however, that he would have rested on his laurels for long. Perhaps he would have gone on that bicycle trip to South America that he had once proposed, or into the bicycle business.

No doubt Lenz would have resumed an active role in the local cycling community. But he hardly would have recognized his old club, the Allegheny Cyclers, whose membership had soared into triple digits. He might also have been surprised at the number of lady riders. Shortly after his departure, his other club, the Keystone Bicycle Club, began to admit women. Reported the *Press* at the time: "The Keystone members all like the idea and they are doing missionary among their lady friends to increase the number."

Yet, as much as the sport had opened up, many were still effectively excluded. Asian cyclists on the West Coast were often harassed, and blacks were formally disbarred from the LAW in 1895. Although the ban came about largely at the insistence of southern whites, anti-black sentiment prevailed throughout the country, Pittsburgh included. Observed the *Press* on New Year's Day 1893: "The wheelmen in all the cycle clubs hereabouts are very seriously opposed to colored men joining the L.A.W. The Keystones would about as soon disband as admit an off-color member."

Perhaps Lenz, who had dedicated his trip to a "more sympathetic appreciation of fellow men" following his near-fatal attack in

China, would have lent his considerable prestige in favor of inclusion. After all, he had spoken eloquently about the virtues of tolerance. And there is little doubt that he would have returned from his great adventures a vastly more mature and thoughtful man.

In sum, Lenz would no doubt have found some creative and profitable way to ride out the great boom. To be sure, he would have had to share the local limelight with George A. Banker, the youngest of the Banker brood, who would take over Zimmerman's place as America's top racer, winning the World Championship in 1898. Lenz, however, would have been elated with Banker's success, having photographed the champion's first race in Brownsville on July 4, 1889—atop a high-wheeler.

With regard to his personal life, Lenz would no doubt have maintained his base in Pittsburgh, to be near his beloved and long-suffering mother. Perhaps he would have married Annie R. Leech, who would live until 1951 without ever taking a husband. Had they had children, he would no doubt have been the kind and loving father he himself had never had.

By the start of the new century, with the bicycle in dramatic and seemingly irreversible decline, Lenz would doubtless have found a new direction. He would have had many attractive options to choose from. Perhaps, like Robert Bruce, who joined the American Automobile Association, he would have worked in the budding field of motor tourism. He had always loved maps and topology after all. Or perhaps he would have found employment in the manufacturing sector, like his old rival A. C. Banker, who made a small fortune developing windshields.

Of course, none of those happy scenarios played out. On the contrary, even his feeble legacy took a severe beating. The brief mourning period had barely elapsed before the press printed unflattering portraits depicting a reckless young man who might even have harbored a thinly veiled death wish. A member of the Hagerstown Bicycle Club recalled a disturbing dialogue with the ill-fated wheelman early in his tour, shortly after he rolled into that city on a flat tire and under a hard rain:

After donning a dry uniform he talked of the big task before him. He took anything but a cheerful view of it. He said he felt that he would never return to this country alive. When told that others had safely accomplished what he intended to do, he replied: "Oh, no they haven't. I propose literally to ride around the globe on my wheel wherever it is possible. Other persons when they struck Asia used the railroads and ships. I expect that my determination will cost me my life. But I fully intend to go ahead." The last words Mr. Lenz said when he mounted his wheel were: "Well, good-bye. I suppose it is forever."

Another cyclist, Charles Fuller Gates, writing in the *Los Angeles Times*, recalled a similarly eerie exchange:

I rode part of the way with Frank Lenz while he was crossing this country. As he was our guest for several days, I had a good chance to study him. He was a persistent fellow and full of courage but with poor judgment. The last time I saw him, I said partly in humor: "You'll surely get killed in Asia, you are so stubborn," or words to that effect. He replied: "I expect to be."

Well before motorized vehicles rendered the notion of a world tour by bicycle laughably quaint, the press had already dismissed its supposed merits. In early 1895, following Lenz's disappearance, *Bearings* articulated the prevailing sentiment.

When Thomas Stevens rode around the world, it had the merit of novelty. But when Tommy returned all the cream had been skimmed from this jar. Nothing was left for his successors but thin milk. Allen and Sachtleben followed him, but although they are only a year or so home, they are already forgotten. Poor Lenz started out on an old and beaten track, and even if he had succeeded the result would have been nil. The bicycle may have a great mission to perform in the world, but bearing a lone man through the wilds of Asia is not part of it.

As the twentieth century unfolded and the bicycle boom became a faint memory, Lenz's name quickly ceased to circulate. In 1923, when eighty-two-year-old Anna Lenz died and was buried beside her second husband in Pittsburgh's St. Mary's Cemetery, not one of the local newspapers recalled that she was the mother of the missing wheelman.

Lenz's cycling contemporaries nonetheless occasionally invoked his memory. Writing for a motorcycle review in the early part of the new century, Robert Bruce recalled his old friend from time to time. When Allen and Sachtleben briefly reunited in 1935, after nearly forty years of separation, they naturally alluded to Lenz. That same year, shortly before he retired to Florida, Charlie Petticord reminisced about his old buddy with a Pittsburgh reporter, showing her the photos and letters he had kept all those years. Ned Friesell described how he had almost become Lenz's escort. "I am still looking forward to that trip around the world," he mused to a gathering of dentists in 1940, "but have given up the idea of doing it by bicycle."

One by one, however, their voices were stilled; Petticord (1944), Friesell (1946), McClarren (1952), Sachtleben (1953), Bruce, Langhans (1954), and Allen (1955). Frank G. Lenz, once one of the world's most famous wheelmen, was "lost" once again—becoming an utterly forgotten figure.

16

REFLECTIONS

O NE MIGHT, OF COURSE, dismiss Lenz's trip as an ill-conceived lark. His various justifications, ranging from the mundane (to test tires) to the sublime (to foster human harmony), were hardly convincing. Yet, however meager its real merits, there is little doubt that a successful conclusion would have accomplished his overriding, if tacit, objective—to get somewhere in life. He knew when he started out that he would never go back to a boring desk job. He was bound for better things. And the fact that he came so agonizingly close to achieving his objectives is proof enough that his calculations were not far off the mark.

Although his vision, courage, and dedication were beyond reproach, his judgment obviously failed him, repeatedly and tragically. For starters, his decision to travel alone, though it was not his preference, placed him in perpetual danger. Notwithstanding Lenz's lame explanation to the *Pall Mall Budget*, Sachtleben was no doubt correct in his observation that an extra pair of eyes would have served the Pittsburgher well.

Lenz's vow never to take a boat or a train from one point to another, if he could theoretically cycle or walk there, further endangered him. Were it possible to circle the globe exclusively under one's own steam, such a rigid policy might have had some merit. But given that even the most ambitious globe girdler had to cover an arbitrary portion of his journey with assistance, all that really mattered in the end was the total distance traversed overland. Clearly, if Lenz had achieved his goal of covering twenty thousand miles and had returned home safely, no one would have cared if he had taken an occasional train or boat ride to get through a problematic stretch or to hasten his pace. Allen and Sachtleben had shown such sensible flexibility on several occasions, and the world thought no less of them for that.

Lenz's stubbornness also endangered the lives of others. If the main purpose of his trip was to prove the practicality of the safety bicycle, what was the point of hiring young men to carry his vehicle over mountains and streams, where one slip could have meant disaster, rather than shipping it ahead to the next bicycle-friendly destination? Had Lenz been more conscientious and prudent, the life of that poor man who drowned in Burma might have been spared.

Despite these pointless impositions, Lenz might well have returned home safely had he not made one glaring oversight: the failure to exercise more caution while traversing Turkey, one of the two countries he himself had identified at the onset as his most dangerous destination. Perhaps, as Bruce suggested, his narrow escape from China, the other country he cited, had lulled him into a false sense of security.

Certainly, as Chambers observed, Lenz should have advised the foreigners living along the caravan route of his approach, so that they could have kept an eye out for him. More importantly, he might have done a better job of concealing his valuables. His fatal error, however, was his failure to rely heavily on zaptiehs, as Allen and Sachtleben had done, even if they were an added expense and often a nuisance, and they might have slowed him down. But at least he would have probably made it to Constantinople.

Mrs. Lenz, of course, would claim that Frank had asked Turkish officials in Dyaden for protection. That does not, however, appear to have been the case. He was known to have disregarded the advice of several foreigners residing in Tabriz to avoid Turkey altogether. There seems little reason to believe that he had at least the prudence to ask for guards while approaching the notorious Deli Baba Pass, or that he would have been refused. Nor is it clear where Mrs. Lenz got the information that her son had wanted an escort. Perhaps it was simply wishful thinking on her part, or a claim she had to make to support the demand for an indemnity.

Still, no matter how much one attributes Lenz's untimely death to his own miscues and misdeeds, his story remains a heart-wrenching tragedy shrouded in mystery. Robert Bruce, for one, would never find closure. "I try to picture the intrepid young American among the barbaric Kurds who slew him—just when and where and how no one knows," he wrote in 1913. "They made away with him so completely that no trace of his body or bicycle or other belongings ever was found. The slayer may yet be holding the miserable secret, or have died with it."

One feels special sympathy for Mrs. Lenz. She had been right, of course. If only her son had heeded her advice and buckled down to the business of life. . . . The world, over time, would have opened up to him in ways he could have scarcely imagined in 1892, with the advent of automobile and jet travel. But the bicycle was Lenz's life, and he would have had it no other way. And so he remains one of those frozen figures, immortalized—ironically—by his premature death. There simply is no other way to picture Frank Lenz but as a young man in the prime of life, beaming with joy as he straddles his beloved two-wheeler.

As sad as Lenz's death was, the search for his remains was no less tragic. Although Sachtleben returned alive—no small feat under the circumstances—and his findings ultimately enabled Mrs. Lenz to collect more than $10,000 in insurance and indemnity payments, the plagued process took a heavy toll on an equally valiant young man. Worse, it claimed the lives of two Armenian captives and caused untold grief to their fellow villagers. In nearly every respect, the search was a colossal failure. Endless delays. No body. No justice. Although Lenz was long gone before anyone could have rescued him, it is fair to ask whether a different approach might have produced more satisfying results.

First, one must acknowledge the obvious shortcomings of the Turkish justice system at that time. The sultan himself had insisted, not unreasonably, that Moostoe's possession of Lenz's inner tubes was not proof of his complicity in the murder. Yet five Armenians were thrown summarily into jail for possessing a handful of screws that allegedly had belonged to Lenz's camera. To secure justice from a system with such a glaring double standard would have been an extremely difficult task even under more tranquil circumstances.

Even so, one might have hoped for better results. The list of bunglers starts with James Henry Worman, who was largely responsible for the investigation's belated start. Even taking into account that transportation and communications were excruciatingly slow by today's standards, a year was a long time to get an investigator to the approximate location of the crime. Sachtleben himself noted that, upon his arrival in Erzurum in May 1895, "the first thing Chambers and Graves asked me was why Lenz's friends had waited so long before investigating."

Given Lenz's previous disappearing acts, Worman might be excused for having ignored the first signs of danger. By the fall of 1894, however, he should have been reporting Lenz missing to the State Department rather than writing the ministers abroad, who were powerless to act without Washington's approval. Contacting the missionary headquarters and cabling their envoys along Lenz's route would also have been a prudent measure. Valuable months might have been gained in the vexing quest to pinpoint Lenz's last known location.

In theory, if Worman had cabled Thomas Cook & Son by early August 1894, with instructions to look for Lenz, the agency might have promptly traced Lenz to Chilkani and gotten native investigators to the site before the outbreak of massacres in that region. Obviously, if they had been able to conduct a discreet search for Lenz's grave at that time, they would have stood a much better chance of finding it than Sachtleben did months later operating in a climate of fear. Presumably, they would also have been in a better position to uncover clues pointing to the murderer or murderers.

But even if Worman had acted with greater alacrity and resolve, he might not have obtained satisfactory results from on-the-spot agents. Certainly, he cannot be faulted for ultimately hiring an out-side investigator, given his obligations to Lenz's family and the fact that Turkish authorities were unlikely to search for the body, let alone the murderers. Still, he managed to drag out the selection process and cause needless strife. And even when he finally settled on Sachtleben after clumsily dropping Bruce, his decision to detain the investigator in Alton while the winter passed in Turkey only riled his man and added further delay.

Terrell, having initially spurned the pleas of Lenz's friends for assistance, is another easy target for criticism. For all his wooing of the sultan, he seems to have had little ability to disrupt the Turks' endless stonewalling and foot-dragging. Still, he was hardly as in-effective as Sachtleben claimed. Turkish records show clearly that he did ultimately take the Lenz matter in hand, if not to heart, and he did push discreetly behind the scenes for Turkish cooperation. And Shakir's intervention probably was the result of Terrell's ma-neuverings, as the minister maintained, though one might ques-tion its ultimate value.

Nor was Terrell devoid of any sensible insights. His advice to Sachtleben—to concentrate on finding Lenz's grave—was sound. Had the wheelman accepted the two zaptiehs the vali initially of-fered in May 1895, he could have gotten to Alashgerd months ear-lier to search quietly for Lenz's remains. Had he found them, he would have accomplished at least one major objective, while per-haps uncovering important clues to the murder. Conceivably, even if he had failed to find the grave, he could still have returned in the fall with Shakir to conduct house searches and make arrests.

Instead, Sachtleben chose to remain in Erzurum and make highly public demands for a small army to enable him to search the homes of the Kurdish suspects, a dangerous task that even he

admitted was unlikely to produce helpful results. Even if Sachtleben had managed to conduct his raids in the summer rather than
the fall, it is doubtful that the outcome would have been any more
satisfying.

In retrospect, one must question whether Sachtleben really was
the best choice—or even a good choice—for an investigator. Certainly his credentials appeared impressive on paper, though he had
no prior experience in criminal investigation or law enforcement.
But as Worman and the State Department quickly found out, he
was a loose cannon whose judgment was not always sound. One
wonders if the jilted Bruce might have done a better job after all,
despite his tender age.

Still, one cannot fairly assess Sachtleben's performance without
addressing a crucial question: Did he get it right? Was Moostoe
indeed the "arch-murderer" of the unfortunate Lenz? Though it
is difficult, if not impossible, to make a conclusive judgment from
this vantage point, one might ask whether Sachtleben's detailed
account was at least a plausible one.

Perhaps the first question to address is this: Why did Graves's
Kurdish informant maintain that Lenz had been shot in the Deli
Baba Pass, near Kourdali, if in fact the wheelman had been slain a
good thirty-five miles to the east, while still traversing the plain?
And why did he cite six Kurds from Dahar if in fact they had nothing to do with the crime? Why, in particular, was Moostoe, the
supposed arch-murder, not on the list?

Of course, we might suppose that the Kurd was simply mistaken,
or that he was deliberately trying to throw Graves off Moostoe's
trail. However, a number of seemingly independent sources originally cited the village of Kourdali in the Deli Baba Pass as the location where Lenz was killed. The various accounts that Lenz's
corpse was left lying on the road seem suspiciously consistent.

To be sure, the finding of various bits and pieces that presumably belonged to Lenz by the Hopuz River outside Chilkani sug-
gests that he was attacked at that spot. But without an eyewitness

to the crime or the discovery of Lenz's body in the vicinity, it does not necessarily follow that he was killed there. One might imagine, for example, that he was robbed and perhaps roughed up, but that he continued afterward in the direction of the pass, perhaps in a weakened state. In that case, he could conceivably have drowned while trying to cross one of the intervening rivers. Perhaps he did in fact wash up near Karakalissa. Or maybe he reached Kourdali later in the day, only to be killed in the manner described by Graves's informant.

Of course, one can point to the lack of Lenz sightings west of Chilkani as evidence that he never made it far out of that village. Yet it is clear that a climate of fear prevailed across the entire region and that villagers were reluctant to step forward with information. Even the residents of Chilkani initially denied that Lenz had stopped there. So the lack of witnesses west of Chilkani does not necessarily mean that Lenz never made it to the pass.

And what about Moostoe? Of course, he could have been lying when he claimed never to have met Lenz. Quite a few Armenian villagers, after all, had signed a petition stating that the Kurd had not only visited Lenz at Parsegh's residence on the evening of May 9, 1894, but had verbally threatened the American. On the other hand, Lenz's host, who freely acknowledged that Lenz had passed the night in his farmhouse, pointedly denied that Lenz had entertained visitors that evening. In any event, it seems unlikely that all twenty-two Armenian signatories were present that evening in the Parsegh home and overheard Moostoe's threats. At least some of them, it would seem, were acting on hearsay or simply cooperating with Der Arsen's request to sign his petition.

Even if Moostoe was present at the Parsegh home that evening, and even if he did accost Lenz, he did not necessarily make good on his threat. Nor was his admitted possession of bicycle inner tubes, presumably once part of Lenz's gear, proof of murder. It may be that Moostoe confiscated the material without killing Lenz, or perhaps he did indeed obtain the tubes, as he maintained, from a third party. After all, his tubes were in theory no more incriminating than the bits and pieces of Lenz's camera obtained by the local Armenians.

Of course, if Moostoe and his son really were in possession of Lenz's gun and clothing, and if the elder Kurd really did openly discuss his involvement in Lenz's murder, the evidence against the Kurd would have been overwhelming. But neither of these points seems to have been established beyond reasonable doubt.

What remains a distinct possibility is this: although Moostoe really was a dangerous and violent character, as Sachtleben maintained, and was roundly despised by the local Armenians, he was not the author of this particular crime. It may be that Der Arsen and local Armenians, under heavy pressure from Sachtleben and anxious to exculpate their fellow citizens, saw an opportunity to pin Lenz's death on the detested Kurd and took it.

Oddly, Der Arsen's oath, as collected by Sachtleben and submitted to Mrs. Lenz, makes no mention of Moostoe or his alleged threats to Lenz. The entire document reads as follows:

> I Der Arsen Hagopian, the priest of Tchelkani, testify that a foreigner traveling on a bicycle came to our village in the later part of April or the early part of May 1894 and remained the night. We had an evening meal and morning meal together, and he gave me some raisins he had with him, and he inquired again and again my name and surname, wrote it in his note book, and after a pleasant visit he started the following morning, shaking hands with me and promising to send me a present from Europe. The following is a description of this foreigner, as near as I can remember. In figure he was strongly built, broad shouldered, the fingers thick and strong, and rather long; his wrists thick and strong, a little taller than Mr. Sachtleben; eyes blue; he wore a small English cap; moustache of a light color and hardly visible; fair complexion; ears large, hair auburn, he wore brown leather leggings. And I positively identify this man as the same one in the attached photograph. At the same time I certify that neither before or after,

until this date, has such a foreigner traveling on a bicycle passed through our village.
signed Der Arsen, November 14, 1895

Moostoe aside, it seems oddly remiss that Sachtleben, so critical of others, never formally retracted the original accusation identifying the six Kurds of Dahar, based on Graves's findings and lodged with the porte. Rather, the American seems to have been fixated on nailing Moostoe at all costs, even if his alleged accomplices mysteriously morphed into a completely different band of men.

Perhaps if Sachtleben had taken a slightly less strident approach, not only with the Turks but also with his own government, and a more critical look at his own behavior, he would have gotten along better with the authorities and achieved better results. One wishes, in retrospect, that he had concentrated on finding Lenz's grave rather than on meting out justice in Turkey. Obviously, the return of the wheelman's remains to Pittsburgh for burial would have given his mother and friends the sense of closure they so badly needed. Such a poignant conclusion to the Lenz affair would also have given Sachtleben the measure of success and satisfaction that his failed mission sorely lacked, regardless of how the legal and diplomatic proceedings played out going forward.

To be fair, Sachtleben faced a colossal and unenviable task in his spirited bid to unravel the Lenz mystery so long after the cyclist's tragic passing, under difficult—if not impossible—circumstances. No one should discount his evident sleuthing abilities. His meticulous notes made in a tiny scrawl reveal a wonderfully sharp and observant mind. To his credit, he was remarkably consistent with his details, even when writing years after the events in question. In my research, I had the pleasure of speaking with two women who actually met Sachtleben late in his life: Relna Wolfe and Nancy Benson. Both recall him as a charming man of extreme intelligence and full of wonderful tales.

If Sachtleben did indeed get anywhere near the truth of the murky Lenz matter—and it is quite possible that he did—that was truly an extraordinary accomplishment, and one that should have enhanced, rather than doomed, his budding career as an investigator and adventurer par excellence. A brave and resourceful man full of noble intentions, he too deserved a better fate.

Notes on Sources

Acknowledgments

Photo Credits

Index

Notes on Sources

Nearly all the quotes in this book are based on written accounts. I frequently edited for clarity but endeavored to preserve the original intent as I understood it.

Prologue

The prologue is based on a lead article in the *Alton Evening Telegraph* of October 28, 1952, describing Sachtleben's surprise visit to the newspaper office. I also used material gathered from other articles appearing in the same paper, notably a letter to the editor from Sachtleben published on April 17, 1943.

Chapter 1 (*Lenz's early years*)

I drew material on Lenz's early years (before 1890) primarily from the cycling column of the *Bulletin*, a social review based in Pittsburgh's East End. The author, Charles F. Seidell, was a member of the Keystone Bicycle Club. Starting in the spring of 1887, shortly after Lenz took up cycling, Seidell made frequent mention of the young cycling prodigy. For reports on the Erie-to-Buffalo race I culled the Pittsburgh papers as well as various newspapers published in the towns along the route. I imagined Lenz's reactions to the bicycles of Lallement and Stevens, which he undoubtedly saw, at the International Industrial Fair in Buffalo. Several articles suggested that Lenz's interest in a world tour dated from about this period, so it is very likely that the sight of Stevens's bicycle either prompted or intensified Lenz's dream of cycling around the world.

To sketch the cycling scene in Pittsburgh at this time, I relied on accounts published in Pittsburgh papers and also reports from Pittsburgh correspondents to cycling reviews. Quotes and information relating to the history of the bicycle I extracted primarily from my book *Bicycle: The History* (Yale University Press, 2004).

I am grateful to the genealogist Suzanne Johnston for helping me piece together Lenz's family roots. Unfortunately, however, some questions remain. We were unable to determine how or when Lenz's biological father, Adam Reinhart, died. It is almost certain nevertheless that it was the death of his father when Lenz was still a toddler that prompted his mother's move from Philadelphia to Pittsburgh. We were also unable to determine Lenz's connection to the Walper family of East Liverpool, Ohio. Although the local newspapers referred to Catherine Walper, John J. Purinton's mother-in-law, as the sister of Anna Maria Lenz, that does not appear to have been the case. According to probate records, the latter was an only child.

We were also unable to find out anything more about Annie R. Leech, who was evidently Lenz's girlfriend at the time when he left on his world tour. (He stipulated that she was to inherit his estate should his mother be deceased at the time of his death.) It is tempting to speculate that Lenz was planning to settle down with her upon his return to Pittsburgh.

Chapter 2 (*Allen and Sachtleben, having ridden across Europe, prepare to enter Asia*)

To recount Sachtleben's winter lull in Athens, I relied on his diary covering January to February 1891. I am grateful to Gia Aivazian for bringing this wonderful document to my attention. It is one of two diaries written by Sachtleben during his world tour that is now held by UCLA Special Collections. (He compiled several dozen notebooks during the three-year trip, but the others are lost.) For an interesting account of how this document was plucked from a Texas bonfire in the 1970s, see Aivazian's chapter, "Sachtleben Papers on Erzurum," in *Armenian Karin/Erzurum*, edited by R. G. Hovannisian (Mazda Publishers, 2002).

I drew additional details about the German cyclist Anton von Gödrich from an article by Wolfgang Schoppe, translated by Renate Franz.

To describe Sachtleben and Allen's trip across Europe, I relied on their reports published in the *Penny Illustrated Paper* of London and *Vélo-Sport* of Bordeaux. I also found good supplemental material in various French and Italian newspapers.

For background information on Allen and Sachtleben prior to their world tour, I mined *Student Life*, the Washington College review, and Alton newspapers.

Chapter 3 (*Lenz's long-distance rides prior to his world tour*)

To trace Lenz's summer trips from Pittsburgh to St. Louis (1890) and from Pittsburgh to New Orleans (1891), I mined papers from Pittsburgh and from the various cities through which the cyclists passed. The cycling literature, which took note of these rides, provided helpful supplemental information. The recollections of Robert Bruce, published in various motorcycling and cycling reviews, also helped me piece together a portrait of Lenz just prior to his departure on his world tour.

Chapters 4, 6, and 8 (*Allen and Sachtleben's ride across Asia and North America*)

To recount the Asian portion of Allen and Sachtleben's world tour, I drew most of my material from their own account in *Across Asia on a Bicycle*. Additional details came from several articles in the colonial newspapers of Peking and Denby's amusing report to the secretary of state. An article published in the Russian periodical *Niva* provided many valuable supplementary details. The author was Ivan Korostovets, a translator at the Russian embassy in Peking who met and interviewed Allen and Sachtleben upon their arrival in that city. I am grateful to Victor Fet for bringing the interview to my attention and for translating it.

To trace Allen and Sachtleben's American tour, I relied mostly on articles drawn from newspapers published along their route.

Chapters 5, 7, and 9 (*Lenz's world tour*)

To chronicle Lenz's journey across the United States and Asia, I consulted both his own accounts in *Outing* and numerous articles published by newspapers in the cities along his route, including English-language newspapers based in Japan, China, Burma, and India. Pittsburgh papers once again proved an excellent supplementary source, as they occasionally published all or part of letters that Lenz sent to his friends while abroad. Cycling literature provided additional information.

Chapters 10 to 14 (*the search for Lenz*)

Lenz's disappearance was extensively covered in the American press, starting with the Pittsburgh papers. I copied numerous articles from the local papers on microfilm (drawn from the *Chronicle-Telegraph, Commercial Gazette, Dispatch, Post, Press,* and *Times*). I also consulted newspapers from all over the country, often with the help of electronic databases.

Files from the State Department, the American Board of Commissioners for Foreign Missions, and the British Foreign Service provided rich sources of information on the search for Lenz. Sachtleben himself described his trip to Turkey in great detail in a series of articles published in *Bearings* in 1897. I gleaned useful information from his account published in the *Alton Evening Telegraph* of April 3, 1953, as well as from the autobiographies of the missionary William N. Chambers and the British diplomat Robert W. Graves. I also benefited greatly from Lewis L. Gould's book *Alexander Watkins Terrell* (University of Texas Press, 2004).

Chapters 15 and 16 (*Epilogue*)

I tracked the Lenz trial and the claim for an indemnity from the Turkish government through State Department files and newspaper articles. Thanks to Candan Badem, I was also able to review extensive files on the Lenz case held in the Ottoman archives of Istanbul.

In researching this book, I consulted the following facilities:

American Bible Society
Amherst College Archives (Talcott Williams papers)
Alabama State Library
Alton (Illinois) Public Library
Arizona State Library
Biblioteca Nazionale, Florence and Rome
Bibliothèque Nationale, Paris
Boston Public Library
British Library, London and Colindale
California State Library
Carnegie Public Library, Pittsburgh
Chicago Public Library
East Liverpool (Ohio) Public Library
Erie (Pennsylvania) Public Library
Heinz History Center, Pittsburgh

Houghton Library, Harvard University (records of the ABCFM)
Idaho State Library
Indiana State Library, Indianapolis
Kansas State Library
Library of Congress
Library of Virginia
Lincoln Library, Springfield, Illinois
Maryland State Archives
Minnesota Historical Society
Missouri History Museum
Montana State Library
National Archives at College Park, Maryland (State Department files)
National Archives at Kew, United Kingdom (British consular records)
New Jersey State Library
New Mexico State Library
New Orleans Public Library
New York Public Library
New York State Library
Ohio Historical Society
Oklahoma Historical Society
Redwood City (California) Public Library
San Diego Public Library
Seaver Center, Los Angeles Natural History Museum
    (Sachtleben papers)
South Dakota State Library
St. Louis Public Library
State Historical Society of Missouri
State Library of Pennsylvania
Tennessee State Library
Texas State Archives
University of California at Los Angeles, Special Collections
    (Sachtleben collection)
University of Oregon, Knight Library
University of Pittsburgh, Archives Service Center
University of Texas at Austin, Center for American History
    (Terrell papers)
Washington State Library
Washington University Archives (*Student Life*)
Wisconsin Historical Society
Yale Divinity School Library (diary of A. P. Parker)

Acknowledgments

SO MANY PEOPLE have helped me with this vast project, in ways big and small, that I hardly know where to start. Kathleen R. McBride provided me, once again, with constant encouragement, insightful criticism, and expert assistance with graphics. As always, my family and friends were extremely supportive.

For the book's conception, I am grateful to the late Irving A. Leonard, who wrote movingly about Lenz's story in *The Wheelmen* magazine, and to John Kelly of the *Washington Post*, who brought to my attention, many years ago, the need for a book on Frank Lenz. I am also indebted to Lara Heimert, then with Yale University Press, for wisely advising me to write a general bicycle history before tackling the Lenz project and for connecting me with my superb agent, Scott Waxman, who helped me shape this book's proposal and land a contract with a top-notch publisher.

My editor at Houghton Mifflin Harcourt, George Hodgman, has been a wonderful mentor and taskmaster, a font of insights and encouragement. I am also grateful to his able assistants, Sasheem Silkiss-Hero, who offered me guidance early on in the writing, and Johnathan Wilber, who helped bring the project to a timely completion. I am equally indebted to my eagle-eyed copyeditor, Cynthia Buck, who offered numerous helpful suggestions, and to Lisa Glover, who oversaw production and helped implement final edits. I also thank Patrick Barry for his wonderful cover design and Melissa Lotfy and Laura Brady for their excellent design and layout work. Finally, I wish to thank my publicist, Megan Wilson, for her invaluable counsel and promotion.

Many individuals assisted me during the long research phase, including several who had done independent work in a similar vein. I am grateful to Geof Koss, who generously shared his findings, and Gia Aivazian, who introduced me to UCLA's rich Sachtleben collection and freely offered valuable insights. Danette Hein-Schneider, an expert on nineteenth-century missionary life, helped orient and inspire me from the start.

I am indebted to all those who facilitated my research or did research on my behalf. Suzanne Johnston of Pittsburgh uncovered many important details about Lenz's family and early life. Cathy Bagby of the Alton Museum of History and Art showed me the town's life-size statue of Robert Wadlow and Sachtleben's boyhood home. I thank the current owner, Eric Stauffer, for kindly opening its doors to me.

Ed and Linda Reusing of St. Louis, Robert and Joan Taylor of Columbus, Sarah Tracy of Oklahoma City, Paul Rubenson of Baltimore, Jill DiMauro of College Park, Maryland, Glenn and Janci Rau of Austin, Amanda Benson and Anthony Forster of Brentwood, Tennessee, Phil Saunders of London, England, Claude Reynaud of Domazan, France, and Fabio Noferini of Florence, Italy, all hosted me for long stretches, enabling me to conduct research in their localities.

I also received considerable help from abroad. In Germany, Renate Franz uncovered and translated a wealth of useful information. Professor Hans Erhard Lessing helped research Lenz's German roots. Chris Barouxis and Raymond Henry found good information about Allen and Sachtleben's stay in Athens. Yasuyuki Matsushima tracked the travels of Lenz and Thomas Stevens in Japan. Victor Fet brought to my attention an important article in Russian on Allen and Sachtleben and translated it for me. Candan Baden scoured the archives of the Ottoman Empire and unearthed, among other valuable contributions, a transcript describing Alexander W. Terrell's meeting with the sultan, Abdul Hamid II, to discuss the Lenz case. Others who helped me pursue, collect, and interpret research from abroad were Antoinette Burton, Norie Lynn Fukuda, Jan Heine, Raymond Henry, Keizo Kobayashi, Anthony Molho, and Rebecca Nickerson.

Many who helped with my research have special ties to the book's main characters. I am especially indebted to John Lenz, the great-grandson of Fred Lenz (the brother of Frank Lenz's stepfather William), who shared two original letters from Frank to Fred as well as dozens of photographs depicting Lenz on his high-wheeler and safety bicycles. John Herron, who inherited the fabulous scrapbook of Charles Petticord, kindly provided another trove of marvelous photographs, mostly taken by Lenz himself during his ill-fated tour. Ann Irvine, granddaughter of the missionary William Chambers, was a huge help. She and her husband, Allen, graciously hosted me in Istanbul. Wink Smith, a great-grandson of John J. Purinton, and his wife, Dorothea, were also extremely accommodating. James L. Judson, whose father, Frank, was Petticord's nephew, unearthed several photographs of interest as well as illuminating documents. Relna Wolfe freely shared her memories of William Sachtleben, whom she met in Columbus in the early 1950s. Her daughters, Jane Wolfe and Mary Crall, were also very helpful.

Here is a partial list of other individuals who provided helpful information about key characters in the book:

Robert Bruce: Ronald Bruce, John Burdick, and C. Don Weston
William Nesbitt Chambers: Robert Chambers
Ned and Charles Friesell: Sandra Friesell
Theodore P. Langhans: Bob Luthultz and Henry Thompson
Frank Lenz: Ed Berry Jr.
W. Nelson Lovatt: Dorothy Gilette and Wayne K. Patterson
Winifred Manatt: Heidi Cavaganaro
Warren T. McClarren: Ralph Gordon McClarren
John C. Mechlin: Jean Overly
Albert H. Overman: Joyce Bowman and Cynthia Sonntag
William W. Peet: Cay Peet
Charles H. Petticord: Judd Lacko
William L. Sachtleben: Carolyn Bening, Scott Sachtleben, and
    Earl Sachtleben
Alexander Watkins Terrell: Lewis L. Gould
William S. Vanneman: William Higdon
William Whipple: Dr. Samir Johna and Dr. John M. Howard
James Henry Worman: Phil Knowles and William McHone

Among the archivists, librarians, and museum professionals who were especially helpful were: John Cahoon of the Seaver Center; Amy

Casamassa of the K. Ross Toole Archives; Joan Duffy of Yale Divinity Library; Simon Elliott of UCLA Special Collections; Lauren Uhl and David Grinnell of the Heinz History Center; Daniel Hope of Bowdoin College; Mary McAndrew of Knox College; Kristin Miller of the American Bible Society; Wendy Pflug of the University of Pittsburgh Archives; Sonya Rooney and Miranda Rechtenwald of the Washington University Archives; Seth A. Smith of the State Historical Society of Missouri; and Jen Teleja of Saint George's Academy. I would also like to thank Nadine Besse, Anne Henry, and Blandine Fond of the Musée d'Art et d'Industrie of Saint-Étienne, France; Brian Johnson of the ABCFM, Istanbul; Paul Smith of the Thomas Cook Archives, Peterborough, England; and Gabriele Wüst of the Landesarchiv Baden-Württemberg, Germany.

I enjoyed expert help amassing and digesting all this research. Professor Elizabeth Thompson, an old college friend, and her colleague Sabri Ates generously shared their knowledge of Ottoman Turkey. Roseanne Freese and Jim Butterworth helped me with Chinese matters, and Professor Thomas Ricks advised me on Qajar Persia.

For additional illustrations, I am indebted to Chris Barbour and his assistant Xu Cheng, who scanned numerous images from original *Outing* issues held by Tufts University, and to John Weiss and Lorne Shields, who provided delightful images from their fabulous collections of bicycle-related photographs.

I am grateful to Gary Sanderson of the Wheelmen for his attentive reading of the manuscript and for his many helpful suggestions. I would also like to thank all those who have helped and inspired me to delve into bicycle history over the years, including fellow Wheelmen, members of the Veteran-Cycle Club of the United Kingdom, and participants in the International Cycle History conferences.

To all these people, and to many others I have neglected to credit, I am deeply indebted. Without their collective help, the compelling stories of Lenz and Sachtleben might have remained untold.

Photo Credits

All photos by Frank Lenz unless otherwise noted.

Courtesy of John Weiss: Lenz with camera (photographer unknown); Lenz
leading Canton Bicycle Club; map of Allen and Sachtleben's route;
cycling review *Bearings*.

Courtesy of John C. Herron: St. Louis Tournament; Lenz moods; Lenz in
Mandarin dress; photographs of Lenz out West, 1892; Lenz aboard
Oceanic; photographs of Lenz in Japan; Lenz crossing very narrow
bridge; Lenz crossing stone bridge; Lenz in city of temples; Lenz in
Agra; Lenz unpacking bicycle parts; Lenz in front of Taj Mahal; Lenz
with camels; Lenz at rest; stamped envelope.

Courtesy of John Lenz: Lenz lounging with friends; McClarren, Petticord,
and Lenz riding; McClarren, Petticord, and Lenz at Wade Park; photographs of Lenz and Petticord on tour from Pittsburgh to New Orleans;
handwritten letter.

*Courtesy of the Seaver Center for Western History Research, Los Angeles County
Museum of Natural History:* Allen and Sachtleben posing in studio (En-
rico Resta); Allen and Sachtleben with flag (Thomas Allen/William
Sachtleben); Allen and Sachtleben posing in Taiyuan (photographer
unknown); calling card; prison at Erzurum (William Sachtleben); contents of Lenz's trunk (William Sachtleben); last known photo of Lenz
(Mozaffar al-Din Shah).

Courtesy of the U.S. Patent Office: Illustrations for bicycle bag patent.

*Courtesy of George Eastman House, International Museum of Photography and
Film:* Early Kodak advertisement.

Courtesy of Musée d'Art et d'Industrie, Saint Étienne, France: Kodak photographs of the Maison Carrée and Coliseum (Thomas Allen/William Sachtleben).

Courtesy of the Bowdoin College Archives, Brunswick, Maine: Portrait of Serope A. Gürdjian (photographer unknown).

Courtesy of Heidi Cavagnaro: Manatt family (photographer unknown).

Courtesy of the UCLA Charles E. Young Research Library Department of Special Collections, copyright © Regents of the University of California, UCLA Library: Allen and Sachtleben in front of gate to Teheran (photographer unknown); Lenz's trunk (William Sachtleben); Armenians burying dead (William Sachtleben).

Courtesy of the University of Southern California, on behalf of the USC Specialized Libraries and Archival Collections: Sachtleben and Allen with the Los Angeles Bicycling Club (photographer unknown).

Courtesy of Archives & Special Collections, Mansfield Library, the University of Montana, 98-0110: Lenz posing in Missoula, August 1892 (William A. Hoblitzell).

Courtesy of Christopher Barbour, coordinator of Special Collections at Tisch Library, Tufts University, and Xu Cheng: Lenz in front of palace; *Outing* page with Lenz and Buddha; Lenz using chopsticks; Lenz resting on milestone; "Around the World" graphic.

Courtesy of the Boston Public Library: Lenz cycling past onlookers in China.

Courtesy of Casey Greene and Adventure Cycling: Map of Lenz's route around the world. Map by Casey Greene.

Courtesy of the Library of Congress, the Abdul Hamid II Collection: Selamlik ceremony (photographer unknown).

Courtesy of Ann Irvine: Reverend Chambers interviewing local residents (photographer unknown).

Courtesy of Candan Badem: Portrait of Shakir Pasha (photographer unknown).

Courtesy of the Print Collection, Miriam and Ira D. Wallach Division of Art, Prints and Photographs, the New York Public Library Astor, Lenox and Tilden Foundations: Portrait of Sultan Abdul Hamid II (W. & D. Downey, London).

Index